CLIMBER'S GUIDE

TO THE

SHAWANGUNKS

THE NEAR TRAPPS
MILLBROOK

Dick Williams

THE
CLIMBER'S GUIDE
TO THE
SHAWANGUNKS

THE NEAR TRAPPS
MILLBROOK

Dick Williams

First Edition 1991

ISBN: 0-9646949-2-1

Written and Edited by
Dick Williams

Design and Layout
Gregory Rukavina

Cover Design
Gregory Rukavina

Sketches and Drawings
Annie O'Neill

Frontispiece
The Shawangunks as seen from within the Skytop Memorial Tower.
Photograph by Dick Williams

Back Cover
Illustration by Tony Angell, from *In the Company of Crows and Ravens*, Yale University Press 2006.

Published by
Dick Williams
Vulgarian Press
510 Mohonk Road
High Falls, NY 12440

DEDICATION

To That Ancient and (we hope) Un-vanishing
Creature: the Trad Climber

And to my son Richard, who continues
his life's adventures

ANTS LEEMETS
1938—2007

In loving memory of a very dear friend and climbing partner. He was an extremely talented, natural athlete who loved climbing, skiing and riding motorcycles to the maximum. We shared many great experiences. The most memorable was climbing El Capitan in 1966–it was our greatest climbing adventure together. Those memories will forever keep me smiling. I miss him dearly.

THE NEAR TRAPPS

OVERLOOK

THE TRAPPS

ROUTE 44/55

CONTENTS

Acknowledgments	i-ii
Area Map	iii-iv
Emergency Information and Disclaimer	v-vi
Introduction	vii-ix
Mohonk Preserve	x-xiii
Appropriate Behavior	xiv-xviii
Climbing Ethics and Style	xviii
Climbing Gear	xix-xx
Ratings and Grades of Climbs	xxi-xxvii
Useful Information	xxviii-xxxvi
Near Trapps Route Descriptions	1-193
Near Trapps Route Photographs	194-227
Millbrook Route Descriptions	228-283
Millbrook Access Map	284
Millbrook Route Photographs	285-303
Appendix A: Near Trapps Route Statistics	305-306
Appendix B: Near Trapps Routes by Grade	307-317
Appendix C: Millbrook Route Statistics	318-319
Appendix D: Millbrook Routes by Grade	320-323
Index of Routes: Near Trapps & Millbrook	326-333
About the Author	334-339
Author's Guide Book History	340-341

ACKNOWLEDGEMENTS

Whatever defects this book may have, it is not for want of preparation. To gather material I led every pitch afresh, or followed a score of climbs that were beyond my leading abilities, and immediately wrote a new description or revised an old one from my previous guides. This on-site reporting will, I hope, make the material--both as to climbs and protection grading–the most reliable ever assembled on the Nears Trapps climbs. For a four-year period I climbed up to four days per week (weather permitting) from spring to fall, accompanied by many, many wonderfully talented, fun-loving and patient partners, among whom I'd like to thank Burt Angrist, Thom Campbell, Elaine Mathews, Chris Moratz, Gregory Rukavina and John Thackray. I would especially like to thank Annie O'Neill, who from the very beginning of this project bravely followed me on so many occasions on some great climbs and on the many scary, dirty, loose rock-hellish climbs. We especially liked to find and put up new little one-pitch climbs and name them (some good and some ridiculous). Special thanks also to Brian McGillicuddy who led many of the very difficult, scary, desperate climbs. Everyone generously gave their time, skills and advice on some many obscure routes and untraveled parts of the cliff. My thanks are also extended to some of the most knowledgeable climbers on these cliffs who helped with important pieces of information, history and photos: Jim McCarthy, Ivan Rezucha and Rich Goldstone.

There was not enough time or personal ability for me to climb the many routes at Millbrook. I therefore took all the routes from my 1992 Millbrook guide and upgraded many of the routes (not all) with new information, especially climb grades and protection ratings, thanks greatly to Rich Romano who almost single handedly put up most of the climbs there.

I would especially like to thank Keith LaBudde who helped in the seemingly endless task of editing.

Special thanks also to Gregory Rukavina, for help in a multitude of areas: editing, layout of the guide and help whenever I had a computer problem or needed help on how to use a computer program. I'd also like to thank the many climbers who gave me information on new climbs or feedback on grades and protection of existing climbs. I sincerely apologize if I've forgotten to credit someone who has been helpful in this process. Last but not least, my gratitude goes to the Mohonk Preserve and its Rangers for their understanding of the Gunks' rich climbing history and the sensitive way they maintain order in this beautiful land, while allowing climbers the immense privilege of being on the finest trad crag on the East Coast. I'd urge readers to check out the Preserve's web site (www.mohonkpreserve. org) for its unique history and for further details on regulations governing access, pets, camping, day use fees, guides, annual climbing passes and much more. Also visit www. gunks.com and www.uberfall.com for general discussion of issues, information on routes, gossip, controversy, popular top ropes and chat rooms.

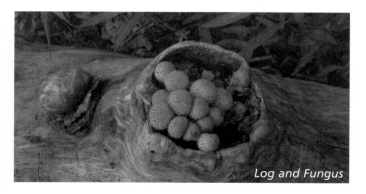

Log and Fungus

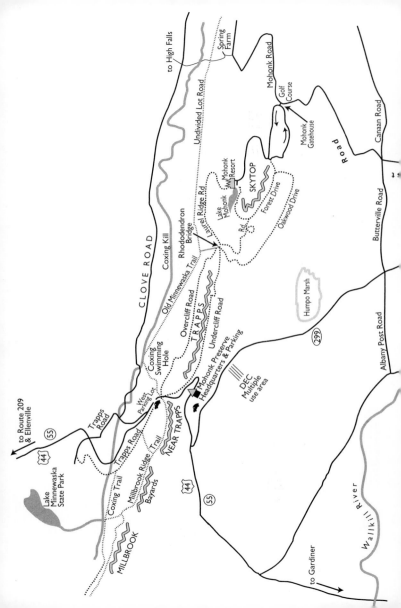

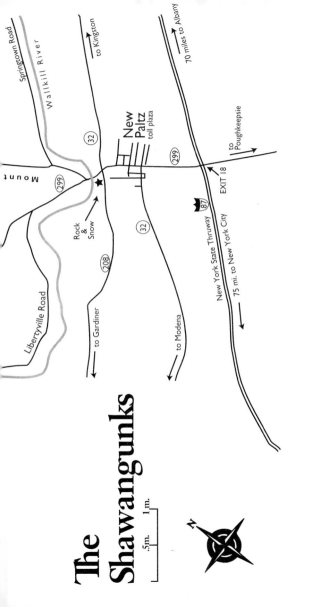

IN CASE OF AN ACCIDENT

GO/SHOUT FOR HELP, LOCATE A RANGER

—*OR*—

CALL THE MOHONK PRESERVE
845-255-0919
(Seasonal)

—*OR*—

CALL THE MOHONK MOUNTAIN HOUSE

845-255-1000
(24/7 All Year)

—*OR*—

CALL 911

Secure and stabilize the injured person as quickly as possible. Hopefully someone with emergency first aid training will be nearby.

Preserve Rangers are usually stationed in a truck parked on the carriage road at the steel bridge and on patrol along the carriage road. There is also a Stokes litter and emergency equipment in the rescue box at the Überfall.

There are public phones at the Mountain Bistro and The Mountain Brauhaus at the intersection of Route 299 and 44-55.

READ THIS WARNING AND DISCLAIMER BEFORE USING THIS BOOK

Rock climbing and any variation of this sport are dangerous; whether you're a novice or an expert, you can be seriously injured or **KILLED.** The author and publishers of this book cannot assure the accuracy of any information contained herein, including but not limited to route descriptions, difficulty ratings, protection ratings or route drawings in the photos.

This book is **NOT** an instruction manual for climbing. For proper instruction refer to books specifically written for that purpose. In addition, it is strongly recommended that those wishing to learn this sport hire an experienced professional guide.

DO NOT DEPEND on any information in this book for your safety and that of your partners. Your safety depends entirely on your judgment and abilities—**NO ONE ELSE'S!**

NEVER ASSUME ANYTHING when you are climbing. Don't trust "fixed" protection such as pitons, bolts, nuts or slings. **ALWAYS** back them up with equipment you place yourself. All leaders should wear helmets. Don't assume you will be able to lead all climbs at a particular grade of difficulty. Remember grades are subjective and relative; i.e., the experience of a 5.7 face move and a 5.7 roof are very different.

If you are frightened or nervous and feel you cannot do a climb without endangering yourself or others, **DON'T DO IT!** The primary virtues of a safe climber are self-control, restraint and knowing one's limits. A failure to possess any of these qualities can have terrible consequences, at best an injury, at worst a future confined to a wheelchair or a coffin.

INTRODUCTION

This Near Trapps guide covers 289 routes, including "Link-Ups." The Millbrook guide covers 95 routes. Some descriptions depart from the once-hallowed practice of tracing the route of the first-ascent party, but instead follow the more popular line that has evolved over time. In most cases, both the original and the "evolved" lines are drawn in on the photo pages. Sometimes there wasn't enough room to do so without creating a confused jumble of lines. These omissions are clearly identified with "not shown." In some instances where the first ascent took a wandering line, I've dubbed this a variation (Original route) that, like all variations that are drawn in, gets tagged with a dotted line. The new, higher quality climb is indicated by a solid line. For example, the Near Trapps route 152: Positively Fourth Street. Another feature of this guidebook are recommended "Link-Up" climbs. These are routes that combine various pitches of different climbs to make for a more consistently graded/quality route. For example, look at Near Trapps route **32a: (LINK-UP) 5.8 PG ★★★ DOG-STICK-RIDGE**. This route combines portions of four separate climbs. Each pitch has a different variety of moves and exposure, all of which makes this a ★★★ route.

This guide book also features an "As a Toprope" designation. On climbs that have great moves but are horror shows to lead and are fairly convenient to set up a toprope on, I've listed "As a Toprope" under the climb's name because I am recommending it as a toprope climb only. For example, look at Near Trapps route 51:

BIRD BRAIN 5.11d X
(As a Toprope)
and route 55:
TO BE OR NOT TO BE 5.12a PG ★★★
(As a Toprope)

From a historical perspective, there have been many changes in the 73 years that these cliffs have been climbed, changes expressed and reflected in guidebooks. When I first climbed here in 1958, there was no guidebook; we used only word-of-mouth information. The first "guide" to appear was mimeographed with hand drawings and printed by the Appalachian Mountain Club. Then in 1964 Art Gran wrote a guidebook with aerial photos and 285 routes in the entire Gunks. This opened many a climber's eyes, for one could clearly see where the routes were and, for the keen route setter, where they weren't. Back then, the consensus in the climbing community was that experience of adventure should be maximized. Route descriptions were brief so that everyone had a taste of some of the uncertainties that the first ascentionist had faced.

Members of the climbing community rarely gave beta on moves or protection. And of course, everyone had to pound in pitons and take them out, just as the first ascent party had done. Some older climbers mourn the passing of that epoch, and lament the altered benchmark of what constitutes an adventure today. The public expects guidebooks to be more and more detailed, which has the effect of squeezing out uncertainty and ambiguity in deciphering a route. Let's face it; a step-by-step guidebook doesn't promote the self-reliance that is such a useful attribute in alpine or high-altitude mountaineering and back-country trekking. Many climbs are tackled today with way more information than is strictly necessary—either through a guidebook or on-line chatter. Guidebook writers are caught in a Catch 22: the more information they offer, the more they condition their readers to be less adventurous.

My wish is that readers will primarily use the cliff photo route line drawings or, from time to time, leave this book in the trunk of their car and walk to some unfamiliar part of the cliff, read the rock, pick out a line, and try climbing it. They will surely learn something—and just might have more fun than the many experienced climbers who now only toprope climbs or continually repeat a dozen favorite routes they have "wired," having repeated them over and over again for many years. Climbing offers many types of adventure that lead to greater self-awarness and experience of nature. Have you ever tried deliberately climbing in the rain? Or when the cliffs are encrusted with January snow? True adventure depends on the imagination and the drive to go where you've never been before.

Peregrine Falcon

THE MOHONK PRESERVE

The Mohonk Preserve and the Mohonk Mountain House resort are separate entities that share a common heritage but are not legally associated with one another. The Mountain House resort was founded in 1869 by the Smiley family, who spent many years acquiring thousands of acres of land in the Northern Shawangunks. In 1963 the Mohonk Preserve (then called The Mohonk Trust) was established and opened to the public for recreational activities compatible with preservation of the area. The Preserve is a nonprofit organization that depends on membership support, grants and charitable contributions from individuals, outdoor conservation groups and businesses.

Today the Preserve contains over 6500 acres of forested lands and old fields, including 25 miles of carriage roads and 40 miles of hiking trails that give access to one of the most beautiful mountain ridges in the Northeast. Each year over 150,000 people visit the area to rock climb, hike, bicycle and cross-country ski, while enjoying the natural surroundings.

Of the four major cliffs (Sky Top, the Trapps, the Near Trapps and Millbrook), only the Trapps and portions of the Near Trapps are completely within the Preserve boundaries. Climbing at Sky Top is only allowed if you are an overnight guest of the Mohonk Mountain House, and only while escorted by an authorized rock climbing guide. For further information, go to their web site www.mohonk.com. Millbrook is divided between the Preserve and several private landowners whose property begins in the valley below.

A day-use pass or annual membership is required to use the Mohonk Preserve. These may be obtained at the Preserve's trailheads, including the Mohonk Preserve Visitor Center on Route 44-55 (see map). Memberships may also be obtained by mail at PO Box 715, New Paltz, NY 12561, telephone 845-255-0919, or by visiting their web site www.

mohonkpreserve.org. The fees are used to defray the costs of maintaining the land and facilities, and to support the Preserve's environmental education and field research programs. Preserve Rangers aim to help climbers in many ways, but they do not instruct or advise climbers, nor are they responsible for warning visitors of dangerous conditions or practices.

The Shawangunks Ridge is a popular area close to a number of large cities and is subject to ever-increasing population pressures. All types of climbers use the cliffs and the surrounding area, along with mountain bikers, hikers, walkers, bird watchers, and fall-foliage leaf-peepers. Climbing is only one facet of the land and its use, and it cannot take place in isolation from the larger community of land users; they deserve our respect, as do the flora and fauna.

PARKING:

On busy weekends in the spring, summer and fall, plan to arrive early to ensure a parking space at one of the Preserve's parking facilities at the West Trapps Trailhead, Warwarsing or Mohonk Preserve Visitor Center parking lots (See map). Please note that parking along Route 44-55 is illegal and dangerous. Also consider carpooling as a way to minimize congestion in the parking lots. Please park as close to other cars as possible so as to maximize space for everyone.

WHERE TO PARK:

The most popular choice for parking when climbing in the Nears is the West Trapps Trailhead parking lot, just a few hundred yards west of the "steel bridge" that goes over Route 44-55 and connects the Trapps and the Near Trapps. The area holds about 120 cars and is open from the early morning to 8 PM daily. It's a very convenient walk along the West Trapps Connector trail to the steel bridge. Be careful crossing the highway and walking down to the Nears trailhead, especially on the weekends. One can avoid crossing the road to the Nears by crossing over the steel bridge and then cut through the campground and down to the Nears' base trail near Kansas City.

The other alternative is to park at the Warwarsing parking lot, but that makes for a long hike to the Nears. The entrance is located about 100 yards downhill from the hairpin turn and just uphill from the Preserve's Visitor Center (look for signs). From here, take the East Trapps Connector trail (otherwise known as "The Stairmaster") to meet the Undercliff Road near the "Strictly From Nowhere" (140) approach trail. If you park at the Visitor Center, the East Trapps Connector trail will take you the to Warwarsing parking lot.

WHERE TO CAMP:

NY STATE DEPARTMENT OF ENVIRONMENTAL CONSERVATION MULTIPLE-USE-AREA: Located on Route 299 just 1/2 mile east of Route 44/55 in Gardiner. Camping is free; however, there are no amenities other than a portable outhouse. It's a first-come-first-served area, so it's best to get there early. This area is threatened with closure by the DEC due to complaints by neighbors of noisy parties and lack of proper toilet facilities. For more information, contact:

DEC Regional Office
South Putt Corners Road
New Paltz, NY 12561
845-256-3000

TRAPPS CAMP:

Commonly known as Camp Slime, is on the Preserve property near the steel bridge on Route 44-55. It is a first-come-first-served area at no additional charge. Directions for use are posted on bulletin board at the camp's entrance. Its features include a short walk to the portable outhouses and to spring water at the Überfall. For more information, contact the Preserve. This campground and the multiple use area may someday be closed if a proposed new campground is developed nearby.

OTHER CAMP GROUNDS:

Creekview Campsites
227 Creek Locks Rd.
Rosendale, NY 12472
845-658-9142
www.creekviewcampsite.com

Tuthilltown Grist Mill
20 Grist Mill Lane
Gardiner, NY 12525
845-255-5695
www.tuthilltown.com

APPROPRIATE BEHAVIOR FOR GUNKS CLIMBERS

As being something of a rebel in my past, I do not enjoy telling others how to behave. But because of the tenfold increase in the numbers of weekend climbers in recent decades (there are over 40,000 climber visits per year), all of us today have a responsibility to be more aware of how personal conduct can affect the pleasure and safety of others, and also the integrity of the environment. To be sure, the Preserve has regulations about climber conduct–i.e. no cutting down trees or rock trundling, no chipping or chopping of holds, no radios—but these don't go far enough.

If the Gunks are to retain a character different from a climbing gym, climbers must voluntarily conduct themselves with courtesy, consideration and an understanding of their environmental impacts. Very small deeds, when multiplied, can have distasteful consequences. For instance, if half a dozen parties climbing within 30 feet of each other all scatter their packs' contents across the base trail, hikers who navigate these litter piles will feel that something of the outdoor experience is being denied them. Moreover, these 'pack dumps' lead to the creation of "rogue" or "maverick" trails which cause erosion. The solution, obviously, is for everyone to keep as much gear as possible in their packs, and to stash them off the trail while climbing. What follows are standards of appropriate behavior which, when adopted, will enhance the pleasure of climbing at the Gunks for everyone.

NOISE: Shouting, whooping and hollering can be great fun. There can also be moments of stress on a climb when screaming to your belayer is absolutely necessary. But many climbers shouting simultaneously give the cliffs the atmosphere of a ballpark. Please limit using the top of your voice. If there is a high wind or a lot of distance between climbers, set up some rope or hand-signals beforehand. Some climbers have diminished the overall noise by use of walkie-talkies. These are especially useful on climbs near the highway and climbs above and opposite the intersection of route 44-55 and 299, the Mountain Brauhaus and Mountain Bistro, when the din of cars, trucks and Harley Davidson motorcycles fills the air

LITTER: When leaving the base of a climb or hiking the trails, be vigilant about picking up litter (whether or not it is yours): climbing tape, cigarette butts, food wrappers, bottle caps, plastic doo-dads.

RAPPELLING: The Nears has only two bolted belay/rappel anchors at this time and they are not identified on the route photos as in The Trapps, but are identified in the route descriptions for Route **35 FAT CITY DIRECT 5.10d PG ★★★**, located near the original second pitch belay spot, and on Route **155 MAIN LINE 5.8 PG ★★★**. Almost all rappels are from trees with fixed webbing/perlon and screw links or rappel rings; some of these are identified in the cliff photos with a letter "R" icon designation. There are too many rappel stations for all to be shown. Do not rappel from trees without using rappel slings; otherwise rope burn will kill the tree. The soil around the trees is easily disturbed, and we should all be careful not to disturb this soil or stand on the roots. It is extremely important to check the webbing/perlon for obvious safety reasons. It is important for rappellers to give adequate warnings to those below and, where possible, lower or snake their ropes down rather than throwing them. Always wait a few seconds after giving verbal warning before throwing your ropes.

DOGS: Preserve regulations say that dogs must be kept on a leash and never left unattended. Preserve Rangers have the right to remove unattended, aggressive, non-stop barking or whining dogs. Aggressive dogs are a particular problem, whether tied up or on a leash; they will often attack other dogs or growl and threaten climbers along the base trail. People with difficult dogs should leave them at home and save everyone from their bad behavior. Remember also that the entire talus slope is in a very precarious condition: a dog that loves to cool down by digging tummy pits contributes greatly to soil erosion.

CALL OF NATURE: At this time there are two portable outhouses located at the Northwest side of the steel bridge (This is the closest location to the Nears). In 2003 a new outhouse was placed alongside the carriage road in the Trapps near the climb Boston (60). It's very important that everyone use these service stations and not relieve themselves randomly in the woods. Should you feel the call of nature while climbing, descend from the base of the cliffs at least 50 feet into a sheltered part of the talus and do your business. Make sure you pack out your used toilet paper.

LEADERS' RIGHTS: Nowadays many climbs are frequently both led and toproped. It happens sometimes that parties using each of these styles arrive on the scene simultaneously. Because this is a trad climbing area, custom dictates that the party that plans to lead has the right to go first. This means that no party that is climbing one route in order to toprope an adjoining route should try to claim that route and stop another party from leading it.

TOPROPERS: If you have led a climb to set up a toprope for your friends, please have the courtesy to not hog or tie up this climb for too long, and never leave your rope hanging there unattended, or you may find it laying on the ground.

PRECEDENCE OF CLIMBERS OVER RAPPELLERS: Should there be a lead climber on the route, rappellers must request permission to rappel and not assume that right. This is both courteous and a good safety practice.

TRAIL EROSION: In recent years the trail along the base of the climbs in the Nears has turned from robust to fragile due to increased climber traffic. Consequently, the Preserve has initiated a long-term rehabilitation program. The beginnings of this effort can be seen in various sections along the entire length of the approach trail. Volunteers have spent literally hundreds of backbreaking hours doing this work. The single largest project in the Nears to date was done at the base of the White Pillar #121. The trails will only survive if climbers use them and do not stray off onto personal detours. Should you wish to volunteer for trail work, please visit the Preserve's web site (www.mohonkpreserve.org) or ask a Preserve Ranger how to sign up.

CHALK: Limit the use of chalk. First, because it is visually ugly and detracts from the natural beauty of the rock. Second, too much chalk makes holds slippery. A climber gets better traction using less, rather than more chalk (think "less is more"). I recommend the use of an inner sock, or chalk ball, inside the chalk bag. If you carry a small brush and see egregious chalk accumulation, remove it. This can easily be done if you are being lowered from a one-pitch climb. Please don't leave tick marks. It's insulting and annoying to those climbers who like to figure out moves for themselves.

BETA: Volunteering beta to climbers on a route is a no-no. Doing so is basically an ego trip, otherwise known as "spraying." Don't volunteer beta unless someone ASKS for it, and then only give it sparingly. Let's keep the challenge pure. Climbers feel so much better when they figure out the moves for themselves.

CELL PHONES: As in the theatre, keep all cell phones turned off. If you must use them, walk away from others and talk as quietly as possible. Ones' private conversations are an inexcusable imposition on other people near you. Remember: in the beginning was silence.

SAFETY: Crowded cliffs mean an increased likelihood of rock fall and pieces of gear coming out of the sky. In heavily traveled areas of the cliff wear a helmet at all times. If you must bring along spectators or dogs or babies, remember they are also at risk.

SMOKERS: Please don't. It's incredibly unhealthy and inconsiderate to your fellow climbers and it's also a fire hazard. If you do smoke, please be thoughtful enough to stand downwind and take your butts back home with you.

CLIMBING ETHICS AND STYLE

ETHICS is about good and bad behavior. In this context "good" ethics reflects a respect for the integrity of the environment—e.g. picking up trash. And bad ethics lead to alteration or damage to the rock and the surrounding environment, such as placing bolts or pitons and chipping or manufacturing holds. The land and cliff owners, the Mohonk Preserve, has firmly stated what the rules of conduct will be: There will be no new placement of bolts or pitons, no chopping of existing bolts, no chipping of holds and no cutting of trees or trundling of rocks or boulders. The Preserve may revoke violators' climbing privileges.

STYLE, on the other hand, refers to the form, philosophy and standards concerning the actual manner in which climbing is done, and is left to the individual. Once upon a time in the Gunks there were strongly held views on the appropriate style. (Would you believe it, from the 60s through the 70s the best style demanded a climber who fell, leading or seconding, be immediately lowered all the way to the beginning of the pitch?) Nowadays there are other choices, including hangdogging, redpointing, toproping and pinkpointing. Anything goes. Even so, climbers should be aware that not all styles are equal. There is a hierarchy. On sight, ground-up leading is clearly the purest style.

CLIMBING GEAR, ROPES, ETC.

All the climbs in the Gunks require technical climbing equipment and knowledge of its use. It is not the purpose of this guide to explain climbing technique or the use of climbing gear.

ROPES: The standard rope today is 60-meters, or 200 feet (up from 50, which was popular some years past). This preference is mainly because some rappels are 100 feet long. Many climbers prefer double ropes (60-meter) for their versatility in reducing rope drag through overhanging sections and on traverses. Double ropes reduce the number of rappels required; you can usually reach the ground in one shot from the Not So Grand Traverse Ledge—written as "NSGTLedge" or "NSGTL" throughout this guide.

GEAR: You'll need a good variety of just about everything from the smallest steel and/or brass wired nuts to the largest. As for camming devices, you'll want to cover the size range from very small to very large cams (0.34 to 0.54 inches up to 2.0 to 3.4 inches). Larger cams are sometimes necessary and are usually mentioned in the route description. Since I mostly use the larger Black Diamond cams, the chart below may be helpful for cam size conversions. Extra carabiners, quick draws, over-the-shoulder runners, etc. are also very necessary.

Climb if you will, but remember that courage and strength are nothing without prudence, and that a momentary negligence may destroy the happiness of a lifetime.

—Edward Whymper, after his rope broke on the Matterhorn.

CHART OF BLACK DIAMOND CAMS		
UNIT	**COLOR**	**RANGE**
.5	Purple	0.75" to 1.25"
.75	Green	0.96" to 1.58"
1	Red	1.19" to 2.0"
2	Gold	1.5" to 2.5"
3	Blue	2.0" to 3.4"
3.5	Black	2.4" to 4.1"
4	Purple	2.9" to 4.9"
4.5	Red	3.3" to 5.8"

NOTE: In the Fall of 2004 Black Diamond released new, redesigned spring loaded camming devices. These new devices may have a range different from those listed in the chart above.

Toad

RATINGS AND GRADES OF CLIMBS

The Yosemite Decimal System (YDS) is used to describe the climb's relative difficulty from 5.0 to 5.13. These ratings are based on a consensus of experienced climbers from all over the world. In the 1970s, Jim Bridwell subdivided grades at 5.10 and above into a,b,c and d sub-grades. (5.10a = 5.10-, 5.10 b/c = 5.10, 5.10d = 5.10+). Generally speaking, if the difficulty of a climb is height-related or if protection is strenuous or difficult to place, it will be referenced as such.

GRADE COMPARISON				
USA	**FRENCH**	**UK**	**AUSTRALIA**	**UIAA**
5.2				II
5.3				III
5.4		D		IV-
5.5		D-VD		IV
5.6		VD-S		IV+
5.7		VS		V-
5.8	5a	VS-HVS-E1		V
5.9	5b	HVS-E1-E2		V
5.10a	5c	E1-E2-E3		V+
5.10b	6a	E2-E3		VI-
5.10c	6a+	E2-E3-E4	18	VI
5.10d	6b	E3-E4	19	VI+
5.11a	6b+	E3-E4-E5	20	VII-
5.11b	6c	E4-E5	21	VII
5.11c	6c+	E4-E5-E6	22	VII+
5.11d	7a	E4-E5-E6	23	VIII-
5.12a	7a+	E5-E6-E7	24	VIII
5.12b	7b	E5-E6-E7	25	VIII+
5.12c	7b+	E6-E7-E8	26	IX-
5.12d	7c	E6-E7-E8	27	IX
5.13a	7c+	E7-E8-E9	28	IX
5.13b	8a	E7-E8-E9	29	IX+
5.13c	8a+	E7-E8-E9	30	X-
5.13d	8b	E8-E9-E10		X

PROTECTION GRADINGS

The protection grades, G, PG, R and X are used to describe the quality and availability of protection for the crux of a particular pitch or climb. Many people think G is for "good" and PG means "protection good or pretty good or even, pretty grim," Not so. These terms come from the Hollywood yardsticks for describing violence or sex in a movie: G is good for "general release" and PG is "parental guidance" suggested. The system's whimsical inventor was Jim Erickson in his Colorado guide of 1980 called Rocky Heights. A protection grade has nothing to do with how difficult or strenuous it might be to place that protection; it is telling the climber about **the level of security that a placement is likely to offer**. When it's unusually difficult or strenuous to place protection, this guide may take note. If certain parts of a pitch are more poorly protected than others, this is usually mentioned; one example is Near Trapps route 42: SHIT FACE. Pitch one's crux is 5.10c PG but there is a 5.8 R section after the crux. Also, given the overhanging nature of some of the routes found in this guide, very long falls may be taken where there is no risk of hitting anything except air and, therefore, may be considered PG.

◆ **"G"** implies good protection that is closely spaced so that only short falls are likely.

◆ **"PG"** implies that the protection is more widely spaced or not so good, and that moderately long falls are likely, up to about 15 feet. Keep in mind that on extremely overhanging climbs, a 50-foot fall is considered PG if there is nothing to hit but air.

◆ **"R"** implies that the protection is widely spaced or relatively poor in quality and that a long fall (over 20 feet) is likely, with a pretty good chance of hitting a ledge or something else and getting hurt, or it could be that a short fall guarantees hitting a ledge. Also many "R" rated routes have unprotected boulder problem starts that can be made safer with a good "spot."

◆ **"X"** Implies there is NO protection to keep you from being very seriously injured or killed. I am not recommending "R-X" or "X" routes.

◆ **DIFFICULT or STRENUOUS TO PROTECT:** Means that it takes a lot of work, strength, energy and/or ability to place protection properly.

ROUTE DESCRIPTIONS

The first feature of the route description is the name line, which includes the number and name of the route, the difficulty grade from (5.0-5.13), the protection grade (G, PG, R, X, or combinations thereof), the quality rating (0-3 stars), and the word "toprope" if the route is a toprope climb or recommended "As a Toprope."

◆ **START:** Identifies the specific feature that marks the beginning of the route and relates it to one or more nearby climbs.

◆ **TOPROPE:** Means that the first ascent put up the route on toprope. For example,

Route 55a: **(TOPROPE)** Believe It Or Not 5.12a

◆ **As a Toprope:** (*The symbol is a grey diamond* "◆") Appears immediately below the route name and means that the route is recommended to be climbed on TOPROPE even though it was originally led. These "As a Toprope" climbs are horror shows to lead. For example,

Route 55: **TO BE OR NOT TO BE 5.12a PG ★★★
(As a Toprope)**

◆ **LINK-UP:** These are climbs that combine various pitches of different climbs to make for a more consistently graded/quality route. For example,

Route **32a (LINK-UP) 5.8 PG ★★★ Dog-Stick Ridge**
Route Descriptions (continued)

This route combines portions of four separate climbs. Each pitch is in the 5.8 range, each with a different variety of moves and exposure, all of which makes this a ★★★ star route.

Most route line drawings on the photo pages are drawn in black, others are also drawn in white or a combination of black and white. The routes are drawn in white because sometimes the black line is very hard or impossible to see in dark/shaded areas.

Copperhead snake

ROUTE QUALITY RATINGS

This guide's star ratings are built on consensus and are not infallible: you won't always agree with it and, as in every climbing area, you may climb an un-starred route and have a great experience.

All recommended routes are printed in **bold** lettering, meaning that the climb is at least average, and therefore worth doing.

★★★ *Three Stars.* A don't miss Gunks classic, great quality, moves, rock and exposure. For example:

Route **22: GRAND CENTRAL 5.9 PG ★★★**

★★ *Two Stars.* Quality route with good/great moves. For example: Route **67: LOOSE GOOSE 5.6 PG ★★**

★ *One Star.* Better than average. For example:

Route **158: INSIDE OUT 5.9 G ★**

No Stars. A climb worth doing. For example:

Route **106: BM 5.8 PG**

Route number in bold (with route name in non-bold) Only certain pitches are recommended. For example:

Route **107**: Slab Shtick 5.8 PG

–or–

A climb or pitch listed in non-bold CAPITAL letters. Once in a while you will see a climb that falls into a grey area–not quite recommendable but not bad either. For example:

Route **109**: HIGHWAY 51 5.7 PG

No bold type. Most people wouldn't like this climb.

For example:

Route 60: CORPORATE CONGLOMERATE 5.9 PG

(NR) *Not Recommended.* Dangerous, dirty or loose rock etc. For example:

Route 69: **(NR)** Ain't This Yab Yum? 5.5 PG

ROUTE DEFINITIONS

CRACK: A vertical crack, seam or fissure in the rock, distinct from a "horizontal crack" or "horizontal" which is always referred to as such.

LEFT-FACING CORNER: The corner's side or face, faces left and can vary in depth from inches to yards.

RIGHT-FACING CORNER: The corner's side or face, faces right, and can vary in depth from inches to yards.

OPEN BOOK: An inside corner that faces straight out, neither left-facing nor right-facing (like an open book that's being read).

OVERHANGS, CEILINGS AND ROOFS: Overhangs vary in size along their length and depth; different parts of them may be referred to as an overhang, a ceiling or a roof. Sizes are approximate. Ceilings and roofs may be tiered and composed of a series of smaller overhangs.

◆ **A BULGE:** Smaller than an overhang, basically the rock face bulges out steeper than the face below it.

◆ **An OVERHANG:** Is described as an "overhang" when it sticks out approximately 3 feet or less in size

◆ **A CEILING:** When it's between approximately 3 and 6 feet in size.

◆ **A ROOF:** When it's greater than 6 feet in size.

TREES: Trees are often used as reference points even though they don't last forever, so use other references as backup.

VARIATIONS: Are variations of an established route. They usually do not have an original start or finish. They are indicated by V1, V2, etc. at the point where they start on the pitch. If a variation has no grade, it means that it is no harder than the grade of the route.

OLD PITONS: Often used to help in route-finding, even though some of these old relics will disappear in time.

FIRST ASCENTS AND FIRST FREE ASCENTS

At the bottom of each route description are the names of those who did the first ascent (FA) and the year in which it was done.

First Free Ascents (FFA) tells who first climbed completely free a route that had originally required some aid, whether it's a shoulder stand, holding on to a piton/nut or using etriers, etc.

A single name on the credit line usually means that the leader was belayed and no one could or would follow, or it was done on self-belay.

NEW ROUTE INFORMATION

Please send new route information, corrections and constructive criticism to:

Dick Williams
510 Mohonk Road
High Falls, NY 12440

Black snake

USEFUL INFORMATION FOR THE VISITING CLIMBER

WHEN TO VISIT AND WHAT TO EXPECT

The best times to climb here are in the Spring and Fall seasons. Spring weather, mid-March to the end of May, is usually dry except for April showers, with a temperature range from about 50 to 80 degrees F. The weather can be a gamble though; it can be exceptionally wet, as in the unusual Spring, Summer and Fall of 2003.

June, July and August can be debilitatingly hot (up to 95-100 degree's or so), with 90% humidity during the worst 3 weeks of Summer.

September to early November is usually great (about 55-80 degrees). October seems to be almost everyone's favorite: comfortable temperatures and spectacular Fall foliage.

BLACK FLIES, SNAKES, DEER TICKS, LYME DISEASE

By June, at about the same time as the beautiful mountain laurels begin to blossom, the nasty, blood sucking black flies and mosquitoes appear. They can make life pretty miserable, but you can get used to them with the help of bug dope.

You may also encounter black rat snakes (non-poisonous), copperheads and the rare timber rattlesnake (both poisonous). People who know where to look can find dozens of them right along the carriage road. Keep a careful lookout when scrambling up the talus trails on the way to and from climbs because these snakes can be well camouflaged in fallen leaves between boulders. Generally they won't bother you if you don't bother them.

Another and growing concern is Lyme disease caused by infected deer ticks. Its incidence has been on the rise throughout the Northeastern U.S. There is a huge deer population in the area surrounding the cliffs—between a low of 600 to a high of 800 by some estimates.

SUMMER HEAT, CHIGGERS, BEES and WASPS

Because July and August can be debilitatingly hot, locals climb early, from 7 or 8am till about 1pm, take a break in the shade till about 4pm and then climb till dark. This is also the time when CHIGGER LARVAE are prevalent (microscopic). They hang out on grassy ledges, and as you climb past they jump onto you, pierce the skin (usually at a hair follicle) and inject into you a salivary secretion containing powerful, digestive enzymes that break down skin cells that they ingest (tissues become liquefied and sucked up). After a larva is fully fed in four days, it drops off of you, leaving a red welt with a white, hard central area on the skin that itches severely. If you scratch them, they will itch even more and will eventually begin to bleed and may become infected. There is no antidote to ease the itching other than not to scratch them. The best prevention I have found to avoid them in the first place is by rubbing some Flowers of Sulfur/Sulfur Sublimed powder around your waist and crotch (where they like to reside—tight, sweaty places). DEET also seems to work.

Wasps and their nest.

More serious than chiggers though are ground-nesting yellow jackets. They have made many vicious attacks on climbers, hikers and dogs. The nests in some seasons can be numerous, particularly when it is dry, so keep a sharp eye out. A good way to check for them is to stand still near where you want to belay and look for a steady stream of bee movement to and from their nests in the ground, usually a small hole near the base of a tree or rock.

Wasps can be a very serious problem while climbing. Many a climber has reached up for an out-of-sight hold and been attacked and stung. Their sting isn't as severe as the ground-nesting yellow jacket's, but all the same, painful, so always keep a sharp eye out for them. Back in the 70s there was a huge infestation of wasps, so bad in fact that many a climber carried a wasp bomb on a sling as part of their lead protection gear so as to destroy the huge dinner-plate-size wasp nests called "death stars."

ANNUAL WEATHER PATTERNS					
MONTH	**MEAN**	**MIN**	**MAX**	**RAIN**	**SNOW**
January	26.4 °F	-17 °F	65 °F	3.38"	16.5"
February	24.2 °F	-20 °F	68 °F	3.49"	15.4"
March	36.5 °F	-8 °F	80 °F	3.71"	11.0"
April	45.7 °F	5 °F	88 °F	4.00"	2.7"
May	57.4 °F	23 °F	91 °F	3.63"	trace
June	65.1 °F	33 °F	95 °F	3.93"	0"
July	69.8 °F	43 °F	96 °F	4.49"	0"
August	67.5 °F	39 °F	94 °F	4.82"	0"
September	61.5 °F	28 °F	93 °F	4.08"	0"
October	50.4 °F	19 °F	84 °F	3.59"	trace
November	40.3 °F	3 °F	72 °F	3.14"	12.9"
December	27.7 °F	-24 °F	63 °F	3.64"	12.6"

NEW PALTZ AREA INFORMATION

New Paltz is the nearest town to the Gunks, located just west of NYS Thruway Exit 18, along Route 299 (Main Street) 6 miles east of the cliffs.

I would highly recommend visiting the local climbing store, Rock and Snow, and talking to the sales people for all kinds of beta on where to eat, sleep and camp. Visit their web site at www.rockandsnow.com. This is the place not only to purchase the latest in equipment and clothing, but to meet your friends and find out the latest about what gear or beta you might need on some climb you're interested in.

ROCK AND SNOW (established in 1970)
44 Main Street
New Paltz, N.Y. 12561
Tel: 845-255-1311
www.rockandsnow.com

◆ For more information about New Paltz, restaurants, hotels, motels, B & B's, camping and much more, go to: www.newpaltzchamber.org. Tel: 845-255-0243

◆ For information on climbing, biking, hiking, etc., go to www.gunks.com

◆ For information about the Mohonk Preserve, including climbing, camping and regulations, go to www. mohonkpreserve.org. Tel: 845-255-0919 or drop by their visitor center on Route 44-55. (See map.)

◆ Also, there is the Ulster County Chamber of Commerce; go to: www.ulsterchamber.org

TRANSPORTATION

Public bus transportation is available to New Paltz from the larger nearby cities. Since there is no public transportation from New Paltz to the cliffs, climbers will have to take a taxi, hitchhike, or try to bum a ride from other climbers going to the cliffs.

PLACES TO EAT NEAR THE CLIFFS

There is a restaurant and a convenience store on Route 44-55, just 2 miles downhill from the cliffs. The Mountain Brauhaus (845-255-9766) restaurant is on the corner of Route 44-55 & Route 299. A deli-type convenience store is just across the road (The Bistro Mountain Store, 845-255-2999). This is a convenient and popular meeting place before and after the day's climbing.

PLACES TO EAT IN THE VILLAGE OF NEW PALTZ

There are too many restaurants and bars to list, so I've just included some of the more popular ones in the downtown (Village) area.

Gilded Otter, (brewery, burgers) 3 Main St.	845-256-1700
La Stazione, (Italian), 5 Main St.	845-256-9447
The Loft, 46 Main St.	845-255-1426
Neko Sushi, (Japanese), 49 Main St.	845-255-0162
Yanni's, (Greek), 51 Main St.	845-256-0988
Bacchus, (Mexican), 4 South Chestnut St.	845-255-8636
Main Street Bistro, 59 Main St.	845-255-7766
Gourmet Pizza, 68 Main St..	845-255-2666
Hokkaido, (Japanese), 18 Church St..	845-256-0621
The Bakery, 13A North Front St.	845-255-8840
Earthgoods, (health food), 71 Main St.	845-255-5858
Jack's Meat & Deli, 79 Main St.	845-255-2244
Mexicali Blue, (Mexican), 87 Main St.	845-255-5551
P & G's, 91 Main St. (burgers).	845-255-6161
Toscani and Sons (Italian Deli), 119 Main St.	845-255-6770

PLACES TO EAT (continued)

Plus, there are some great places to eat in Kingston, Poughkeepsie and High Falls; check the yellow pages for more information.

MOVIE THEATERS

New Paltz Cinema   845-255-0420

INDOOR CLIMBING

The **INNER WALL**, has over 4000 square feet of climate controlled climbing, a cave and a lead wall, known as the "wave." Located on Main St. behind the Rite Aid Pharmacy. Tel: 845-255-7625 (ROCK).

LOCAL ROCK CLIMBING GUIDES

Approved by the AMGA (American Mountain Guides Association) and The Mohonk Preserve.

ALPINE ENDEAVORS
P.O. Box 58, Rosendale, NY 12472
Tel: 845-658-3094
www.alpineendeavors.com

EASTERN MOUNTAIN SPORTS (EMS)
Route 44-55 at Route 299, Gardiner, NY 12525
Tel: 800-310-4504
www.emsclimb.com

HIGH XPOSURE ADVENTURES
8 Nichols Road, Armonk, NY 10504
Tel: 800-777-2546
www.high-xposure.com

MOUNTAIN SKILLS
P.O. Box 991 New Paltz, NY 12561
Tel: 845-853-5450
www.mountainskills.biz

THE GUNKS GUIDE
134 Minnewaska Trail, Kerhonkson, NY 12446
Tel: 888-812-0345
www.thegunksguide.com

THE NEAR TRAPPS

The Near Trapps is the second most popular cliff in the Shawangunks because of its ease of access and the high quality of its clean and colorful rock--at least on the northern section, between Kansas City and Loose Goose. The quality deteriorates/degenerates in the central section but with exceptions. The quality returns again on the southern section, beyond Interlewd, and stays good to the end of the cliff (with exceptions of course). There is a ledge system that traverses the cliff beginning near where Birdcage (53) tops out and goes all the way to where Parsifal and Potato Chips finishes (131), but it varies dramatically, and for the greater part there are only short sections one can comfortably traverse without great concern about knocking off loose rocks and boulders. I have dubbed this ledge system The Not So Grand Traverse Ledge or NSGTL.

Rockfall, especially in the central section (almost always above the first pitches, and more recently near Gelsa (56) and Lonely Challenge (67) (spring 2006) and near Rock Around The Clock (89) and Flake, Rattle, and Roll (90) (2007), can be a definite hazard because the approach trail runs directly along the base of the cliff. Climbers high above and way out of sight could easily dislodge a deadly rock missile onto you or your partner's head. Many climbs are the "trust but verify" type of climbs; some holds look good but aren't and visa versa. The loose rock will probably never clear up as well as it has in the Trapps (there wasn't as much loose rock there in the first place), even after more of the climbs have been traveled. Climbers should always exercise great care and caution when climbing or when using the trail along the base of the cliff; many people think it's good idea to always wear a helmet. The Nears is nothing like the Trapps once you move south of Bird Land; it is complicated with route finding problems, lichen and loose rock. This area is NOT for the sport climber or the novice trad-climber. Beware!

The trail, which extends along the entire cliff, starts between the telephone pole and the road sign on the south side of Route 44-55, just east of the steel bridge and approximately 285 feet uphill from the scenic overlook on Route 44-55. Follow the trail 200 feet past boulders to the base of the cliff near Kansas City (1).

To descend from most of the climbs between Kansas City and Birdland, follow the "blue trail" that runs along the top of the cliff north to an unmarked descent trail that cuts down to the approach trail near Kansas City. To descend from climbs on the southern end, walk south to a gully between the Near Trapps and Bayards (Smede's Cove) that leads down to the base of the southern-most end of the cliff (there is a spring there). Then follow the cliff-base trail back north to other climbs.

There are many rappel trees on routes and at the top of the cliff. Some of these rappel trees or threaded rap stations are identified by the "R" symbol on the route photos. Please note that not all rappel stations are listed; there are just too many to identify and would clog up the route line drawings.

It's recommended to use double ropes on the multi–pitch climbs, especially along the highest part of the cliff, not only for rope management but also for the rappels. You may want to carry a small day pack or summit pack with some goodies, like food and water (especially on those long hot summer days) and maybe even bring a wind or rain shirt depending on the time of year. It is always a good idea to bring some extra webbing and descending rings on the not so popular climbs and/or multi-pitch routes.

During the week in Spring through Fall, there is tremendous noise from trucks, and during the weekends, from motorcycles and general busy traffic. It's a good idea to bring walkie talkies when climbing between Kansas City and the White Pillar.

This guide took an especially long time to compile because of all the route-finding adventures on so many of the climbs that I needed to do to make this guide book as accurate as possible. Also in that process many new one-pitch climbs were put up adding to the mix.

There were some climbs or pitches that I attempted but did not climb or refused to climb owing to their poor quality: all three pitches of Three Generations, pitch two of Easter Time Too, Day Tripper, You're In The Wrong Place My Friend, Vulgatits as well as others.

I apologize for the inaccuracy in some route line-drawings where the cliff features were obscured by shadows formed by trees, making it difficult to accurately draw in the route lines.

Black bear

Photo: Lararne Mai

Black Turkey Vulture

The first three climbs described here are to the *RIGHT* of *Kansas City* and *Topeka*, just right of where the approach trail meets the cliff. They were supposedly first climbed in the 1950s or 60s. No soft iron pitons were found and no chromolly piton scars were found. The climbs are pretty much fun depending on one's individual tolerance for dealing with lichen and vegetation.

B-RIGHT   INDEPENDENCE 5.4 G
    START: 15 feet right of Topeka at a short seam with ferns and a laurel bush about 8-10 feet up.
    PITCH 1: 5.4 G Climb to a good right-pointing flake-like hold (crux), then up past overhang to a black birch tree. Continue up past a laurel bush and right-facing corner to the overhang. Move around left and go up into the open book. Climb its right face past a football-size chockstone to the top. (50 ft.)

C-RIGHT   ST. LOUIS 5.5 G
    Some good moves at the beginning and finish.
    START: 37 feet right of Topeka and 22 feet right of Independence at a short hand-crack below a left-facing corner capped by an overhang.
    PITCH 1: 5.5 G Climb crack and corner to the overhang. Step up right and up easiest way to final overhang. Move left and work past left-leaning, right-facing corner (crux, blue Camalot) to the top. (50 ft.)

D-RIGHT   WICHITA 5.3 PG
    Start: 53 feet right of Topeka and 15 feet right of St. Louis at a four-foot high crack below two right-facing flakes which are at the far right end of the cliff.
    Pitch 1: 5.3 G Climb past the major left-jutting flake to the overhang, step/move left up past easy overhang and move up onto slab. Step up (crux) and run it out to the top. (45 ft.)

Matt Jasinsky, Vadim Marcovallo and Tim Kelly on *Kansas City 5.12b (Route 1)* Photo: Mike Freeman

A1　　　　　　　**TOPEKA 5.10a G ★**

Good climbing via the route described. Originally, a variation that began at the retreat/back-off anchors at base of Kansas City's roof. Best guess is that it was first climbed with aid back in the 50's.

START: At the first, large, blocky left-facing corner below the first roof in the Nears. This corner is where Kansas City originally started.

PITCH 1: 5.10a G Follow corner to final overhang that's about 10 feet below roof. Work straight up past overhang and corner (old pin) to the roof. Then finger traverse right (crux) to the nose and climb straight past overhang (long reach) to the top. (60 ft.)

1　　　　　　　**KANSAS CITY 5.12b G ★★**

Strenuous, sequency and wild. There was a time when some found it easier to do barefoot–ouch!

START: The original start was in the left-facing corner described in Topeka. One can also start 10 feet left of Topeka or start on Outer Space.

PITCH 1: 5.12b G Climb one way or another up past overhangs to the base of roof and retreat/back-off anchors. Climb crack in roof to the top.

FA 1962: Dick Williams and Dave Craft

FFA 1973: John Bragg

Success is not the key to happiness.
Happiness is the key to success.
If you love what you are doing,
you will be successful.
　　— Albert Schweitzer

2   **OUTER SPACE 5.8 PG ★**

A pretty neat climb, it's harder than it looks and has some good moves. The Direct Finish is pretty wild, often reached by starting on Le Plie or Crass.

START: 20 feet left of Topeka's blocky left-facing corner, below a short slab and just left of a large three-forked oak tree.

PITCH 1: 5.8 PG Climb past a bulge to the overhang with jutting block. Make a move straight up and clip a fixed angle pin (V1), then step back down. Diagonal left on small edges and up to a good horizontal at the ceiling, traverse left to the notch and then move up to the roof (**V2**). Traverse left again for about 20 feet to a sloping platform belay/rap-station (this is where Infinite Space finishes). (80 ft.)

PITCH 2: 5.4 PG Move up left to small ledge, then climb straight up to the top. (40 ft.)

Variation 1: 5.9 PG Make the thin traverse left to good horizontal.

Variation 2: 5.10b PG (**Direct Finish,** drawn in w/dotted line) Work up past the left side of the jutting overhang (crux), then up a bit right to the top.

FA 1959: Art Gran and Jim Geiser

FA (V2) 1970's: John Stannard

3   **EASY RIDER 5.9- G ★★**

Not a good climb to do on a busy weekend because of crossing other parties and their ropes. The route originally finished on Yellow Ridge. It has some fine features, a good deal of exposure, and many possible starts and finishes, including numerous rappel spots for getting back to the ground. Most of the route stays dry when it's raining, and the photographic possibilities are excellent along the way. The pitches are relatively short to enhance communications and reduce rope drag.

START: Same as for Outer Space.

PITCH 1: 5.8 PG Climb the first pitch of Outer Space. (80 ft.)

PITCH 2: 5.6 G Climb diagonally up left for about 25 feet and then traverse left about 60 feet, following a horizontal

Lynn Hill on *Kansas City* 5.12b (Route 1)

crack system to the Broken Sling notch. Climb the notch and belay. (110 ft.)

PITCH 3: 5.7 G Step down and traverse left under the overhangs. Then reverse the Disneyland traverse and continue left until below the Swing Time open book, just right of the Te Dum crux. Climb up to the Swing Time/Te Dum belay. (90 ft.)

PITCH 4: 5.7 G Step down and left to a small ledge, and traverse left and around a nose to a ledge above the Inverted Layback crux. Then continue left to the large Layback ledge. (50 ft.)

PITCH 5: 5.1 G Traverse about 40 feet straight left along a horizontal crack to the Grand Central belay. (40 ft.)

PITCH 6: 5.9- G Traverse left under the ceilings past two fixed pins to the Alphonse open book. Then continue left along the lower horizontal crack of Alphonse, past the Alphonse optional belay, to the cramped and blocky Yellow Belly belay. (80 ft.)

PITCH 7: 5.6 G Step down and traverse left under the overhangs for about 25 feet, then move up to the Yellow Ridge belay. (30 ft.)

PITCH 8: 5.7 PG Traverse left (following Yellow Ridge) and climb up to the two fixed pins on the Yellow Ridge arête. Move left and down to a short slab and then back up left to a long overhang with flakes stuck up under it. Traverse about 10 feet left and then downclimb 15 feet to a ledge system that is followed to the Baskerville Terrace belay. (60 ft.)

PITCH 9: 5.3 PG Climb 10 feet up Baskerville Terrace to the first overhangs and two old pins. Then traverse about 60 feet left, across Requiem to the Fat City bolt anchors. From here, take the Fat City exit by traversing left, climbing diagonally down left along a ramp to a narrow ledge system that leads 25 feet to a belay in the Gelsa corner. (120 ft.)

FA 1969: Joe Kelsey and Roman Laba

FFA 1981: Mark Robinson and Russ Clune

4   **LE PLIE 5.7- PG ★**

An awkward crux move, even if you're not tall.

START: 35 feet left of Outer Space and 20 feet right of Crass, at the short crack in the slab.

PITCH 1: 5.7- PG Climb crack and slab to the left side of the large wedged block that forms an overhang. Work up past left side of block (crux) and make the very awkward crab-crawl-like traverse left about 10-15 feet to a ledge. Then an easy traverse left about 15 feet to a bulge/small overhang. Move up to a slab and crab-crawl left again to a ledge with some boulders. (90 ft.)

PITCH 2: 5.6 PG Climb up left to the small overhang and then move up to a stance on the slab (crux), move up to the overhangs and traverse right about 20 feet to easier rock and on to the top. (70 ft.)

FA 1957: Art Gran and Roman Sadowy

FFA: Unknown

5   **(LINK-UP) 5.10b PG ★**
CRASS/OUTER SPACE DIRECT FINISH

Good sustained climbing.

START: On Crass, about 20 feet left of Le Plie at a crack that leads up and breaks the ceiling 15 feet up.

PITCH 1: 5.10b PG Climb straight past crack in ceiling (crux-1) to a stance. Then diagonal up right to the large wedged block on Le Plie. Climb past right side of block and diagonal up right to the notch (5.8 R). Then up notch to the roof and move left a few feet. Work straight up past the left side of the jutting overhang (crux-2) and up a bit right to the top. (60 ft.)

Just worry about what you can control.
    — Nicky Hayden, 2006 World Motorcycle GP Champion

5a   CRASS 5.10b PG

START: About 20 feet left of Le Plie at a crack that leads up and breaks the ceiling 15 feet up.

PITCH 1: 5.10b PG Climb straight past crack in ceiling (crux) (V1) to the roof and base of big, but short right-facing corner. Move up corner to roof (V2) and hand traverse left and up to ledge to join Le Plie.

Variation 1: 5.9 PG Traverse left 5 feet and then up right to corner.

Variation 2: 5.11a R (Totally Crass) Work straight past roof and up to the top.

FA 1976: Ivan Rezucha and Kevin Bein

FA (V1 on Toprope) 1977: Kevin Bein

FFA (V2) 1989: Rich Gottlieb and Tom Spiegler

5b   Infinite Space 5.12a PG ★★ (Variation)

A great variation that's incredibly clean and finger-friendly. You may think you've got it made till you get to the last crux move and realize "it ain't over yet baby." A real endurance test piece.

Pitch 1: 5.12a PG Start on Crass or Le Plie and climb past the block to the notch and horizontal crack. Hand traverse left about 20 feet and then work up past the thin cracks (crux) that break the final roof to the rap-station.

FA 1981: Rich Romano and Chuck Calef

5c   DOUBLE CROSS-ISSIMA 5.12d R

Start: 10 feet left of Crass, 15 feet right of Iron Cross below vertical seam that breaks the first overhang.

Pitch 1: 5.12d R Climb past seam to second overhang. Work past it at its widest point, then continue up past final overhangs to short face. Move up left to Iron Cross's anchors. (50 ft.)

FA 2007: Andy Salo and Scott Barocas

Jim Strickler on *Infinite Space*, 5.12a (Route 5b)
Photo: Mike Freeman

6 **IRON CROSS 5.12d PG**

Height-related, long reach, very sequency, technical and strenuous.

START: 25 feet left of Crass/Outer Space Direct, and a few feet right of Criss, at thin cracks that rise up through a ceiling to a short right-facing corner capped by a roof.

PITCH 1: 5.12d PG Climb into the corner, pass the roof above from the outside corner, then up to the next roof at a thin crack. Work up crack and do the "iron cross move" (crux) and up to the jugs and rap-station. (80 ft.)

FA 1978: John Bragg

7 **CRISS 5.11a PG**

A fairly popular lead boulder problem that often winds up turning into a **toprope** problem. In 1985 it became a grade harder due to a flake breaking off.

START: About 30 feet left of Crass/Outer Space Direct, below a right-facing corner that begins 8 feet up.

PITCH 1: 5.11a PG Start on the right and diagonal up left to the corner (harder if you climb straight up) then work up to the roof and the rap-station (30 ft.) **or** continue straight up and follow a small, short right-facing corner past an overhang and up to join Criss Cross, which is followed to the Le Plié belay. (50 ft.)

Pitch 2: 5.10c PG Climb straight up to the overhang at a tiny right-jutting flake, move up to some edges and work up a bit right to a stance (crux: strenuous). Finish by climbing past the next overhang at a short right-facing corner to the top. (40 ft.)

FA 1967: John Stannard and Willie Crowther

8 **CRISS CROSS 5.10a PG**

Start: Same as Criss Cross Direct

Pitch 1: 5.10a PG Jam and layback the crack, then straight up past a fixed pin to a long, sharp horizontal crack that leads to the right. Follow the crack for about 10 feet and work up to a small overhang. Step right to the top of a left-facing corner and move up (5.7 R) and a bit right to a tree and another left-facing corner. Ascend this corner till it ends, exit right and move up to the Le Plié belay. (120 ft.)

Pitch 2: 5.7 G Traverse right about 20 feet to a fault that breaks the overhang. Finish by climbing the fault and stepping right and up to the top. (40 ft.)

FA 1959: Jim Andress and Doug Tompkins

FFA 1963: Jim McCarthy

9   CRISS CROSS DIRECT 5.10a PG ★★★

The original route, Criss Cross, begins with a strenuous layback but traverses right after the beginning crux move that was first free-climbed by Jim McCarthy in 1963. The direct continuation is a superior line with excellent moves and is now considered a classic that should not be missed. Too often, the second pitch is not climbed.

START: About 25 feet left of Criss, at a 10 foot high right-facing corner with a hand crack that breaks the bulging overhang above the corner.

PITCH 1: 5.10a PG Jam and layback the crack, then straight up past a fixed pin (crux) and a series of small overhangs to a small stance (optional belay/rap-station. (60 ft.)

PITCH 2: 5.10a PG Step left and climb up just right of a small left-facing corner (5.8 R). Continue past an overhang and move slightly right till beneath a block in the final ceiling. Move out and right along the edge of the block and climb past the overhang (crux) to the top. (70 ft.)

FA 1971: Pete Ramins and John Stannard

10   BETWEEN THE LINES 5.11a/b R

A much less demanding but popular first pitch link-up is to do the first pitch of Broken Sling.

Start: At a small, rounded left-facing corner about 12 feet high, 12 feet right of Broken Sling.

Pitch 1: 5.11a/b R Gain the corner and step right onto the face. Climb face and bulge (no pro) to the overhang, clear the overhang and then climb up left to join Broken Sling. (90 ft.)

PITCH 2: 5.10d PG Traverse left about 15 feet to a prominent nose. Continue left around the nose a few feet and then climb the face past a notch in the overhang. Continue to a small crack and on up to the top. (90 ft.)

FA 1973: John Burns and Gordon MacLeod

11 (**TOPROPE**) Sling Line 5.11a
Start on the face midway between Between the Lines and Broken Sling and climb the face.

12 **BROKEN SLING 5.8 PG** ★★★
A committing, bouldery start. Both pitches have quite a lot of variety; pitch two is particularly thin and intricate.

START: 30 feet left of Crass, at a short nose below a short right-facing corner. There is a massive triangular roof just to the left, about 15 feet up.

PITCH 1: 5.8 PG Work up into the corner and first overhang (V1), then climb straight up crack in overhang to the next overhang. Step right and up the short crack to small ledge and make a belay. (75 ft.)

PITCH 2: 5.8 PG (V2 & V3) Move up a few feet and make the thin, 20-foot traverse right to better holds. Climb past tiny corner to the overhang, then traverse left and climb past a notch and easier rock to the top. (65 ft.) (This pitch was first climbed as a variation to bypass the aid used on the off-width crack on the original route.)

Variation 1: (Original Route) 5.8 PG Step left around the corner and up to a short thin crack. Then step back right to the crack to the regular route.

Variation 2: 5.9+ PG Climb the flaring off-width crack above past the roof, then traverse left and up to the top. (60 ft.)

Variation 3: 5.10b PG (original aid line) Climb to the off-width, traverse right, then up to the notch on the regular route.

FA (Original aid line) 1956: John Turner and Craig Merrihue

FA 1962: (As described) Jim McCarthy
FFA (Original aid line) 1970: Kevin Bein

12a   (**TOPROPE**) Bumkey 5.12a
   Start by climbing the first pitch of Broken Sling. Traverse left about 10-15 feet till below a left-facing corner. Climb the corner to its top, step right and work past two over-hangs to a good stance. Do not exit left here, continue straight up past the final overhang to the pine tree. FA 1994: Dave Lanman

13   SQUAT THRUST 5.12a PG
   Start: Same as Broken Sling.
   Pitch 1: Follow Broken Sling till it traverses right. Then diagonal up left to brightly colored rock at a left-facing corner and work up to a stance. Continue past overhang following a small, overhanging right-facing corner (5.10+ R). Pass the next overhang at thin cracks, traverse right under a third overhang to another thin crack and on to the top. (110 ft.)
   FA 1986: Russ Clune and Jeff Morris

14   **DISNEYLAND 5.6 PG ★★★**
   A great old classic climb. Many people do the whole climb in one pitch with double ropes.
   START: At the left side of the huge triangular roof, 35 feet left of Broken Sling, below huge open book with grass bogs in it.
   PITCH 1: 5.6 PG Diagonal up right to base of short, thin crack with old pin (**V1**). Move up to overhang and fixed pin, then hand traverse right around nose and mantel up to small ledge and make a belay (optional). (40 ft.)
   PITCH 2: 5.5 G Move left and climb to the top of the corner and roof (**V2 & V3**), then traverse right about 20 feet and up the face, going up a bit left **or** straight up to the top. (100 ft.)

Jason Kahn on *Disney Point* 5.10d, Variation 3 (Route 14) /
Photo·Dave Karl

Variation 1: 5.6 G (Original Route) Traverse right around nose at thin left-facing flake to a thin stance and old fixed pin. Move straight up to ledge and join the regular route.

Variation 2: 5.8 G (Sling Time) Step around left and crank straight past notch in overhang (crux, long reach) and up corner and face to the top.

Variation 3: 5.10d PG ★ (Disney Point, drawn in w/dotted line) Traverse left to the large flake stuck under the roof. Take a deep breath and hand traverse out to the point and work straight up (crux) to a stance on the face, then up easier rock to the top.

FA 1959: Dave Craft and Eric Stern
FA (V3) 1978: Kevin Bein

15 **SLING TIME 5.11d G**
All yours if you've got the strength and technique.
START: Same as Swing Time, 5 feet left of Disneyland at a thin crack that leads to the roof that's about 30 feet up, usually marked by retreat/pro slings.
PITCH 1: 5.11d G Climb to the roof (same as Swing Time), then jam out right along the crack (crux) in the overhang and up to a belay/rap-station. (70 ft.)
PITCH 2: 5.8 G Finish up the face and crank straight up past notch in overhang (crux, long reach) and up corner and face to the top. (90 ft.)
FA 1964: Dick Williams and Jim McCarthy
FFA 1973: John Stannard

16 **SWING TIME 5.11a PG ★★**
This climb begins with an exciting move at the first roof, not to mention the wild last pitch that will take your breath away.
START: 5 feet left of Disneyland at a thin crack that leads to the roof, same as Sling Time.

PITCH 1: 5.10b PG-R Climb to the roof and work up left at the break (crux) and up past the left side of a series of overhangs to a belay in an open book. (100 ft.)

PITCH 2: 5.11a PG Climb up a bit left to the imposing crack in the ceiling, crank past it to the final overhang. Then make the wild, difficult and cramped crux traverse right, then on to the top. (50 ft.)

FA 1964: Ants Leemets and Elmer Skahan

FFA 1968: John Stannard

17   LEFTOVERS 5.7 PG

A contrived route with some interesting climbing.

START: At the first, short left-facing corner capped by large overhang, 10 feet left of Swing Time and 13 feet right of Te Dum.

PITCH 1: 5.7 PG Move up corner to first horizontal, move right around nose and diagonal up left to short right-facing flake, then up left to a stance. Move up to overhang, exit right and climb face to small overhang and Te Dum's nose. Climb short face using nose/arête to belay/rap-station just below corner. (80 ft.)

PITCH 2: 5.5 PG Move up and traverse left 6-8 feet on narrow ledge then up face to right-facing flake at left side of roof (**V1**). Step left and go straight up to left side of overhang to finish on Inverted Layback's left-facing flakes to the top. (70 ft.)

Variation 1: 5.9 G Move up and traverse right and up to finish on Swing Time.

FA 1981: Russ Clune and Rosie Andrews

FA (V1) 1992: Ivan Rezucha

18   TE DUM 5.7 G ★★

Good route, especially if the direct start is dry.

START: 45 feet left of Disneyland at the deep, wide crack, just left of an often wet, left-facing corner/open book.

PITCH 1: 5.7 G (V1) Follow the crack 25 feet to a stance where the crack flares, then traverse right past the corner to a ledge. Climb straight up the face to the right side of the roof, move right (crux) and up to a belay in the open book. (120 ft.)

PITCH 2: 5.4 PG Diagonal up right to the edge of the roof and to the top. (50 ft.)

Variation 1: 5.6 PG ★ (Direct Start) Start at the broken left-facing corner, 10 feet right of the crack. Climb up about 20 feet, step right then up left-facing flakes to join Te Dum.

FA 1949: Hans Kraus and Roger Wolcott
FFA 1958: Art Gran

19   **INVERTED LAYBACK 5.9 PG ★★★**

Quite a climb in 1959 and still is; varied, technical and strenuous. On the first ascent, Craft free-climbed the inverted layback section but then used a point of aid on the bulging crack section just above. The variations leading to the inverted layback are fun and it's easy to escape left to Layback and its easy finish.

START: At the crack in the nose, 10 feet left of Te Dum's wide crack and 10 feet right of Layback.

PITCH 1: 5.9 PG (V1 & V2) Climb crack to a ledge 20 feet up. Either climb straight up and move right up into the deceptively difficult crack and squeeze chimney (5.8 PG) or move right on ledge and climb straight up to chimney. Climb chimney or face on right (easier) to horizontal (V3). Move right and climb up into the inverted layback crack. Psych up and make the strenuous inverted layback moves out right (crux) and up to a belay under the roof. (100 ft.)

PITCH 2: 5.8- PG Traverse right to the nose and climb a thin crack (crux), then up face to the top. (60 ft.)

Variation 1: 5.6+ PG (Drawn in w/dotted line) Start on Te Dum and continue up the right set of cracks past a small jutting flake to the inverted layback.

Variation 2: 5.7 PG (Not drawn in) Start on Te Dum. Climb to ledge and middle crack, then continue up to the offwidth and up to the inverted layback.

Variation 3: 5.1 PG (Exit Left, drawn in w/dotted line) Diagonal up left to join Layback.

FA 1959: Dave Craft and Pete Geiser

20 BURNING BABIES 5.11b/c PG

Start: At a vertical seam on the face between Layback and Inverted Layback.

Pitch 1: 5.11b/c PG Climb face and nose above to broken ledges. (70 ft.)

FA 1983: Mike Law

21 **LAYBACK 5.5 PG ★★**

A fun climb with lots of variety, blue Camalot or larger cam helpful.

START: 10 feet left of Inverted Layback at the chimney with a large chockstone in it, 15 feet up.

PITCH 1: 5.5 PG (V1) Work up the chimney and gain the top of the chockstone, then climb the face up left to the lip of the layback crack. Climb the crack/corner to the broken ledges and belay at threaded rap-station. (60 ft.)

PITCH 2: 5.1 PG (V2) Diagonal up right about 40 feet to the nose, then up to the overhang, step right and up to the top. (60 ft.)

Variation 1: 5.7 PG Climb thin crack 5 feet left of the chimney to the first overhang and fixed pin (one can move right here to the chockstone in chimney). Step left and move up to the next overhang, step left again and move up short corner to ceiling. Step right to join Layback.

Variation 2: 5.7 PG (Portland) Hand traverse left along the obvious horizontal for about 30 feet to join Grand Central.

FA 1941: Fritz Wiessner and George Temple

You can observe a lot just by watching.
— Yogi Berra

Elaine Matthews on crux of *Inverted Layback* 5.9 (Route 19) Photo: Dick WIlliams 1995

21a   BA-BA MORAN 5.11a PG ★

A height-related crux with a wild finish. Named in part after the Beach Boys song–you know the one.

START: On the rounded nose, 5' right of Grand Central.

PITCH 1: 5.11a PG Climb the nose past a short, shallow left-facing corner to meet the seam at the roof. Work your way past the roof (crux) at the small, right-facing flake at the lip to a small, but welcomed stance. Continue straight up the face past some small overhangs to a short right-facing corner. Step left and go straight up to a whitish overhang, move right and belay on the Layback ledges. (60 ft.)

PITCH 2: 5.10b/c PG Move back left and climb past right side of overhang, then back up left to finish at the first break/crack in the ceiling (crux) at the left side of the huge triangular roof. (90 ft.)

FA 1991: Dick Williams and Barb Moran

22   GRAND CENTRAL 5.9 PG ★★★

What a great classic this is, varied and interesting. The final overhang crack move is height-related, the shorter you are, the harder it will be–between grades 5.7 to 5.9. Often done in one pitch with double ropes or combining pitch one and two or pitch two and three. Variation one is excellent.

START: At the large open book with two cracks, 25 feet left of Layback.

PITCH 1: 5.6 PG (V1) Climb corner and cracks to the roof, traverse left to a small optional belay ledge left of the nose. (60 ft.)

PITCH 2: 5.9 PG Climb up about 10 feet to a horizontal and traverse right around the nose to a good stance. Climb the steep face (crux) till better holds lead up to a sloping ledge below the final overhang and crack. (60 ft.)

PITCH 3: 5.8 PG (V2) Jam past the crack (crux) and up past the overhangs to the top. (40 ft.)

Variation 1: 5.9 PG ★ (Drawn in w/dotted line) Start in the left-facing corner immediately left of Penn Station and 15 feet right of Alphonse. There are two stacked blocks at base of corner. Climb corner (crux-1) to final overhang, then hand traverse right (blue Camalot) about 15-20 feet (crux-2) to the nose and small pedestal to join Grand Central.

Variation 2: 5.6+ PG (Drawn in w/dotted line) Make the airy traverse left under overhang and past pointy nose for about 12 feet, then climb straight up past small overhangs to the top.

FA 1947: Bonnie Prudden, Hans Kraus and Dick Hirschland
FFA 1963: Jim McCarthy
FA (V1) 1973: Jim Kolocotronis and Herb Laeger
FA (V2) 1986: Todd Swain and Andy Schenkel

23   PENN STATION   5.10b/c PG

Start: At the first crack just past the nose, 10 feet left of Grand Central.

Pitch 1: 5.10b/c PG Climb crack and the short open book above to the overhang. Move right and continue up face past a small tree to the roof. Traverse right, then climb past the next overhang to join Grand Central below its crux. Follow Grand Central to a belay below overhang and crack. (100 ft.)

Pitch 2: 5.10b/c PG Climb back down and traverse right about 15 feet to finish at the first break/crack in the ceiling (crux) at the left side of the huge triangular roof. (70 ft.)

FA (P1) 1981: John Stannard, Rich Goldstone and
Steve Wunsch
FA (P2) 1981: Ivan Rezucha and Mike Sawicky

The arc of a climbing career is much like the arc of life. If you climb long enough, the climbs that tested you when you were starting out return to test you in old age.
    — Richard Goldstone

24   **ALPHONSE 5.8 G ★★★**

A great route in a wild atmosphere of beautiful rock and huge roofs with a neat exit crux. Often done in one pitch with double ropes to avoid the cramped belay below the crux.

START: There are two, broken left-facing corners immediately left of Grand Central. Alphonse begins at the 2nd one, which is 30 feet left of Grand Central.

PITCH 1: 5.6 G Climb to the first overhang (about 20 feet up) (V1), step left and climb the broken cracks, to the big ledge. Climb the great corner (5.6 G) till just below the giant roof (**V2** & **V3**), traverse left about 25 feet to a small, awkward belay. (100 ft.)

PITCH 2: 5.8 G Step right and work past the notch (crux) to the overhang (**V4**), traverse right and up to the top. (50 ft.)

Variation 1: 5.6 PG (Original Route) Move right and up to a small stance at a small pine tree. Then move up thin face (crux) moving left at the overhang and up to the ledge.

Variation 2: 5.9- G (Reverse Easy Rider) Traverse right under ceiling past two old pins and up right to join Grand Central at final overhangs.

Variation 3: 5.10d/11a PG (The Olde 40, drawn in w/dotted line) Move up to the roof and crab-crawl right to nose, then up face to final roof. Work past roof (crux) and up to the top.

Variation 4: 5.10a PG (Sissy Boys) Step left and work straight up past crack in overhang at notch to the top.

FA 1948: Ken Prestrud and Lucien Warner

FFA 1950's: John Turner

FA (Pitch 1, broken cracks variation) 1983: Ivan Rezucha and Annie O'Neill

FA (V3) 2007: Wes Converse and Mike Lillis

FA (V4) 1986: Jason Kahn and Eugene Pulumbo

25   SISSY BOYS 5.10d R

The climb originally started about 10 feet to the left of Alphonse, but a hold broke. Pitch one has some fun climbing, especially its 5.8 variation. Pitch three is a variation on Alphonse and is exciting.

START: Same as Alphonse.

PITCH 1: 5.9 PG With hands at the first horizontal, diagonal up left past crack/seam (**V1**) to short horizontal to meet No Slings Attached. Then climb straight past right side of small tree and thin crack above to ledge and belay/rap-tree. (40 ft.)

Pitch 2: 5.10d R Step right and climb a thin crack past a small bulging overhang. Continue up to the left of a mossy streak and past another small overhang to the Alphonse belay ledge. (70 ft.)

PITCH 3: 5.10a PG Follow Alphonse past the notch to the overhang. Step left and work straight up past crack in overhang at notch to the top. (40 ft.)

Variation 1: 5.8 PG Follow thin crack and seam to a good stance (small tree is about 4 feet to the left). Work straight up the unprotected pebbly face past right side of pointy block to ledge.

FA 1986: Jason Kahn and Eugene Pulumbo

26   NO SLINGS ATTACHED 5.10b/c R

All pitches are very demanding and scary to lead. Pitch one has no pro for the first 20 feet, therefore it's recommended as a **toprope**, good moves (cheater stone should be helpful for those under 5'9").

START: 15 feet left of Alphonse, at the base of a small sentry box-like open book capped by a triangular ceiling.

PITCH 1: 5.9 R (As a Toprope) Work up into the open book, then exit right and up to a stance (crux). Diagonal left and climb white nose to the ledge and belay tree/rap-station. (50 ft.)

Pitch 2: 5.10a R Go up left on ramp about 1/2 way and then up face (blue Trango Ballnutz) to ceiling. Work right to nose and up face to a thin stance (5.9+ PG-R) and step up to good holds at small overhang. Clear overhang and work straight up past small, blocky right-facing corner (crux) to jugs and Alphonse. One can make a belay here or further to the left. (50 ft.)

Pitch 3: 5.10b/c R Move left to an ill-defined corner-flake system in the bulge/overhang. Climb this, move left, and continue past a second overhang to the top. (40 ft.)

FA 1977: John Bragg, Mark Robinson and Russ Raffa

27   BONGOS AND BEACHED WHALES 5.10a R

The second pitch crux move is very committing and involves a long reach, would be a bad fall.

Start: Same as Yellow Belly, at the thin crack just right of the corner that rises to the overhang.

Pitch 1: 5.7 PG Step up crack and move right at first horizontal and climb face past right side of small tree to a stance. Move up to overhang and exit right to Alphonse's ledge and tree belay. (50 ft.)

Pitch 2: 5.10a R Follow rising ramp up left and move up to ceiling and wide crack, then move left to Yellow Belly's nose. Work straight up right side of nose (crux) to wide horizontal. (This is where you can step left to finish on Yellow Belly). Hand traverse right about 20 feet to join/finish on last pitch of Alphonse or No Slings Attached.

FA 1983: Russ Clune and Pete Black

28   YELLOW BELLY 5.8 PG ★★

A great climb, the face moves on pitch two are exciting with a neat crux move out of the alcove. All the variations are good.

START: 35 feet left of Alphonse, at two parallel cracks, one in the open book and the other one (very thin) on its right face. Begin at the thin crack.

PITCH 1: 5.8 PG (V1) Climb crack and face to the overhang (**V2**), clear this overhang (crux) and the next one, then up corner/crack to a belay at the nose. (70 ft.)

PITCH 2: 5.8 PG Move up nose, step left and move up

Jimmy Dunn on
Pitch 3 crux of *Yellow Ridge* 5.7
(Route 29)
Photo: Dick Williams

onto thin face to a tiny stance. Work up face near nose (crux-1) and up past some blocks into the cramped alcove under the roof. Exit left (crux-2) and up past a short left-facing corner to the top. (90 ft.)

Variation 1: 5.11a PG (Underbelly) Start about 5 feet left of the thin cracks and climb the short open book to ceiling. Step right to nose and crack, and follow crack to the first horizontal. Then move left and continue up to the overhangs, where the regular route is joined.

Variation 2: 5.7 G (Original Route, drawn in w/dotted line) Hand traverse left about 12 feet around and up to join Yellow Ridge to a belay on small ledges below an open book. Then go up about 20 feet to the overhang and broken crack (**V2a**). Climb crack past small overhang to a small tree, diagonal up right and up into Yellow Belly's alcove.

Variation 2a: 5.7 G-PG From right side of overhang, climb up short open book to overhang, then step left to crack or climb up right with optimism past the overhang to the blocks and up into the alcove.

FA 1957: Jim McCarthy, Bob Larsen and Ken Prestrud
FFA 1958: John Turner
FA (V1) 1986: Rich Gottlieb and Teri Condon

29   **YELLOW RIDGE 5.7 PG ★★★**
Another Wiessner classic with an atypical offwidth crack and an exciting and airy final pitch. The variations are good and may be a bit confusing; I'm hopeful the line drawings will help.

START: 5 feet left of Yellow Belly at the short left-facing corner just right of the nose which is below an offwidth crack and 50 feet right of Fat Stick.

PITCH 1: 5.7 PG (V1 & **V2**) Climb the short corner just right of the nose to the roof, traverse left to the nose and move up to and climb the offwidth crack (crux) to an optional belay ledge. (50 ft.)

PITCH 2: 5.5 PG Climb the corner above for about 20 feet to an overhang and broken crack. Diagonal left on left-leaning/ascending ledges **(V3)** about 40 feet to a belay on a ledge at a wide horizontal or belay further left at a left-facing corner. (70 ft.)

PITCH 3: 5.6 PG (V4) Traverse left on ledge, then diagonal up left to the nose, make the airy moves up (crux) then on up past the juggy overhangs to the top. (80 ft.)

Variation 1: 5.7 PG-R (Original Route, drawn in w/dotted line) Just left of the nose, from atop blocks, directly below an open book that has an overhang about 20 feet up. Step up to wide horizontal and make the thin traverse right to the nose, then work up to the offwidth.

Variation 2: 5.8 PG (Drawn in w/dotted line till traverse) Move up the open book to the overhang **(V2a)**, make the thin traverse right (crux) to the offwidth crack.

Variation 2a: 5.8+ G-PG (Drawn in w/dotted line) Make a small step right then up left (crux) past the short right-facing corner to the roof. Exit right to Yellow Ridge.

Variation 3: 5.9 G-PG (Drawn in w/dotted line) After you have diagonalled up left from the broken crack about 15 feet, move up to good finger horizontal and traverse right about 6-8 feet to old Gerry pin. Climb straight up past bulge to a wide horizontal (some loose rock in crack). Step right and work past overhangs at notch (crux: long reach) to wide horizontal (blue Camalot helpful) and a stance. Move left about 6 feet to a short left-facing corner with old waffer-like piton, step right and move up to overhang. Then either diagonal up left on dirty rock to the top **or** (best to do) traverse right to left-facing corner and join Yellow Belly to the top.

Variation 4: 5.6 G (not drawn in) Traverse right along lip of overhangs about 10 feet to a short left-facing corner and old waffer-like piton (joining **V3**), step right (crux) and move up to overhang. Then either diagonal up left on dirty rock to the top **or** (best to do) traverse right to left-facing corner and join Yellow Belly to the top.

FA 1944: Fritz Wiessner and Ed and Ann Gross

FA (V2a) 2004: Dick Williams and Annie O'Neill

30 FAT STICK DIRECT 5.10b PG ★★★

A great route with lots of exciting moves.

START: At the base of the open book, immediately left of the prominent nose, 40 feet left of Yellow Ridge, same as Fat Stick.

PITCH 1: 5.8 G-PG (V1) Climb the open book/flakes/face to a stance below the V-notch in the overhang. Climb past notch (crux), then work your way up past an awkward move to the overhang, move left to belay stance at belay/rap-station. (60 ft.)

PITCH 2: 5.10b G (Direct) Climb the overhang directly above into the short left-facing corner (crux), exit right onto the face and continue up a bit right to a belay on the ledge below the left-facing corner (same as Yellow Ridge). (60 ft.)

PITCH 3: 5.9+ PG-R Climb face and corner above to the overhangs. Diagonal steeply up right, then straight to the top. (60 ft.)

Variation 1: 5.6 PG Diagonal up right to the nose and up it to the V-notch.

FA (P1) 1957: Jim McCarthy and Hans Kraus

FA (P2 & P3) 1968: John Stannard and G. Livingston

31 FAT STICK 5.8 G-PG ★

An old classic, and quite the lead in the piton days of old; there was no pro from the V-notch to the anchors. Thank God we have cams and nuts now.

START: At the base of the open book, just left of the

prominent nose, 40 feet left of Yellow Ridge.

PITCH 1: 5.8 G-PG (V1) Climb the open book/flakes/face to a stance below the V-notch in the overhang. Climb the notch (crux), then work your way up past an awkward move to the overhang, move left to a belay stance at belay/rap-station. (60 ft.)

PITCH 2: 5.7 PG Traverse left about 30 feet to a right-facing corner, which is followed to its top. Then move left and up to a ledge, and continue diagonally up left to a belay stance. (110 ft.)

Pitch 3: 5.5 PG Climb a small right-facing corner to the overhangs, traverse right about 20 feet and then finish up past an inside corner to the top. (100 ft.)

Variation 1: 5.6 PG Diagonal up right to the nose and up it to the V-notch.

FA 1957: Jim McCarthy and Hans Kraus

32   GENERATION GAP 5.11b/c PG

Ever since a crucial hold broke off in 1985, the crux sequence has been tough to figure out. Test yourself, see if you can do it without any visual or verbal beta! You won't have to wait on line to lead this one, even if it's dry.

START: At a broken crack that leads to a notch in the ceiling 25 feet up, 30 feet left of Fat Stick and 15 feet right of The Hounds.

PITCH 1: 5.11b/c PG Climb broken crack and maneuver up past the notch (crux). Then follow Fat Stick's right-facing corner till near its top. Step right, move up face past a right-facing flake w/crack to alcove under roof. (60 ft.)

PITCH 2: 5.6 PG Traverse right under roof following horizontal to the arête/nose, then up it to join Yellow Ridge straight up past overhangs to the top. (60 ft.)

FA 1968: Jim McCarthy and Dick Williams

FFA 1969: John Stannard and Howie Davis

Dick Williams on Pitch one of *Fat Stick* 5.8 (Route 31)
Photo: Richard Goldstone

32a   (LINK-UP) DOG-STICK-RIDGE 5.8 PG ★★★
HOUNDS/FAT STICK/GENERATION GAP/
YELLOW RIDGE

A great combination of various routes' pitches, lots of variety with exposure.

START: Same as for The Hounds, 15 feet left of Generation Gap and 25 feet right of Baskerville Terrace. In the chimney formed by the right side of Requiem's huge block that leans against the cliff.

PITCH 1: 5.8 PG Climb chimney to top of block, diagonal up right passing an overhang (crux) to an open book that forms a finger crack. Follow crack to overhang and exit right to a nose, move up this and go right into Fat Stick's right-facing corner. Near the top of the corner, step right to join Generation Gap. Move up face past a right-facing flake with crack to alcove under roof. (90 ft.)

PITCH 2: 5.6 PG Move up and traverse right under roof following great horizontal to the arête/nose, then up it to join Yellow Ridge straight up past overhangs to the top. (60 ft.)

32b   THE HOUNDS 5.10b PG

START: 15 feet left of Generation Gap and 25 feet right of Baskerville Terrace. In the chimney formed by the right side of Requiem's huge block that leans against the cliff. Same as for Dog-Stick-Ridge link-up #32a.

PITCH 1: 5.10b PG Climb chimney to top of block, diagonal up right passing an overhang to an open book that forms a finger crack. Follow crack to the overhang, step left and work up the steep face past fixed pitons (crux), then continue up to join Fat Stick. (90 ft.)

Pitch 2: 5.9- PG (V1) Follow Fat Stick till 10 feet along its final traverse, then climb some loose blocks/flakes to clear the overhang and continue up the face to the top. (80 ft.)

Variation 1: 5.6 PG Continue right to finish on Fat Stick.

FA (P1) 1986: Todd Swain and Mark Wallace

FA (P2) 1982: Brett Wolf and Dave Cason

33   REQUIEM FOR A HEAVYWEIGHT 5.12d PG-R

A wild route that is not often climbed; it has a long involved history of attempts with different parties, with an original victory via Fat City Direct variation. First rated 5.12a before a handhold broke in 1987.

Start: Immediately right of Baskerville Terrace at the left side of the huge block leaning against the face, 20 feet left of The Hounds.

Pitch 1: 5.10a R Climb to top of block and continue up face past a thin crack and seam to the huge open book. (70 ft.)

Pitch 2: 5.12d PG-R Climb open book to black rock on the left, then climb up and left to the second crack that goes through the ceiling. Follow crack to the next ceiling. Traverse left (V1) 10 feet and climb past ceiling and bulge (crux) to a belay stance. (70 ft.)

Pitch 3: 5.10d PG (V2) Climb face past overhangs to a short, broken left-facing corner capped by a ceiling. Climb corner (V3) and weave up past the overhangs to the top. (120 ft.)

Variation 1: 5.10d PG (Method) (Original Route, includes first complete ascent) Traverse left about 20 feet to the fault that goes up left (Fat City Direct). Follow the fault for about 10 feet and traverse back right about 30 feet to a belay on the regular route.

Variation 2: 5.11b/c PG (Drawn in w/dotted line) Diagonal up right, pass the first roof at small triangular point and then continue up past ceilings and overhangs just left of outside edge.

Variation 3: 5.8 PG Climb about 30 feet up right and around onto face and head straight for the top.

FA (V1 and complete route ascent) 1981: Ivan Rezucha and Don Lauber

FA (V2) 2005: Cody Sims and Jack Jeffries

FFA 1982: Russ Clune and Russ Raffa

Bruce Justusson on
Pitch 2 crux of *Fat City Direct*,
with Elaine Mathews.
5.10d, (Route 35)
Photo: Dick WIlliams 1995

34 BASKERVILLE TERRACE 5.7 PG ★★

A good climb with an interesting crux. Be careful of the tricky climbing up to the crux corner.

START: Below a short, shallow groove/open book capped by an overhang 15 feet up, immediately left of Requiem's huge block leaning against the cliff.

PITCH 1: 5.7 PG (V1) Climb the groove to the overhang, step left and move up short, thin crack to a stance at the small, short left-facing corner. Move up, step right (crux) and up to a belay in the huge open book. (60 ft.)

PITCH 2: 5.5 PG Step right and climb face past some cracks and at the overhang, move right to nose and step up right to small ledge to join Fat Stick. Diagonal up left to a stance (optional belay). Climb the small right-facing corner to the overhangs. Traverse right about 20 feet and continue up past a left-facing corner to the top. (150 ft.)

Variation 1: 5.7 PG-R Climb the slabby grey face at thin crack, 8 feet to the left.

FA 1958: John Wharton and Dave Isles
FFA 1961: Jim McCarthy

34a (LINK-UP) BASKING RIDGE 5.7 PG ★★★
BASKERVILLE TERRACE/GENERATION GAP/
YELLOW RIDGE

A nice, old combination of routes' pitches. Basking Ridge is the name of a town in New Jersey where on Friday Dec 13, 1776 General Lee was captured by the British cavalry during the War of Independence.

START: Same as Baskerville Terrace, below a short, shallow groove/open book capped by overhang 15 feet up, immediately left of Requiem's huge block leaning against the cliff.

PITCH 1: 5.7 PG Climb the groove to the overhang, step left and move up short, thin crack to a stance at the small, short left-facing corner. Move up, step right (crux) and up to an optional belay in the huge open book. (60 ft.) Step right and climb face past some cracks and at overhang move right to nose and up to small ledge that goes right. Traverse right about 15-20 feet to a small ledge in the open book capped by huge roof to join Generation Gap. (130 ft.)

PITCH 2: 5.6 PG Move up and traverse right under roof following great horizontal to the arête/nose, then up it to join Yellow Ridge straight up past overhangs to the top. (60 ft.)

35   FAT CITY DIRECT 5.10d G-PG ★★★

A wild, very popular classic route that weaves through the fantastic, giant kaleidoscopic overhanging roofs. One can make the clip before making the move or make the move and then clip; either way it's hard and scary. Using a long stick clip from directly below the old pin makes it safer. If you just want to do some good 5.9 climbing, do pitch one and (**V1**) to the bolt anchor/rap-station.

START: About 20 feet left of Baskerville Terrace and 20 feet right of Gelsa, at the first left-facing corner below a roof that's about 45 feet up, split by a crack. There is a little tree in the roof.

PITCH 1: 5.10d G-PG Climb the corner and work past the roof (5.9 PG) to a small optional belay stance at a short pointed nose (**V1**). (70 ft.) Climb straight up to a tiny alcove, step left and work up left to big holds (crux) (**V2**). Continue straight up to left side of ceiling and work past the old pin (5.10b R) to a stance (**V3**). Continue up a bit right and weave your way past the overhangs (5.8 PG) to the top. (160 ft.)

Variation 1: 5.6 PG (Original Route, drawn in w/dotted line) Diagonal up left about 25 feet to belay/bolt anchor/ rap-station, placed in 2005 (**V1a**).

Variation 1a: 5.10b R (Original Route, drawn in w/dotted line) Diagonal up right to the short, slanting left-facing corner, move up right (crux: old pin clip) and up to a stance.

Variation 2: If you want to break up the pitch, traverse left 20 feet and move down to belay/bolt anchor/rap-station.

Elaine Mathews on
Pitch 3 crux
of *Fat City Direct*
(Route 35)
Photo: Dick Williams 1995

Variation 3: 5.9 PG (Original Route, drawn in w/dotted line) Traverse left about 25 feet to a small ledge below an overhang. Climb past the old "spinner" bolt up steep whitish rock to a ledge (**V3a**), diagonal up left (passing the roof on the left), and continue to the top. (80 ft.)

Variation 3a: 5.11d/12a PG-R (Drawn in w/dotted line) Climb pretty much straight up past the widest part of the overhangs in roof past some fixed gear to the top.

FA 1966: Dick Williams and Dave Craft
FFA 1968: John Stannard and Gary Brown
FA (Direct) 1970: John Bragg and John Stannard
FA (V3a) 2005: Cody Sims and Joe Frankel

36   GELSA 5.4 PG ★★★

THE classic 5.4 in the Gunks! Has lots of variety.

START: From a pile of blocks (with black birch tree) at the base of a short crack, 20 feet left of Fat City.

PITCH 1: 5.4 PG Climb crack (**V1**), then move up to the overhang and fixed pin (**V2**), traverse left 25 feet, passing two short, right-facing corners to an optional belay ledge and dying oak tree. From the left end of ledge move up a bit left to the overhang (**V3**), then traverse left about 30 feet to the nose, then up it to make a belay at ledge below the roofs. (110 ft.)

PITCH 2: 5.4 PG Climb about 10-15 feet (**V4**) then diagonal up right and climb the corner to the top. (90 ft.)

Variation 1: 5.9 PG (Drawn in w/dotted line) From the top of the crack, move right and up face to a stance above the nose. Work up face (crux-1) to the second overhang and base of shallow right-facing corner. Work up to top corner (crux-2), traverse right about 6-8 feet and up groove/crack to right side of roof. Then diagonal left to Fat City's belay/bolt anchor/rap-station placed in 2005. (100 ft.)

Variation 2: 5.7 G ★★ Step left and up to the right-facing flake/fin. Climb past flake and crack (crux), then past some small right-facing corners to the base of a large, short left-

Hans Kraus on second
ascent of *Gelsa* 5.4
(Route 36)
(1942 or 1943)

facing corner. Work up corner to the overhang and step around right and up crack/face to the Fat City belay/bolt-anchor/rap-station placed in 2005. (100 ft.)

Variation 3: 5.4 PG-R (Drawn in w/dotted line) Pass the overhang, step right and climb the face to a small overhang. Move left, then diagonal up left to the ledge.

Variation 4: 5.4 PG (The Appie Way, drawn in w/dotted line. Diagonal up left (past loose rock) around outside corner and up the face to the top. (100 ft.)

FA 1942: Fritz Wiessner, Beckett Howorth and George Temple

37   LAND OF THE GIANTS 5.10a/b PG

The first pitch is highly recommended. Climbers inadvertently pulled off some big rocks/flakes on the second pitch in 2004, which may have changed its grade from 5.11X to 5.10a/b PG. **HOWEVER**, there may still be lots of loose rock up there in the ceilings; there was huge rock fall as recently as May 2006.

START: Same as Gelsa.

PITCH 1: 5.7 G ★★ (V1) Climb Gelsa to the overhang (fixed pin), step left and up to the right-facing flake/fin. Climb past flake and crack (crux), then past some small right-facing corners to the base of a large, short left-facing corner. Work up corner to the overhang and step around right and up crack/face to the Fat City belay/bolt-anchor/rap-station placed in 2005. (100 ft.)

Pitch 2: 5.10a/b PG Climb up and slightly right past the ceilings, joining Fat City's original route near the end of its traverse and finish up past the left side of the roof. (80 ft.)

Variation 1: 5.8 PG (Original Route, drawn in w/dotted line) Climb the short face from the block immediately left of Gelsa's start.

FA 1985: Jeff Gruenberg and Scott Franklin

37a (LINK-UP) G-STRING GIANTS 5.8 G ★★
G-STRING/LAND OF THE GIANTS

A real fun climb with lots of interesting and varied climbing. Bring lots of long slings.

START: (Same as G-String) 15 feet left of Gelsa, from a small ledge at the base of a small ramp that leads up left to a flaring chimney/crack.

PITCH 1: 5.8 G Climb flared chimney/crack to last overhang, finger traverse right about 5 feet to "feel-good" holds (crux). Then work up slab to the wide horizontal (intersecting Gelsa). Traverse right about 10-12 feet to right-facing flake/fin and crack. Climb past flake and crack, then past some small right facing corners to the base of a large, short left-facing corner. Follow corner to the overhang and step around right and up crack/face to Fat City's belay/bolt-anchor/rap-station placed in 2005. (100- foot rappel)

38 G-STRING 5.9 PG

Good climbing on both pitches, airy and thoughtful; the second pitch is not as scary as it looks but has a committing start. Two ropes a definite and lots of duplicate gear really helps, like 2-Black, 3 Blue, 4 Green and 3 Yellow Aliens, plus lots of long slings. The rock is solid, with bits of shale on bigger holds here and there.

START: 15 feet left of Gelsa, from a small ledge at the base of a small ramp that leads up left to a flaring chimney-crack.

PITCH 1: 5.8 G ★★ Climb flared chimney/crack to last overhang, finger traverse right about 5 feet to "feel-good" holds. Then work up slab to the wide horizontal (intersecting Gelsa) (V1). Follow Gelsa's traverse left past two, short right-facing corners and up to the overhang. As with the Gelsa variation, move up right and follow a vertical fault and go up right to overhang with small rounded flake at lip. Climb straight past overhang to a belay at a 4-foot high left-facing corner and old lost arrow pin. (A ramp begins at its top and goes up right to Fat City's original route pitch one belay/bolt anchor/rap-station placed in 2005) (90 ft.)

PITCH 2: 5.9 PG Move up right onto ramp, step up and traverse left 5 feet, then follow best holds up a bit right to a horizontal shale band (5.7 R) (V2). Move up to good holds (white horn) and short horizontal to the right (red Camalot specific). Work straight up (crux) and a bit right passing overhangs about 10 feet left of Fat City's old crappy "spinner" bolt up to the right side of triangular roof to join the last 20 feet of Fat City up left to the top. (90 ft.)

Variation 1: 5.10a R (Original Route) Climb straight past overhang at thin seam.

Variation 2: (grade and pro unknown at this time) (Geisha) Climb the steep, dark face up left, staying right of Gelsa.

FA 1973 (including variations): Jim Kolocotronis and Bob Jahn

39   PAIN STRAIN 5.11a/b PG

The original second pitch was basically a very short 5.9+ variation on Gelsa that joined Gelsa's old 5.4 variation called Appie Way. A more interesting and challenging second pitch is now described in the link up of Roseland/Pain Strain/Appie Way (42a).

Start: On the face 15 feet left of G-String.

Pitch 1: 5.11a/b PG Climb to a 2-foot-high right-facing flake, step left, and work up past the overhang and bulge above, joining Gelsa at its nose, then up to Gelsa's belay ledge. (100 ft.)

Pitch 2: 5.9+ G Hand traverse immediately left onto face a few feet, then work up to a stance on small slab (crux). Step right at short horizontal and crank up to jugs and blocks. Step left and up the easy face, (old 5.4 variation to Gelsa called The Appie Way, drawn in w/dotted line) to the top. (100 ft.)

FA 1983: Russ Clune, Russ Raffa, Pete Black, Kevin Bein and Barbara Devine

40 **(TOPROPE)** Forbidden Zone 5.12a/b
Climb face and thin crack midway between Pain Strain and Eraserhead. FA 1986: Russ Clune

41 ERASERHEAD 5.11d/12a R
Start: Same as Shitface
Pitch 1: 5.11d/12a R Follow Shitface for 15 feet up left to a good horizontal, then work up right to small left-facing flakes at the left side of the overhang. Work past the bulging face left of the flakes (crux), then to Roseland's bolt anchors. (70 ft.)
FA 1983: Russ Raffa and Russ Clune

42 **SHITFACE 5.10c PG ★★**
This is a sustained route with a pumpy crux, plus a thoughtful, runout move after the crux. A crucial hold broke when Jim Andress followed this on the first ascent, making it about a grade harder.
START: On the bulging, polished face about 55 feet left of Gelsa and about 25 feet right of Roseland.
PITCH 1: 5.10c PG Boulder up the polished face about 15 feet to the first horizontal, step left and work up vertical fractures to the thin pointy flake under the overhang. Crank past the overhang (crux) and then straight up (5.8 R) to Roseland's bolt anchors. (60 ft.)
FA 1963: Jim McCarthy and Jim Andress

43 REVOLVING EYEBALLS 5.10b/c R
Start: On the face 5 feet right of Roseland.
Pitch 1: 5.10b/c R Climb up right about 10 feet to a hole with protruding flakes. Move up left and then climb face to the right of the nose to a stance farther up left (at the same level as the Shitface flake and overhang). Continue past a short nose and up right to intersect Roseland about halfway along its traverse (a few feet right of the first piton). Work past small, right-jutting flake at short nose to

a stance in the corner at the overhang. Move up right to Roseland's bolt anchors. (90 ft.)

FA 1983: Russ Clune

44 ROSELAND 5.9 PG ★★★

Beautiful corner and crack climbing on Pitch One and Pitch Two's crux corner is exciting. For variety, try doing the excellent variations sometime. This is one of the best 5.9s in the Gunks.

START: About 25 feet left of Shitface below the impressive and beautiful open book that has an overhang in it, half way up.

PITCH 1: 5.9 PG Climb the crack and open book to its top, traverse right (crux) **(V1)** about 15 feet, then up to bolt anchors. (90 ft.)

PITCH 2: 5.8 PG Climb straight up from left side of bolt anchors, up the crack till near the overhang, **(V2)** move left and work up short face to the base of the acute, slightly overhanging right-facing corner. Work up the wild corner (crux), then up face about 20 feet to a blocky ledge and cedar tree. (60 ft.)

PITCH 3: 5.7 PG Continue up another 30 feet to a ledge, then diagonal up right and pass overhangs (Trango Ballnutz and blue Camalot helpful) and top out at a small point. (70 ft.)

Variation 1: 5.9 PG ★ (Revolving Eyeballs) From about half way along the traverse (a few feet right of the first piton), work past small, right-jutting flake at short nose to a stance in the corner at the overhang. Move up right to Roseland's bolt anchors.

Variation 2: 5.9+ G ★ From good holds just above the crack, reach up left to a pocket-like bucket, then work straight past steep rock to a stance on small slab (crux). Step right to short horizontal, and crank up to jugs and some blocks. Step left and up the easy face (old 5.4 variation to Gelsa called The Appie Way, drawn in w/dotted line) to the top. (110 ft.)

FA 1958: Jim McCarthy and Hans Kraus
FFA 1960: Jim McCarthy

45   BOOGEYMAN 5.11d R
(As a Toprope)

Pitch one has power moves with long reaches. It has been said that pitches two and three are dirty with loose rock and are therefore not recommended. The entire climb is drawn in on the cliff photo.

START: Same as Roseland.

PITCH 1: 5.11d R From the boulder at base of Roseland's open book, move up left to the short ramp of El Camino Real. Then move up to the horizontal, step right and up to overhang. Work straight past the green streak and the small overhang and left-facing corner to the wide overhang. Traverse left to the rap-station. (70 ft.)

    FA 1983: Jeff Gruenberg, Russ Clune and John Meyers

45a   (TOPROPE) Dyno-Soar 5.13a

Start between Boogeyman and El Kabong (V1). A contrived crux consists of a long dyno near the start, ignoring good footholds on the left-intersect with El Kabong. Go straight up face (right of El Kabong) and climb the face right of El Kabong's corner. FA (Toprope) 1994: Jordan Mills.

Variation 1: (**Toprope**) 5.12c (Statosaur) Use the good footholds on the left, avoiding the dyno; the rest is the same. FA (V1) 1994: Russ Clune

46   EL CAMINO REAL 5.11b PG ★★

VERY popular as a **toprope**. It's a rare site to see someone leading it onsight, or leading it period!

START: Same as Roseland.

PITCH 1: 5.11b PG From the boulder, move up left along the ramp, then diagonal up left about 15 feet to the imposing face just right of Trans Con's nose (not fair to rest on Trans Con). Work straight up the face (crux) along the green streak, then right to the rap-station. (80 ft.) Continue past the overhang and work up to a small belay ledge and tree. (120 ft.)

Pitch 2: **(NR)** 5.10b/c PG Climb the face and clear the large overhang. Then diagonal up left (crossing Transcontinental Nailway) and continue up past the big overhangs to the top. (80 ft.)

FFA 1982: Alex Lowe, Dan McMillan and Russ Clune

47 EL KABONG 5.12b/c R

Start: On the highest block under the overhang between El Camino Real and Transcontinental Nailway, slightly left of the thin right-facing flakes that are about 20 feet up.

Pitch 1: 5.12b/c R Climb face and thin flakes straight up crossing El Camino Real. Work straight up to the base of a right-slanting left-facing corner. Climb corner and up to a horizontal and move right to the anchors.

FA (Toprope) 1985: Jeff Gruenberg

FA (Lead) 1989: Gene Smith, Timmy Harder and Guenther Mann

Trust but verify.

Think of President Reagan's famous quote when climbing. Always be suspicious of pitons and all other kinds/types of protection as well as handholds and flakes.

Barb Moran on
Pitch one crux of *Birdland* 5.8
(Route 52)
Photo: Gregor Halenda 1995

48 TRANSCONTINENTAL NAILWAY 5.10b PG ★★★

This is a great route known as Trans Con with many quality moves. The crux two/three finger layback tweaker hold had a pebble in it when McCarthy first climbed it free; Jeff Poffett wiggled it out in 1974, so it's a bit easier now.

START: 45 feet left of Roseland, behind a tree, below a short, slabby ramp broken by a thin crack about 20 feet up.

PITCH 1: 5.10b PG Make the difficult move past the crack in slab to horizontal and step right to fixed pin. Work straight past overhang (crux) to great horizontal and then do one more taxing move up to a good stance. Follow the open book to it's top. Step right, move up, then make the exciting move left and up to the bolt anchors. (80 ft.)

PITCH 2: 5.7 PG Climb up right past fixed pins to a small ledge. Continue up face past right-facing flakes to a ledge with loose rocks. Climb left-facing flakes, then the face up right to small platform. Step right and diagonal up right to small ledge and make a belay. (70 ft.)

Pitch 3: 5.7 PG Diagonal right and follow ledges to join Roseland or the Appie Way variation to the top

FA 1961: Joe Fitschen and Art Gran
FFA 1965: Jim McCarthy

The next three one-pitch climbs are very popular **toprope** climbs.

49   ROAD WARRIOR 5.11d R
(As a Toprope)

START: Same as Trans Con.

PITCH 1: 5.11d R At crack in the slab, move up left to the second overhang. Swing right and crank your butt up onto the face and up past a small, short right-facing corner. Then straight up the face past the overhang (10 feet left of Trans Con) to the bolt anchors. (80 ft.)

FA 1983: Russ Raffa

50   (**TOPROPE**) Slammin' The Salmon 5.12b

Start by climbing the face between Road Warrior and Bird Brain till you meet Bird Brain at the final headwall, move left and finish on the steep orange face past a nose to the anchors. FA 1985: Russ Clune

51   **BIRD BRAIN 5.11d X**
    (As a Toprope)

Excellent climbing workout, seems like you always find the same people toproping it.

START: From the small ledge 15 feet right and downhill from the Birdland's huge open book.

PITCH 1: 5.11d X Diagonal right to the weakness in the overhang, then climb straight past this overhang to the next one. Crank up on the "tweakers" past the overhang (crux) to a welcomed stance below Slammin's bulging orange face. Traverse right about 8 feet to the pebbly triangular overhang, then finish up the black streak near a very thin crack to Birdland's bolt anchors. (80 ft.)

FA (Toprope) 1974: Steve Wunsch
FA (Lead) 1983: Russ Raffa and Russ Clune

52   **BIRDLAND 5.8 PG ★★★**

This is a beautiful climb, a classic, rarely to be found unoccupied on the weekends.

START: At the base of the large, magnificent open book 45 feet left and uphill from Trans Con.

PITCH 1: 5.8 PG (V1) Move up a few feet, then traverse right to a good horizontal and fixed pin. Work straight up to crimpers and step right and up face past another pin to very small right-facing flake (Yellow and Blue aliens helpful). Work past flake (crux), step right and continue up face past thin crack to horizontal, move up right to bolt anchors. (90 ft.)

PITCH 2: 5.8 PG Climb straight up face to steep left-facing corner. Work up corner (crux) and either continue straight up past the overhangs (5.9 PG) **or** escape right around the overhangs to the top. (115 ft.)

Variation 1: 5.7 G (Direct Start) Begin 5 feet right of corner and climb straight up to the horizontal.

FA 1958: Jim McCarthy, John Rupley and Jim Andress

53 BIRDCAGE 5.10b PG

Great first pitch climbing in the corner and on the wild crux roof. The second pitch is best done via variation two from pitch two of Farewell To Arms.

START: Same as Birdland.

PITCH 1: 5.10b PG ★★★ Climb corner to stance below the roof (5.9 PG), then move up and make the difficult traverse right about 10 feet to the cleft at the lip of the ceiling (V1). Work past cleft (crux) to a crouched and welcomed rest. Exit right and move up about 10 feet to a horizontal and a hanging belay/rap-station (100 ft.) or continue (original route) just above the crux overhang, diagonal up left to base of broken right-facing corner. Climb corner and move up a bit left till below short, red left-facing corner. (110 ft.)

PITCH 2: 5.7 PG Climb a short, red left-facing corner and a short, white left-facing corner to overhang with white jutting block. Move right and climb straight up to the top. (60 ft.)

Variation 1: (Escape) Exit right to Birdland.

FA 1971: Dick Williams, Steve Arsenault and Wil King
FFA 1972: Henry Barber and Bob Anderson

53a (**TOPROPE**) Birdjuice 5.12a

Start below the fault that diagonals up left and crosses Farewell To Arms. Climb fault till it meets Farewell, then climb the overhanging face and overhangs to join Birdcage.
FA 1990: Al Diamond

Dave Steres on
crux of *Birdcage* 5.10b
(Route 53)
Photo: Dick Williams 1995

54   **FAREWELL TO ARMS 5.8 PG ★★**

A tricky first move, with nice rock and a pumpy crux. This is the easiest access climb for all those who want to toprope To Be Or Not To Be. Pitch two is good (pro is good but spaced out) with a little bit of route-finding challenges. Variation two is especially good passing the upper corners.

START: Same as Birdland.

PITCH 1: 5.8 PG (V1) Climb the open book for about 10 feet and follow the horizontal out left (crux-1) about 20 feet to the crack/fault, then climb straight up to the top of the corner (crux-2), exit left, then up to the bolt anchors. (80 ft.)

PITCH 2: 5.6 PG (V2) Climb straight up passing old piton anchors on the right (crux), then go up left past overhang and then back right. From here one climbs pretty much straight up passing old piton scars along the way, finishing to the right of the impressive triangular summit roof. (140 ft.)

Variation 1: 5.11d R (Farewell To Fingers, drawn in w/dotted line) Begin on the face 20 feet left of Birdland and about 10 feet right of To Be Or Not To Be. Move up to a horizontal (and old bolt scar), then climb the difficult short face to join Farewell.

Variation 2: 5.7 PG (Link-up to Bird Cage's pitch two) Climb straight up passing old piton anchors on the right to the overhang (about 20 feet) (V2a). Hand traverse right along blocks and then climb up to broken left-facing corner. (You are now on the original pitch two of Bird Cage) Climb corner and up a bit left till below a short, red left-facing corner and old angle piton. Climb past it and a short, white left-facing corner to overhang with white jutting block. Move right and climb straight up to the top. (120 ft.)

Variation 2a: Instead of traversing right, clear overhang and climb up a bit right till below red corner.

FA 1960: Jim McCarthy and Al DeMaria
FA (V1) About 1960: Unknown
FFA (V1) 1970: Rich Goldstone and Dick Williams

54a   **(TOPROPE)** The Boys From Above 5.11d

Start from the top of Farewell To Fingers, move up left and climb face using the arête. FA about 1985: Kevin Bein

55   **TO BE OR NOT TO BE 5.12a PG ★★★**
(As a Toprope)

A great route that's rarely led and highly recommended as a **toprope** because it's 5.11d R to get to the final 5.12a PG direct finish crux. This climb basically follows the fall line of the rappel from Farewell To Arms and To Be's bolt anchors.

START: On the face below a good, narrow horizontal about 10 feet up between some small, right-facing flakes, almost 30 feet left of the Birdland/Birdcage open book.

PITCH 1: 5.12a PG Climb to the short left-facing corner, step up left and up to the bucket, move up (1st crux). Step right and work past the bulge and move left to better holds (2nd crux). Move up (V1) to thin horizontal, then step right and crimp/crank your way up to the bolt anchors (final crux). (80 ft.)

Variation 1: 5.11b R (Original finish) Move left and up to a small stance above overhang. Then continue up to easier rock to the bolt/anchors. (80 ft.)

FA (Toprope) 1983: Russ Clune

FA (Lead) 1983: Russ Raffa, Russ Clune and Lynn Hill

55a   **(TOPROPE)** Believe It Or Not 5.12a

Start next to a short, shallow open book next to a small laurel bush, 6 feet left of To Be or Not To Be. Climb steep bulging face directly past small overhang and a short rounded nose (crux) between To Be or Not To Be and To Have or Have Not to the bolt-anchors. FA 2000: Mike Siacka

56   TO HAVE OR HAVE NOT 5.12a/b R

Some climbers have said the protection is better than R, possibly PG-R.

Start: At a short left-facing corner that begins 6 feet up,

25 feet left of To Be or Not To Be.

Pitch 1: 5.12a/b R Climb corner past red rock to a horizontal. Traverse right about 10 feet and move up and right to a small overhang and a groove with a white streak. Follow groove past the overhang and climb to a ramp (from which climbers can rappel) that leads up right. Then continue up to a ledge. (100 ft.)

Pitch 2: (**NR**) (Unrated) Climb straight past overhangs to the NSGTL, then to the top. (150 ft.)

FA 1966: Pete Carman and Jim McCarthy

FFA 1973: John Stannard

57   SON OF STEM 5.11d R

Start: Same as To Have or Have Not.

Pitch 1: 5.11d R Follow To Have or Have Not for 20 feet to the horizontal. Continue straight past a bulge and overhang into a short left-facing corner. Climb up left to an alcove, then exit right to a belay in a shallow corner system. (80 ft.)

Pitch 2: (**NR**) (Unrated) Continue up face to the top between To Have or Have Not and Grease Gun Groove.

FA 1983: Mike Robin, Stokie Baker and Bruce Breslau

58   SOYLENT GREEN 5.11a R

Start: On face below some right-facing flakes about 20 feet right of Grease Gun Groove and 6 feet left of To Have or Have Not.

Pitch 1: 5.11a R Climb past flakes and a scoop to a shallow, very short left-facing corner. Continue past a short, shallow right-facing corner to a small ledge and then climb easier rock to Grease Gun Groove's pine tree on the left. (90 ft.)

FA 1983: Mike Robin, Stokie Baker and Ed Fripps

59   GREASE GUN GROOVE 5.6 PG ★★

Pitch one is really good and has become very popular despite the old school 5.6. It was first climbed in the rain (therefore its name). There is now a much nicer direct finish. If you plan to go to the top, two 60-meter ropes will juuust get you back to the start in one rappel thanks to rope stretch.

START: About 60 feet left of the Birdcage open book, at a low angle left-facing corner with an overhang about 20 feet up.

PITCH 1: 5.6 PG (V1 & V2) Move up corner to a stance (crux-1), then continue up corner past overhang to a ledge. Climb the next corner to the overhangs, exit right and move up to a stance below a short face (V3). Climb straight up (crux-2), then up left to pine tree belay/rap-station. (75 ft.)

PITCH 2: 5.6 PG Continue up a bit right and move up into the left-facing corner (crux). Follow corner to its top (V4) and then climb straight up to some small ledges below overhangs formed by large blocks. Climb the left side of blocks (or right) and up to the top and pine tree belay/rap-station. (110 ft.)

Variation 1: (**Toprope**) 5.11a Start 8 feet right of GGG and work straight up steep face past right side of overhang 15 feet up.

Variation 2: 5.9+ G Step right and climb the left-leaning flake to the corner (easier if tall).

Variation 3: 5.8 G (Drawn in w/dotted line) Diagonal up left to the crack in the overhang (which can be climbed at 5.8 G), traverse left around onto the face and up to the pine tree belay/rap-station.

Variation 4: (**NR**) 5.4 R (Original Route, drawn in w/dotted line for historical purposes) Diagonal up left on dirty, loose rock to the NSGTLedge if you dare. From here climb blocky white corner past tons of loose rock and up right to the top. (50 ft.)

FA 1958: Gary Hemming, Art Gran and Roger Chorley

59a **TULIP MUSSEL GARDEN 5.10d G ★**

This climb may not suit everyone's taste. There are some good moves with a well-protected sultry crux that will either wet your lips or make them very dry. Height-related, harder for shorter people.

START: 10 feet left of Grease Gun Groove, below a small overhang that's only 8 feet above the ground.

PITCH 1: 5.10d G Climb straight past overhang, the seam, the tiny right-facing flake/corner and short open book with a crack to a stance atop a block. Work up steep orange face (crux) to a short left-facing corner and up to the belay/rap station. (80 ft.)

FA 1989: Dick Williams

59b BROKEN SPRING 5.11a PG-R

The suspicious looking tri-cam held leader falls on the first and second ascents, if it doesn't hold it's R.

Start: Same as Corporate Conglomerate

Pitch 1: 5.11a PG-R Follow Corporate Conglomerate to the big block on the ledge. Move up the short corner and diagonal right past the right side of the second tiered overhang to the third and largest overhang. Work past the crux overhang (ingenious tri-cam placement just above lip) and move up to a small, short left-facing corner. Then continue straight up steep face to a pine tree. Watch out for loose rock at ledge.

FA 1992: Tom Spiegler and Howard Meltzer

60 CORPORATE CONGLOMERATE 5.9+ R

Not recommended because of the dirty and often wet start and the 5.7 R/X section on pitch one. Pitch two is dirty with some loose rock. Pitch three wanders a bit but has a wild and burly "R" runout.

Start: At the right hand (left-facing corner) of two opposing corners, about 55 feet left of Grease Gun Groove. The right-facing corner just to the left is very grungy.

Russ Raffa on
To Be or Not to Be
5.12a (Route 55)
Photo: Dick WIlliams 1995

Pitch 1: 5.9 PG Climb up right following the path of least resistance past a couple of ledges to a block sitting on a large ledge directly below a short left-facing corner with a small bush in it. Move up corner and then diagonal up left to a right-facing flake and keep moving up to stance (crux) (from here it's a 5.7 R-X runout to the ledge). Continue straight up to a small stance, then move up again, step left and climb to the loose rock-filled ledge. Go right about 10 feet to a pine tree belay/rap-station. (70 ft.)

Pitch 2: (**NR**) 5.5 PG Step right of tree and climb almost straight up to the first overhang. Step up left and up to next overhang, move up right and up face to the boulder- filled NSGTLedge and make a belay below open book/right-facing corner. (90 ft.)

Pitch 3: 5.9+ R Climb to top of open book and traverse left past lots of loose rock to a whitish, blocky pinnacle with a boulder sitting on its top. Traverse left again about 10 feet and begin in earnest by cranking straight up, layback-ing a fin-like protrusion past the burly notch at the lip of the final overhang (crux) to the top. (90 ft.)

FA 1981: Ivan Rezucha and Don Lauber

60a   (**TOPROPE**) Quack'n-Up 5.9+

Some good moves but it's a pain to set up the toprope anchors. To do this, it's easiest to climb Grey Gully or Fat and Weak to the first ledge and belay/rap-anchors. Go right to ledge at the right side of a bushy tree. Good cams in horizontal above ledge. Start climbing 15 feet left of Corporate Conglomerate and 10 feet right of Fat and Weak below a crack that diagonals up right. Climb crack to its top, step left and climb face to anchors. One can set up a TR from a small pine 20 feet higher but it's not worth the effort because of all the dangerous loose rock on ledge near pine tree. FA 2006: Dick Williams and Annie O'Neill

60b   FAT AND WEAK 5.7 PG-R
Good climbing till the second pitch which is a bit scary getting to the thin crack.

START: About 35 feet left of Corporate Conglomerate, 15 feet right of Grey Gully and immediately left of a short, ramp-like right-facing corner.

PITCH 1: 5.6 G ★ (V1) Go up ramp-like corner and follow crack up into a right-facing corner (crux). Move up corner to overhang, step around left and up face (old pin on Grey Gully) to small platform/ledge to meet Grey Gully and belay/rap-station. (50 ft.)

Pitch 2: 5.7 PG-R Move up left past a small tree till your feet are at wedged-block level. Move right to the thin crack (crux, Trango Ballnutz helpful), then climb pretty much straight up to the big ledge and pine tree belay/rap-station. (40 ft.)

Variation 1: 5.8 PG Start about 8 feet left and climb straight up crack.

FA 1991: Joe Bridges, Barbara Hart and Dick Williams

60c   **GREY HAIR ARETE 5.6 PG**
While climbing this new route, an observing passing climber said to their partner "a lot of grey hair here." Trango Ballnutzs were the only useful pro in thin horizontals.

START: At the short nose a few feet down and to the right of Grey Gully.

PITCH 1: 5.6 PG Move up nose to small ledge and small white pine. Work up face to the first thin horizontal (crux), then move up onto nose. Climb straight up nose to ledge and belay/rap-station. (50 ft.)

FA 2007: Dick Williams, Joe Bridges, Al Limone and Keith LaBudde

61   GREY GULLY 5.8 PG-R
Pitch one is pretty good if dry, pitch two has an exciting crux passing the rounded holds. Pitches three and four are

not recommended; they have incredible amounts of dangerous, loose rock and are recorded for historical reasons only.

START: On face just right of ferns below a broken right-facing corner with bushes and trees, 15 feet left of Fat And Weak and 25 feet right of Lonely Challenge.

PITCH 1: 5.5 PG Step right and climb face right of ferns up and into corner at first tree (crux). Climb corner to large laurel bush, step right and move up to ledge and belay/rap-station. (50 ft.)

PITCH 2: 5.8 PG-R Step right and move up on good incuts to bucket. Make a long reach up right to rounded holds on nose, work/step right and up face to a stance (crux). Then up to ledge with lots of loose rock. Traverse left about 25 feet to Lonely Challenge's pine tree belay/rap-station. (60 ft.)

Pitch 3: (**NR**) 5.0 R-X (Drawn in w/dotted line) Scramble up left, then up a left-facing corner that ends at a dirty, loose ledge. Diagonal up right (lots of dirty and loose rock here) about 45 feet to a small ledge full of loose rocks/blocks and make a belay at a block below an overhang. (100 ft.)

Pitch 4: (**NR**) 5.0 PG-R (Drawn in w/dotted line) Step right till the overhang can be climbed easily. Then diagonal way left to a tree in a short, broken right-facing corner. Continue up a bit left and up to the right side of a long overhang and an old pin, exit right to the top. (100 ft.)

FA 1959: Hans and Madi Kraus

61a   BACK TO THE FUTURE 5.8 G ★

This is a nice old climb that somehow got lost in the history books. There is some good climbing on it. It's not clear where the FA party went after the stance above the crux so there is a variation to choose from.

START: On the pebbly face immediately left of Grey Gully and just right of Princess Leia's broken arête/nose.

PITCH 1: 5.8 G Climb straight up the pebbly face to the obvious crack formed by a thin, right-facing flake. Work up into a short left-facing corner with two old pins, and step up right to a good stance (crux) (V1). Continue straight up passing the overhang to a good stance, then diagonal left to join Princess Leia at final pointed overhang on nose. (80 ft.)

Variation 1: 5.7 PG Move up right to small alcove and triangular overhang. Carefully move up face (staying just right of small unprotectable groove) passing right side of small pointy overhang to ledge and to Lonely Challenge's pine tree belay/rap-station. (80 ft.)

FA 1950's: Judging by the old ring pin at crux.

61b   PRINCESS LEIA 5.9 PG-R
Named in memory of my precious loving dog.
START: On the broken arête/nose just right of Lonely Challenge.
PITCH 1: 5.9 PG-R Climb straight up nose and face to a white bulge with a shallow open book which forms a seam. Work past seam (crux) to a horizontal with blueberry bushes. Diagonal up right around a small overhang, then up slightly left to pass the final pointy overhang on nose to the pine tree belay/rap-station on Lonely Challenge. (80 ft.)

FA (Toprope) 1991: Joe Bridges with Barbara Hart
FA (Lead) 1991: Dick Williams and Joe Bridges

62   **LONELY CHALLENGE 5.6 PG**
The first pitch of this climb isn't impressive looking from the ground but is pretty good. Variation one is quite interesting albeit a bit contrived and named after one of Williams's two dogs, Cruz. In the spring of 2006 there was a lot of rock fall and lots of rock scars on the slabs. The rockfall was from just below the NSGTLedge just left of pitch two's highest cedar tree. It has been cleaned up somewhat on rappel, but one should be very cautious on pitch two.
START: 25 feet left of Grey Gully, at the base of a trough formed by grey slabs on either side. The right slab is steeper and has a crack which diagonals up left to overhangs and small tree.
PITCH 1: 5.5 PG (V1) Climb left slab or the crack for about 20 feet to overhangs and fixed piton. Step/move right, then up right on steep rock past birch tree to blocky left-facing

corner. Diagonal up right on steep rock to the ledge and pine tree belay/rap-station. (80 ft.)

PITCH 2: 5.6 PG (V2) Step right of tree and basically climb straight up passing cedar tree and flake to small ledge and another cedar tree (this is Horney's pitch two belay). Continue straight up and when about 15 feet below the NSGT-Ledge and large cedar tree, diagonal right to right side of tree. (80 ft.)

PITCH 3: 5.6 G-PG Step right and diagonal up right to some overhangs, step/move right and up passing small tree on left (to avoid rope drag) up to a larger tree in a short, broken right-facing corner. Continue up a bit left and up to overhang that forms a nose with short crack. With optimism, climb up right on jutting dinner-plate-like flakes to a stance on lip at widest point of overhang and rounded holds (crux). Then step up and finish on smooth slab to the top. (100 ft.)

Variation 1: 5.8 PG (Cruz Queen) Either go up the obvious slab or force your way up the short left-facing corner to the first horizontal and foot traverse right to the polished overlap and crack. Diagonal up left to first bush, move up face on right to small grassy ledge. Move right to blueberry bush and thin crack at left side of overhang. Move up crack and step right onto pointy arête, then straight up joining Princess Leia past pointiest part of overhang at nose to the ledge and pine tree belay/rap-station. (80 ft.)

Variation 2: **(NR)** 5.0 R-X (Original Route, drawn in w/dotted line–Not Recommended–dirty, loose rock) Step right and climb face and broken, left-facing corner to a loose ledge to join Grey Gully. Diagonal up right about 45 feet past dirty, loose rock to a ledge full of loose rocks/blocks and belay at a block. (100 ft.)

FA 1965: Art Gran and Joe Kelsey

FA (V1) 2004: Dick Williams and Annie O'Neill

FA (P3) 2005: Dick Williams and Al DeMaria

Old Timers still hanging in there and crankin' down in the Nears, Joe Bridges, John Bragg, Claude Suhl, Richard Goldstone and Patty Matteson. Photo: Dick Williams 2007

63   **HORNEY 5.7 PG**

Despite the indirect line, there's quite a bit of variety and some good variations. The second pitch is exciting, especially if you go directly past center of overhang. Pitch three is OK and the new pitches four and five are good (pitches can be combined) or you can finish on the last pitch of Lonely Challenge at 5.6 PG. All making for an adventure. Two ropes best and bring lots of long slings plus a summit pack with some water in summer time. At the top there is an ash tree rap-station about 70 feet left, on grassy ledge near lip of roof. Same rap as for Up Yours and Loose Goose.

START: Same as Lonely Challenge.

PITCH 1: 5.5 PG Diagonal up left on slab to low angle corner with hand crack that leads up right (one can climb straight up to here starting on Wildmere). Climb crack (crux) to small ledge directly below blocky/flaky right-facing corner with questionable rock and make a belay here or 6-8 feet right at old pin. (60 ft.)

PITCH 2: 5.6 PG (V1) Step right and climb face immediately left of old pin to small ledge. Step right again (old pin) and climb straight up past small overhang and up to whitish overhangs with jagged left-facing flakes and wide horizontal undercling crack. (If you climb straight up here, it's 5.7 PG). Step left and then move up to ledge formed by block (blue Trango Ballnutz helpful here for directional, the original route climbed straight up to the NSGTLedge from here, **NR**). Then traverse right about 30 feet to cedar tree and belay/rap-station. (100 ft.)

PITCH 3: 5.5 PG Climb straight up and when about 15 feet below the NSGTLedge and large cedar tree, diagonal right to right side of tree. (35 ft.)

PITCH 4: 5.7 G (V2 & V3) Climb straight up following a left-slanting right-facing corner past very short blue Camalot-size hand crack (crux) to ledge and up right to highest pine tree and belay. (40 ft.)

PITCH 5: 5.7 PG-R Continue up left on low-angle slab and at the first opportunity step left to outside edge of slab. Ease your way up very exposed arête (crux) to the top. You can avoid the arête's exposure by following the corner past block (5.3 PG) and exit left to the top. (100 ft.)

Variation 1: 5.5 PG   Climb corner to its top and then traverse right about 12-15 feet to another old pin to join regular route.

Variation 2: 5.3 PG (Original Route, drawn in w/dotted line) Traverse left about 25 feet and climb to some overhangs. Step around right on great holds to old pin, then up past overhangs on jugs at jutting rock (crux) to a stance. Diagonal right to the highest of two pines. (90 ft.)

Variation 3: 5.2 PG (Original Route, drawn in w/dotted line) Finish by diagonalling up right to overhang that forms a nose. Keep traversing right crossing Lonely Challenge past break (**V3a**) at old pin at right side of nose and around right to the top. (50 ft.)

Variation 3a: 5.5 PG Move up left to point at lip and widest part of overhang to rounded holds. Step up (crux) and finish on smooth slab to the top. (80 ft.)

FA 1965: Art Gran and Pete Vlachos
FA (P 4&5) 2005: Dick Williams, Annie O'Neill and Al DeMaria

64   **WILDMERE 5.10a PG-R**
The first pitch is so much better than it looks. It has multiple, challenging, good moves up to the NSGTLedge. The last pitch is pretty wild and burly; it's just amazing that it goes at this grade.

START: From left side of the 8 foot-high detached block that's about 40 feet left of Lonely Challenge and 20 feet right of the Bee Bite.

PITCH 1: 5.8 PG Work your way to top of block, then up slab to join Horney at low angle ramp with crack. Move up a bit left and follow crack/seam that diagonals up right to a stance, then up face past right side of cedar tree to small ledge and large block (5.8 PG optional belay-black Camalot helpful, 100 ft.). Continue straight up to first overhang, move up a bit left to next overhang (Trango Ballnutz helpful). Work past overhang (crux) and up to lower angle rock and small ledge. Step right and climb to the NSGTLedge with big stacked blocks (black Camalot helpful). (180 ft.)

PITCH 2: 5.10a PG-R Step right and climb pretty much straight up past first overhangs (about 20 feet), then up a bit right before working/moving left to a right-pointing/jutting flake (5.10a PG-R). Then work up to good stance and welcomed rest spot. Climb straight up on good holds to buckets at lip of roof, then make the strenuous traverse left and crank up past break to finish (5.10a G). (70 ft.)

FA 2005: Brian McGillicudy, Gerry Keiffer and Jerry Freeman

64a   BEE BITE 5.7 G-PG ★★

I am recommending this climb for those who may be looking for a taste of the mountaineering experience. Quite an interesting total climb but especially at the offwidth on pitch one, which involves calmness and good hand jamming technique (one black Camalot can be leapfrog'd or better yet, bring two). This climb is usually dry by summer and should be in the shade by 10 am. If the corner is wet, climb variation two (Hornet Rocks). The slabs dry up quicker than the corner. There is some loose rock high up in and above the final corner. All the belays are in the shade and makes for a nice outing. Variation three was put in on Williams' birthday.

START: 60 feet left of Lonely Challenge in a short right-facing corner that's below the huge right-facing corner system with the all to obvious offwidth crack that begins about 40 feet up.

PITCH 1: 5.7 G-PG (V1 & V2) Work up the corner (crux-1) for about 20 feet to large ledge (**V3**) and optional belay at tree to the right. Climb up into corner and crack (crux-2) then up to the imposing offwidth. Technique your way up the crack to jugs (crux-3) and up to top of slab and overhangs (optional belay). Then up the blocky, loose-looking corner. Climb/stem up (crux-4) till some jutting, blocky overhangs force you left to a small grassy ledge. Continue up dirty ramp/gully to a large ledge with pine trees and threaded belay/rap-station. (130 ft.) Two 50-meter ropes will get you back to the ground at base of Elder Cleavage Direct. One 60-meter rope gets you down to Loose Goose's belay/rap-station.

PITCH 2: 5.4 PG Go straight up 15 feet to large, NSGT-Ledge, then straight up past breaks in overhang at a notch and up to large white overhangs. Traverse/diagonal left to left-facing corner. Continue up face past the left-facing corner (**V4**) to finish on the short head wall to the top. (100 ft.) There is an ash tree belay/rap-station on ledge down to the right, which takes you directly (about 80 foot rap) to the threaded rap-station at end of pitch one.

Variation 1: (**NR**) 5.5 R Climb the dirty face about 15-20 feet to the left to meet Horney at the white buttress.

Variation 2: 5.5 PG (Hornet Rocks) The start is the same as for Lonely Challenge and Horney, 60 feet to the right. Diagonal up left on the slab past a white buttress (with crack in it that diagonals right) to some grass hummocks. (The next section is drawn in w/dotted line) Up hummocks and move left and up short grey face (crux) to a sloping ledge and make a belay (blue Camalot helpful). You are now about 15 feet right of Bee Bite's huge blocky corner that begins above the offwidth crack. (100 ft.)

Variation 3: 5.7 G-PG (Born On The 4th Of July) Traverse left along horizontal to stance on sloping ledge (crux-1) below short, low-angle ramp that leads up right to crack. Step left and climb to body-height right-facing corner and move right to crack. Climb crack past wild flake to good stance (crux-2) below block with tree above it. Begin the easy but neat/exposed traverse left at good horizontal for about 12 feet, then up and left crossing Up Yours to join Loose Goose's pine tree belay/rap-station. (80 ft.)

Variation 4: 5.8- G-PG (Drawn in w/dotted line) Climb up corner or move right into corner to great horizontal, then move right on jugs and up arête to the ledge, go right to belay/rap-tree.

FA: Unknown
FA (V2) 1959: Art Gran and Gary Hemming
FA (V3) 2005: Dick Williams and Annie O'Neill

64b BORN AGAIN 5.10b/c G-PG

Great technical moves, strenuous at times, good pro. There are some people who might ask their "higher power" for the strength to make it past the various cruxes.

START: At Bee Bite's sharp outside corner.

PITCH 1: 5.10b/c G-PG Step left using outside corner to small stance at small right-facing flakes. Move up to overhang, then work up to good holds at base of slab (crux). Work up again to stance on slab, then up to final slab to join Born On the 4th. Continue up to body-height right-facing corner, step up to good holds and exit left around onto face. Climb straight up face and follow broken crack to horizontal and Born On the 4th's traverse. Traverse left about 5 feet, then up and left crossing Up Yours to join Loose Goose's pine tree belay/rap-station. (80 ft.)

FA 2006: Brian McGillicudy and Dick Williams

65 ELDER CLEAVAGE DIRECT 5.10b PG ★★★

One of the best climbs in the Nears. Pitch one is demanding and exciting with tricky gear placements. The last pitch is really wild and was an old climb done with aid back in the 1950s.

START: 100 feet left and downhill from Lonely Challenge there is a boulder that stands just inches from the cliff; the Direct begins about 10 feet left. Two ropes helpful, especially on the last pitch.

PITCH 1: 5.10b PG (V1) Boulder straight up to the crack (crux) and small overhang, step left and up (5.9- PG) to a slab and optional belay. Climb the left-facing flakes up left

Brian McGillicuddy on
final pitch of *Wildmere* 5.10a
(Route 64)
Photo: Dick Williams 2006

to the overhang, step right and work up to the pine tree belay/rap-station. (80 ft.)

PITCH 2: 5.4 PG Traverse/move right and join Up Yours straight past the ledge with pine tree belay/rap-station (same as for Loose Goose) to the highest ledge (NSGT-Ledge). Then walk right about 20 feet to pine tree just left of a pile of stacked blocks below a right-facing corner. There is a small oak tree about 20 feet up. (160 ft.)

PITCH 3: 5.10b PG (V2) Climb straight up to the short left-facing corner to crack in the roof and exit right at the first opportunity, then up to the top and pine tree belay. (80 ft.) Best to rappel from ash tree to the left, about an 80-foot rappel to Bee Bite's threaded rap-station.

Variation 1: 5.8 PG (Original Start) From top of boulder, just 10 feet right of the direct start. Move up to the first horizontal (V1a) and traverse left about 10 feet to join the direct.

Variation 1a: (**Toprope**) 5.12a (Carlos Buhler's Day Off) Continue straight up following a thin seam-like crack.

Variation 2: (**Toprope**) 5.11a (Cat on a Hard Ten Roof) Start on Elder Cleavage and follow it till directly below some large left-facing blocks/flakes (a bit loose). Climb straight up till standing atop the flakes, then traverse left about 5-8 feet till directly below a V notch. Climb straight up through notch, past a crack in the next overhang to the top and large pine tree.

FA 1980: Ivan Rezucha with Annie O'Neill
FA (V1a) 1986: Michael Dimitri
FA (V2) 1993: Peter Darmi and Dick Williams

Unadulterated difficulty unencumbered by concerns of mortality is the province of sport climbing.
— Rich Goldstone

66   **UP YOURS 5.7+ PG ★**

Pitch one has excellent climbing, lots of places for pro if you need it. The name of this climb originated when some passing climbers asked the "Vulgarian" first ascent party: "what climb are you on?"

START: 30 feet left of the Cleavage boulder and 20 feet from Elder's direct start, below the S-shaped crack that is just above the overhang and arches up right to a slab.

PITCH 1: 5.7+ PG Work up the crack to a stance (crux-1) (V1), then diagonal up right to far right side of slab. Climb the broken, left-facing corner (crux-2) and up face and crack to ledge and pine tree belay/rap-station. (same belay as for Loose Goose) (100 ft.)

PITCH 2: 5.3 PG Go back right and continue up the face on easier rock to the second highest ledge and belay on Bee Bite at the threaded belay/rap-station (about 15 feet below the highest large ledge (NSGTLedge). (70 ft.) Two 50-meter ropes will get you back to the ground at base of Elder Cleavage.

PITCH 3: Finish on Loose Goose (5.5 PG) or Bee Bite (5.4 PG). (100 ft.) There is an ash tree rap-station on ledge down to the right.

Variation 1: 5.9+ PG-R (Younger Cleavage) Climb straight up short crack to slab. Then climb steep face to Elder's left-pointing flake and overhang (crux). Climb straight past overhang, then up face past short left-facing flake and up to Loose Goose's pine tree belay/rap-station.

FA 1961: John Weichsel and Bill Goldner
FA (V1) 2005: Rich Gottlieb and Felix Modugno

66a   **BOOB JOB 5.10b PG ★**

A good last pitch climb from the NSGTLedge. For those climbing at this level, one can climb Elder's last pitch and rap down to do this one too. The crux has a long reach and pro is strenuous to place.

PITCH 1: 5.10b PG From the threaded belay/rap-station on Up Yours, scramble up 15 feet to the NSGTLedge. Climb fault and short left-facing corner. Then straight up into V notch in roof, exit right and up (crux) to the top.

FA 1998: Mike Cherry

66b **(TOPROPE)** Nice Job 5.11a

Start on the face a few feet right of Loose Goose and climb the short, steep face. Then go up to a ledge directly below a steep, rounded nose. Climb nose (crux) to finish. FA 1991: Dick Williams with Joe Bridges

67 LOOSE GOOSE 5.6 PG ★★

Good climbing, especially on the first and last pitches.

START: 10 feet left of Up Yours, at the right side of a blocky, broken-up area.

PITCH 1: 5.6 PG Climb straight up to a slab, then past a bulge and short open book till (crux1) below the prominent 5.8 PG crack variation (**V1**). Move up right and climb the left-facing corner with hand crack (crux-2) to a ledge. Go right to pine tree belay/rap-station. (100 ft.)

PITCH 2: 5.2 PG Diagonal left about 15 feet and then straight up face past a couple of pines on the left to large tree and boulder filled ledge. (60 ft.) Then go up left about 20 feet to large NSGTLedge and pine tree belay directly below a left-facing corner that's about 40 feet up. (80 ft.)

PITCH 3: 5.5 PG Climb straight past notch in small overhang (crux), then up joining Bee Bite on face past the left-facing corner (V2) to finish on the short head wall to the top. (80 ft.)

Variation 1: 5.8 G ★ (Crack Variation, see 67a) Follow crack past bulge (crux) to a stance. Continue up face and corner calmly passing questionable rock to pine tree (there is a rap tree about 15 feet to the left on Swissair). Continue up further to another big ledge and belay at Loose Goose's pine. (100 ft.)

Variation 2: 5.8- G-PG (Drawn in w/dotted line) Climb corner or move right into corner to great horizontal, then move right on jugs and up arête to the ledge, go right to belay/rap-tree.

FA 1942: Fritz Wiessner, Beckett Howorth and Hans Kraus

67a   **5.8 CRACK CLIMB 5.8 G ★**

If you are not up to snuff on cracks/offwidths, no worry, this climb has wonderful in-cut buckets inside the crack. Pitch two was an old variation to Loose Goose and it now has its own first pitch. This pitch one also makes for a more direct start, albeit with a 5.4 R-X section. **Loose Goose** is still the nicest way of getting to this pitch two crack climb.

START: 25 feet left of Loose Goose, below Swissair's steep dirty gully. Go right 10 feet to obvious jagged off-width crack.

PITCH 1: 5.6 G Climb crack (crux) and short slab to ledge (last pro placement). Then up slab (5.4 R-X) a bit left of center, then a bit right and up to join Loose Goose at ledge below crack. (60 ft.)

PITCH 2: 5.8 G Follow crack past bulge (crux) to a stance. Continue up face and corner, calmly passing questionable rock to pine tree (there is a rap tree about 15 feet to the left on Swissair). Continue up further to another big ledge (NSGTLedge) and belay at Loose Goose's pine. (100 ft.)

PITCH 3: 5.5 PG Climb straight up finishing on Loose Goose which joins Bee Bite. (100 ft.)

FA (P2): Early 60's

68   SWISSAIR 5.8 PG

If you do this entire climb, you will most likely never do it again. Pitch one is bad, pitch two is good, pitch three is ugly, pitch four is good. Variation one avoids the dirty gully but has a 5.4 R-X run out, best to start on Loose Goose.

Start: At a gully just past a broken area, 25 feet left of Loose Goose. Above the gully are two corners that face each other, there is a ledge with a pine tree about 40 feet up.

Pitch 1: **(NR)** 5.5 PG (V1) Scramble up the steep, dirt-filled gully about 25 feet (V2) and climb the corner/fault system that goes up right to a ledge, then move left to the pine tree belay. (60 ft.)

PITCH 2: 5.8 PG Continue to the overhang, move up right following a right-facing flake to a small ledge. Work past overhangs and go straight up to a good-sized pine tree and belay. (50 ft.)

Pitch 3: **(NR)** 4th Class Work up past an unpleasant series of ledges full of dirt, loose rock, dead branches, trees and bushes to the NSGTLedge and oak tree below the base of the huge slabby-looking, right-facing corner (V3). Go right to a belay at pine tree that angles out from cliff or at Loose Goose's pine tree (about 15 feet further right). (50 ft.)

PITCH 4: 5.8 G Climb pretty much straight up about 15 feet to right-facing flakes/blocks (5.4, first pro). Then gain top of flakes (V4) and continue up and left to ledge and bushy oak tree and corner. Work up corner past overhangs (5.7 G) to a stance (V5). Continue up corner to small overhang. Step left (crux) and up to the top. (80 ft.)

Variation 1: 5.6 G (Same first pitch as for 5.8 PG Crack Climb, 67a) Instead of going up steep gully, go right 10 feet to obvious jagged offwidth crack. Climb crack (crux) and short slab to ledge (last pro placement). Then up slab (5.4 R-X) a bit left of center, then a bit right and up to join Loose Goose at ledge below 5.8 crack. Walk/go left about 20 feet to Swiss Air's pine tree belay rap-station.

Variation 2: **(NR)** 5.7 PG Climb straight up the broken corner to the left side of the pine tree (loose rock).

Variation 3: **(NR)** 5.4 PG (Original Route, drawn in w/dotted line) Move up dirty corner, step right and up past nasty grassy bogs to belay at bushy oak tree.

Variation 4: 5.4 PG (Ain't Dis Yab Yum, drawn in w/dotted line) Step right to small birch tree cluster and diagonal up right and around onto face to join Loose Goose and Bee Bite below corner.

Variation 5: 5.0 PG (Escape route and optional belay, drawn in w/dotted line) Traverse left about 12-15 feet to small tree (optional belay) and then up past flake and blocks to the top.

FA 1981: Todd Swain, Kurt Graf and Max Strumia

69 (**NR**)   AIN'T DIS YAB YUM? 5.5 PG
This route is only written for historical purposes. If you have any sense at all, you will stay off this mess of a climb and leave the vegetation, chiggers and loose rock alone. The variation is interesting and unusual but not worth recommending.

Start: At a low-angle face with a short, wide crack that begins 20 feet up, 50 feet uphill to the left of Swissair. The face is bracketed by very large opposing corners.

Pitch 1: (**NR**) 5.5 PG Climb past the crack heading straight up (V1) to a grass filled vertical fault/broken crack system just left of the big corner. Work up this (crux) past a dead, hanging cedar tree to large sloping, chigger-filled grass ledge. Make a belay on the face about 10 feet above ledge. (80 ft.)

Pitch 2: (**NR**) 5.5 PG Climb straight up to large block pointing left, step right and climb past an overhang at a left-jutting flake (crux) and up to chossy ledge. Then diagonal up right on an incredibly loose dirt and rock-filled ramp to the NSGTLedge and pine tree. Go further right 20 feet to next pine tree. (same as for Loose Goose) (80 ft.)

Pitch 3: Finish on Loose Goose.

Variation 1: 5.7 G-PG (Not So Yummy, drawn in w/dotted line) At the top of the initial crack, continue up a bit and then diagonal up right through trees to the base of narrow chimney and chockstone. Work straight up into chimney and move up to very small ledge on left face. Step right into short, steep left-facing corner and work up to make a belay at chockstone near ledge and cedar tree. Either rappel from tree or chockstone, or scramble up low-angle face and finish on Ain't Dis Yab Yum or traverse left about 50 feet to the cedar tree belay/rap-station on Where The Wild

Things Are.
FA 1973: Ted Dillard and Eric Lucas
FA (V1) 2005: Dick Williams and Annie O'Neill

70   WHERE THE WILD THINGS ARE 5.10d PG
START: On the right side of a short slab that measures about 20 feet high and about 20 feet wide at its base, 30 feet left of Ain't Dis Yab Yum?

PITCH 1: 5.10a PG Climb slab and move up left to the first horizontal break in the middle of the roof. Hand traverse out left to the lip and work up to stance (crux). Then continue up right to the outside corner and climb to a ledge and cedar tree belay/rap-station. (70 ft.)

Pitch 2: **(NR)** 5.7 R Climb up a bit left, then up right and then straight up to right-jutting flake. Climb pretty much straight past small overhang and face (crux) and up to first pine tree and dirt ledge. Continue up face to the large NS-GTLedge and large pine tree (this is your last chance to retreat comfortably). (70 ft.)

Pitch 3: **(NR)** 5.10d PG Walk right about 30 feet over boulders and loose rock till below the scene of a big/massive rock fall area below reddish rock. Climb up right past reddish rock to the ceiling. Work past weakness/break to stance at low angle rock (crux). Move up to overhang, traverse left around corner and up to the top. (100 ft.)

FA (Pitch 1 & 2) 1987: Mike Steele and Nick Mickowski
FA (Pitch 3) 1986: Mike Steele and Bill Ravitch

Age is an issue of mind over matter.
If you don't mind, it doesn't matter.

— Mark Twain

70a   **PREYING MANTLE 5.10a PG**

A surprisingly good climb, curiously demanding moves. It's helpful to have extra red and gold Camalots plus Trango Ballnutz and a micro cam.

START: On slab below vertical seam immediately left of Where The Wild Things Are.

PITCH 1: 5.10a PG Climb slab to roof and make the awkward move left to the left-most flake under roof. Hand traverse left to lip and move up to a good stance at white streak. Work up past tiny pebbly overhang and bulge on rounded holds to another good stance (crux: reachy). Then climb to final overhang and great horizontal. Pass overhang and up low angle slab to the top of the dirt ledge and put in a directional (red Camalot). Go down right to cedar tree belay/rap-station. (100 ft.)

FA 2006: Brian McGillicuddy and Dick Williams

70b   **PREDATOR 5.10a PG-R**

Star-quality moves but not clean enough yet at the beginning or on the second pitch till it has seen more traffic; then it should get an overall star rating. Using variation two makes pitch one a G-protection crux. It is recommended to use double ropes.

START: About 10 feet right of Vultures Know below a short thin crack.

PITCH 1: 5.10a PG-R Climb past crack and face to large oak tree, then move up past short crack to a stance at slabby face. Climb straight up to horizontal break (V1), traverse right about 6 feet to white rock and steep face below overhang. Climb straight up to jugs (long reach) and step up to the overhang (V2). Step left onto nose and work up past overhang to a stance (crux). Move up to ledges and go left about 5-8 feet to place directionals at short horizontal (red Camalots). Diagonal up right to grassy ledge and further right to a (shady) belay at Where The Wild Things Are cedar tree with rap-station. (140 ft.)

PITCH 2: 5.7 PG Traverse back (about 30 feet) up left along top of ledge till above pitch one crux overhang. Climb pretty much straight up (crux about half way up) to (shady) belay at highest pine on the NSGTLedge. (80 ft.) There is a huge pile of very scary precariously stacked blocks 15 feet to the left; don't want to be near or below it when they let loose.

PITCH 3: 5.10a PG From tree, step left and climb broken rock to the base of jutting block, step left and move up into short right-facing corner and roof (black Camalot helpful). From jugs, step left to point and reach way up to holds at lip (gold Camalot above lip) and then work up to a stance above lip (crux). Best to make a belay to the left near lip of roof.

Pitch 4: 4th Class Climb up and left and follow dirt ramp past trees and bushes to the top. (60 ft.)

Variation 1: 5.7 G (Escape Left) Traverse left to join Vultures Know

Variation 2: 5.10a G (Escape Right) Traverse right about five feet to break in small overhang, then crank up to a stance and to ledges.

FA 2005: Brian McGillicuddy and Eric Terzini
FA (V2) 2006: Brian McGillicuddy and Dick Williams

71   VULTURES KNOW 5.10b/c R-X

Pitch one looks so yukky from the ground, but there is actually some very good climbing on it. If pitch one had a nice belay/rap-tree before the 40-foot long, dirty traverse right, it would be very popular; since there is no tree there, make sure to save or have an extra green and or red Camalot for a needed directional (a blue Camalot works but not great). Pitch two is too dirty but has some neat moves with some great holds. Pitch three has no crux pro; it's hard, scary, technical, strenuous and dangerous.

Brian McGillicuddy, on final pitch of Predator's Lair (Route 70b)
Photo: Dick Williams 2006

START: 45 feet left of Where The Wild Things Are, below a series of broken, vegetated left-facing corners, 20 feet right of Yum Yum Yab Yum.

PITCH 1: 5.7 G Follow the corner past trees to a nice crack, up this (crux), then up to top of last corner. Step around right and up to small ledges and short horizontal for needed (red Camalot) directional. Carefully traverse right and up to grassy ledge and shady cedar tree belay/rap-station. (same belay as for Where The Wild Things Are). (140 ft.)

Pitch 2: (**NR**) (Unrated) Climb the face to the right of the jagged right-facing corner to large NSGTLedge with lots of boulders, go right to large pine tree. (60 ft.)

Pitch 3: 5.10b/c R-X Climb the face behind the tree and up a bit left into the blocky overhang in the corner. Move up to the roof, stem and layback up right to small crumbly holds, and if they don't break off continue working up to better holds at lip. If you still have any gas left, crank up to a stance, put in your first pro and take a big sigh of relief. Then up through the jungle to the top. (100 ft.)

FA 1979: Don Perry and Maury Jaffe

72   **AFTER YOU 5.7 PG-R**

Was the first ascent party looking for a leader? Seriously though, this climb has some good climbing. Pitch one has some good thin climbing, a bit necky. Pitch two is an adventure, and if it were climbed more, it would be cleaner and more popular. First two Trango Ballnutz helpful on Pitch one and two. Pitch three's crux overhang is pretty wild for its grade.

START: The same as Yum Yum Yab Yum or on the face just to the right.

PITCH 1: 5.7 PG-R Climb the slab and thin face with short seams just right of nose/outside corner till one can step left to Yum Yum's pine tree belay/rap-station. (60 ft.)

PITCH 2: 5.7 PG Climb straight up left-facing flakes above or step back right onto face and climb to alcove below overhang. Climb past the right edge of the overhang (crux) to a grassy ledge (grass hand holds). Go left about 15 feet and climb the face past a short, right-facing flaky corner. Then up the face past a second, flaky right-facing corner to ledge on left and a pine tree belay/rap-station (same as for Yum Yum). (90 ft.)

PITCH 3: 5.5 PG Follow Yum Yum past right-facing flakes to ledge and oak tree cluster (optional belay, 25 ft.) Step right and climb the overhang that is 10 feet up at a finger crack. Continue up right into a right-facing corner and move up to the crack that breaks the ceiling. Hand traverse left on jugs past an old fixed angle pin and up to a stance (crux: long reach). Either climb up left and finish on Yum Yum or continue straight past an overhang and finish up the right-hand of two short right-facing corners to the top. (150 ft.)

FA 1962: Bill Goldner and Muriel Mayo

73   **YUM YUM YAB YUM 5.3 PG ★★★**

A delightful climb with a wild last pitch traverse, double ropes recommended. If you want to finish on something more exciting, climb the 5.7 last pitch variations.

START: On face just right of low-angle left-facing corner that begins 20 feet up, 20 feet left of Vultures Know. There is a pine tree belay/rap-station about 60 feet up.

PITCH 1: 5.3 G (V1) Diagonal up left and follow the low-angle left-facing corner to ledge and pine tree belay/rap-station. (60 ft.)

PITCH 2: 5.3 PG Diagonal right about 10 feet or so and work left to base of left-facing corner (crux). Climb corner to its top and then go straight up face to ledge, and go right about 5-10 feet to pine tree belay/rap-station. (120 ft.)

PITCH 3: 5.1 PG Climb straight past right-facing flakes to large ledge and oak tree (about 25 feet). Diagonal left to large ledge and make a belay below a large open book. (60 ft.)

PITCH 4: 5.3 G (V2) Climb straight up the open book (crux) to the overhang, move up right and up to old fixed angle piton (**V3**). Then make the long, 35-foot traverse right (**V4**) and up past a groove to the top. (80 ft.)

Variation 1: 5.5 G (Drawn in w/dotted line) Start about 25 feet to the left, at the first left-facing corner that begins on a small grassy ledge about 10 feet above the ground. Climb/stem the corner till near its top and exit right onto face and up and right to join the regular route at the pine tree belay/rap-station.

Variation 2: 5.7 PG ★ (Taste of Yab Yummy, drawn in w/ dotted line) Go back right on ledge about 10 feet and climb broken face and short left-facing corner to large overhang and finger crack that leads right. Traverse right onto face and up to a stance (crux-1). Then climb straight up (crossing Yum Yum's traverse, to join **V4** called Yab Yummy) past overhangs at the obvious break to a stance at a very small pine (crux 2, blue Camalot helpful). Finish on the short face to the top. (60 ft.)

Variation 3: 5.0 PG (Yabba Dabba Do,drawn in w/dotted line) Diagonal up left to roof and traverse left all the way to the large pine tree belay/rap-station. There is one spot of totally avoidable loose rock.

Variation 4: 5.7 PG ★ (Yab Yummy, drawn in w/dotted line) About halfway along the traverse, climb straight up past overhangs (blue Camalot helpful) and steep face to the top.

FA 1960: Art Gran and Al DeMaria
FA (V1 and 3): old variations
FA (V2) 2005: Dick Williams and Gregory Rukavina
FA (V4) 1980's: Bill Ravitch and Mike Steele

After you have chickened out and backed off of a climb, don't despair: you have just had a successful reconnaissance.
    — Joe Bridges

73a　　　　　**SILVER BULLET 5.7 G**

Nice climbing in corner and slab. Creative gear placements with small wires and Trango Ballnutz makes it "G" pro.

START: 35 feet left of YumYum Yab Yum and 5 feet right of B.Warewolf below shallow left-facing corner capped by an overhang.

PITCH 1: 5.7 G Climb corner to top, step up right and up slab to ledge and B.Warewolf's pine tree belay/rap-station. (60 ft.)

FA 2005: Dick Williams and Annie O'Neill

74　　　　　　B.WAREWOLF 5.8 PG

If it weren't for the unprotected start on pitch one and the possibility of hitting the ledge on the second pitch, this could be popular. Pitch three is exciting and well worth the doing, two blue Camalots helpful.

Start: On the face 5 feet left of Silver Bullet below a left-facing corner that begins about 20 feet up, 40 feet left of Yum Yum Yab Yum.

Pitch 1: 5.7 PG-R Boulder up the face about 12 feet to a flake (Trango Ballnutz, blue and red helpful), then up to a stance next to small tree near base of corner. Climb to tree in corner (V1), move right around corner onto bulging face. Work straight up (crux) to ledge and pine tree belay/rap-station. (60 ft.)

Pitch 2: 5.7 R Step right and from the top of flake/rock on ledge, move up a bit left to a stance. Work straight up to a blocky jug and then up to a stance (crux). Continue to the V-notch in small overhang. Above notch, step right to small, right-facing corner and tree. At top of corner, step left and climb past right-facing flakes to large NSGTLedge filled with bushy oak trees. Go right about 35 feet to YumYum Yab Yum. (110 ft.)

PITCH 3: 5.8 PG About 25 feet straight above you are some rust-colored, short left-facing corners. Step right and climb the overhang 10 feet at a finger crack (same as for After You). Continue up and left to a stance on a rock-filled ledge and first left-facing corner. Climb to the roof and work up left passing overhangs to the final overhang and wide crack (crux). Exit right to a stance. Diagonal up left to finish on Yum Yum Yab Yum to the top. (100 ft.)

Variation 1: 5.5 PG (Original Route) Struggle up corner past tree and up to pine tree belay.

FA 1981: Todd Swain and Brett Wolf

If climbing Eenie Meenie, Curly, Larry or Moe, beware of anyone rappelling down Eenie Meenie because the rappellers or their ropes could knock down rocks along the way.

74a   CURLY 5.4 G-PG

START: About 15 feet left of Silver Bullet, at right side of wide block leaning against the face. Walk up left to the small right-facing corner.

PITCH 1: 5.4 G-PG Climb corner and short slab to tree and belay/rap-station. (45 ft.)

FA 2007: Dick Williams and Annie O'Neill

74b   (**TOPROPE**) Larry 5.9

Start at left side of wide block leaning against the face, immediately right of the gully-like area that one third-classes up to climb Eenie Meenie and My-Knee Moe. Step up right onto left side of ledge, begin climbing straight up, then up left, then right in a zig-zag fashion to the short face, then work straight up onto slab (crux) and to the oak tree rap-station. FA 2007: Dick Williams and Annie O'Neill.

74c   MOE 5.8 G

START: Below a thin crack/seam from atop a block/boulder that is partway up the gully-like area that leads to Eenie Meenie and My-Knee Moe.

PITCH 1: 5.8 G Move up crack/seam to thin horizontal, then make long reach or dyno to jugs (crux), then place pro (strenuous to place) for next move. Continue straight up past rounded overhang and another seam to the slab. Go up, place directionals, then go right to oak tree rap-station. (45 ft.)

FA 2007: Dick Williams, Annie O'Neill, Keith LaBudde, Rich Goldstone and Joe Bridges

75 EENIE MEENIE 5.7 PG

Exciting climbing on pitch one's suspicious looking/ sounding hollow flakes. Even today with modern gear it is quite the lead. Try to imagine doing it back in 1959 with pitons. It takes a considerable mountaineering mentality to enjoy this type of climbing. Pitch two is OK till the rock quality deteriorates near belay ledge. Pitch three is short so as to reduce rope drag, but with double ropes pitch three and four can be combined. Pitch four's not bad except passing the tree on the traverse, better to finish on YYYY or on its variations. Highly recommended to do with double ropes to alleviate rope drag, plus it's much more convenient for the rappel.

START: Below a large, orange, loose-looking right-facing corner that begins 30 feet above a boulder and dirt-filled gully-like area, 80 feet left of Yum Yum Yab Yum.

PITCH 1: 5.7 PG Scramble up and right, past large blocks to the ledge and tree below the huge corner. Don't go up the corner, cautiously work your way up the right-facing flakes just right of the corner (crux about half way up). At top of flakes at large red overhang (V1), diagonal up right in blocky right-facing corner about 20 feet to old ring pin, then diagonal up left to huge, precarious-looking block and threaded belay sling/rap-station. Either belay/rap from here or carefully squeeze up left behind the block to make a belay at small ledge and old pin. (120 ft.)

Pitch 2: 5.3 PG Climb pretty much straight up the face passing angle piton till the quality of rock degrades. Then up a bit right to large, chossy NSGTLedge and oak tree belay/rap-station. (70 ft.) Two-60-meter-rope rappel from here gets you back to the ground.

Pitch 3: 5.0 PG Climb straight up whitish pointed nose above and go right to YYYY's large ledge belay below open book. (30 ft.)

Pitch 4: 5.4 PG (High Suspension) Move up the open book about 10 feet to wide horizontal and traverse left about 25 feet to (white) black birch tree. Thrash past tree and then continue traversing past a shale sill/horizontal (crux) to the left side of the roof. Climb up and a bit right to large pine tree belay/rap-station. (70 ft.)

Variation 1: 5.7 PG Hand traverse left 5 feet to a stance, then up to small ledge left of huge block.

FA 1959: Al DeMaria and Art Gran

FA (High Suspension, pitch 4) 1942: Fritz Wiessner, Hans Kraus and Beckett Howorth (The original pitches leading up to this last pitch have been lost over time)

FA (V1) 2005: Gregory Rukavina and Dick Williams

76   MY-KNEE MOE 5.9 G-PG ★

Great first pitch, technical and sustained. Pitch two isn't so bad (it's different and better than where first ascent party went). First half is OK–then it deteriorates–but it leads to an exciting last pitch and in my view is better to do than the rappel options from pitch one.

START: Below Eenie Meenie's huge, orange, loose-looking right-facing corner. There is a steep boulder and dirt-filled gully-like area, 80 feet left of Yum Yum Yab Yum. Scramble up this to big dirt ledge and walk left to a belay at a huge oak tree directly below right-facing flakes/cracks or do the nice direct start variation up to the oak tree.

PITCH 1: 5.9 G-PG (V1) Work your way up the steep flakes (crux) and corners to a belay on grassy ledge at scary, threaded belay/rap-station. (blue Camalot helpful) (90 ft.) If one doesn't want to do pitch two and doesn't like the rap-station there are two other "not so great" options to get down. One is to traverse left about 20 feet to rap-station on small tree above left side of ledge or diagonal up right about 15 feet to Eenie Meenie's pitch one threaded rap-station.

PITCH 2: 5.2 PG (Original Route, drawn in w/dotted line w/no written description) Step/move right and climb straight up following right-facing features passing a small oak tree with rap-station (original pitch one belay) off to the left. Continue up past right-facing flakes to loose rock and a broken ledge system that leads up left. Go up these to a comfortable ledge and pine tree belay/rap-station in a blocky left-facing corner. (90 ft.)

PITCH 3: 5.6 PG (V2 & V3) Climb up left to the roof and make the long, exposed traverse right (about 20 feet) to a good stance at lip, then onward to the top (60 ft.) or from stance at end of traverse, move up about 15 feet and then traverse right on bushy oak tree ledge to the pine tree belay/rap-station on Eenie Meenie. (90 ft.)

Variation 1: 5.7 G (Direct Start, drawn in w/dotted line) Start about 20 feet left of Eenie Meenie's gully, below a short, shallow, right-facing corner about 6 feet up. Climb straight up to great horizontal. Then climb past thin crack (crux) to large ledge and huge oak tree belay/rap-station and base of pitch one. (40 ft.) One can also begin on the sharp left-facing flake immediately to the right (easier).

Variation 2: 5.10b PG-R From the pine tree, climb straight up past an old angle piton to the roof, then traverse right 10 feet and up to the top.

Variation 3: (**NR**) 5.9+ PG (Drawn in w/dotted line) Diagonal up left on reddish, low angle right-facing corner and traverse left to black birch tree below obvious crack in overhang. Work past lip to lower angle dirty rock to the top. (This variation can also be reached from By The Toe.)

FA 1965: Dick Williams and Hilton Long
FA (V1) 2005: Dick Williams and Annie O'Neill
FA (V2) 1960's: Dick Williams
FA (V3, Toproped) 1979: Rod Schwartz

76a   CATCH A TIGER 5.5 PG

A short but cute first pitch and a nice variation one. Pitches two and three are not recommended. Pitch two is dirty and grungy with loose rock. Pitch three is dirty with loose rock and it's really run out after the crux if you don't save larger cams for the upper corner and flakes.

START: About 35 feet left of where you would scramble up to start Eenie Meenie and My-Knee Moe, below an open book with cracks in the left face/slab. There is a large tree about 10 feet up.

PITCH 1: 5.5 G Go up to tree, then move up (**V1**) face/slab and corner to the right-hand crack. Climb crack (crux) to horizontal holds that lead left. Move left and up to pine tree belay/rap-station. (50 ft.)

Pitch 2: (**NR**) 5.5 PG Scramble up past tree and climb a few feet left of the large left-facing corner. Continue up corner near its top (crux) to grassy ledge and small black birch belay/rap-tree that is 7-8 feet above ledge. (60 ft.)

Pitch 3: (**NR**) 5.5 PG Step right and climb face to left-jutting flake/block. With hands on top of flake, traverse right about 6 feet and continue up (crux) past left side of cedar tree and ledge with scary loose blocks. Then follow right-facing flakes/corners to large grassy NSGTLedge and bushy oak trees. Continue straight up and right to pine tree belay/rap-station on My-Knee Moe. (70 ft.)

Pitch 4: Finish on My-Knee Moe.

Variation 1: 5.6 G Step left to join Left Meets Right's crack and climb straight up to the pine tree belay/rap-station.

FA June 1994: Todd Swain, Donette Smith and Randy Schenkel

76b   **LEFT MEETS RIGHT 5.8 G**

Good climbing, a bit sequency at the crux unless you have a long reach.

START: Immediately left of Catch a Tiger, from the left side of a small ledge just off the ground.

PITCH 1: 5.8 G Climb right-facing flakes to thin horizontal at overhang, then work up right (crux) to great layback hold and step up right (you can keep laybacking straight up crack: harder) to a stance. Step up left and climb crack straight up (5.6 G) to the pine tree belay/rap-station. (50 ft.)

FA 2005: Dick Williams and Annie O'Neill

76c   **(TOPROPE)** 5.11d/12a
Start immediately to the left of Catch a Tiger on the left side of a small ledge that's just off the ground (same as for Left Meets Right). Climb right-facing flakes to thin horizontal at overhang. Diagonal up left to tiny right-facing flake and work up to the anchors.

77   BY THE TOE 5.9+ PG
Great pitch one climbing that is star quality, especially due to this new direct start. The second pitch has good, adventurous climbing except for the last 30-40 feet where the climbing gets very dirty, plus it's scary getting up onto the large dirt NSGTLedge that's full of dangerous loose rock. Pitch three is hard to recommend; it's strenuous, technical with long reaches and the climbing after the crux is real dirty.

START: Below a left-facing corner about 10 feet up, 20 feet left of Catch A Tiger and 10 feet right of By The Toe's original start which is at two small boulders leaning against the face, one atop the other, the top one covered with ferns.

PITCH 1: 5.9 G ★ (Direct Start) (V1) Climb straight up and work past overhang (new crux) to a stance in the corner. Step left to the bulge with thin crack/seam. Work past bulge (old crux, 5.9 PG) to the corner (V2). Continue up face following corner system till same level as ledge on left with trees. Traverse left to ledge and Catnip's pine tree belay/rap-station. (80 ft.)

Pitch 2: **(NR)** 5.7 PG Traverse back right and move up to a stance on nose above corner. Climb pretty much straight up to small ledge and thin flaky crack (original FA pitch one belay). Work straight up past fractured overhang (crux-1)

Dick Williams on
By The Toe "Direct" 5.9
(Route 77)
Photo: Joe Bridges 2007

to small grassy ledge and move right a few feet (optional belay). Work up obvious fault (crux-2) to stance (from here on it is very dirty). Angle up left and gain dirty loose rock on the NSGTLedge (crux-3) just left of large boulder and oak tree. (140 ft.)

PITCH 3: 5.9+ PG From tree, diagonal up left past blocky rock (V3) to a short face capped by ceiling (just left of corner). Move up face to ceiling and horizontal. Hand traverse left till holds peter out and meet piton scars, then work up into right-facing corner (crux, harder if short), exit up right to the jungle and the top. (60 ft.)

Variation 1: 5.9 PG (Original Start) At two stacked boulders 10 feet to the left. Go up corner to a stance on ledge. Step left, move up, and diagonal up right to bulge with thin crack/seam.

Variation 2: Make the easy traverse right to pine tree belay, rap-station on Catch A Tiger.

Variation 3: (**NR**) 5.9+ PG Diagonal up right past blocks to horizontal and obvious crack in overhang to join variation three of My-Knee Moe. Work past lip to lower angle dirty rock to the top.

FA 1965: Dick Williams and Bill Goldner

FFA (P 3) 1973: John Stannard

FA (Direct Start) 2005: Gerry Keiffer, Rod Schnier and Brian McGillicuddy

77a   **CATNIP 5.6 G ★★**

Great fun climbing on clean rock. The crux reminds me of Snooky's Return in the Trapps, straight up harder than stepping right.

START: Below a short, blocky right-facing corner, 15 feet left of By the Toe.

PITCH 1: 5.6 G Climb corner past overhang to blocky ledge and black birch tree about 20 feet up. Diagonal up right a bit and climb past a short left-facing corner (crux), then right-facing flake, then wide crack and laurel bush to a small ledge. Go up left to pine tree belay/rap-station. (70 ft.)

FA 2005: Dick Williams and Annie O'Neill

77b   (**TOPROPE**) Bridges To Knowhere 5.10a
      The start is the same as for Catnip. Step left and climb past right-facing flake and overhang to ledge. Continue straight up and work up face immediately left of Catnip (not touching Catnip) to the pine tree anchor. FA 2007: Ethan Ladof, Dick Williams, Elaine Mathews and Joe Bridges

77c   BY THE CLAW 5.10b G
      Good climbing on two sections, too bad it is broken up in the middle. The first section is technical and it's strenuous to place protection (don't be tempted to use the tree, it's out of bounds) The upper crack tests your ability not to be pulled north. If you use the tree it's 5.8, if not it's 5.10a.
      START: 10 feet left of Catnip's deep, 10-foot-high right-facing corner capped by a ceiling.
      PITCH 1: 5.10b G Climb the sharp, shallow right-facing flakes to good horizontal, step right and work up the thin crack (crux-1) to a stance at a flake in corner. Step left and go up rounded nose to dirt ledge and obvious crack. Climb crack to pine tree, step right and work up (crux-2) to large ledge and pine tree belay/rap-station. (70 ft.)
      FA 2005: Dick Williams with Annie O'Neill

77d   NUTZVILLE 5.9 PG
      Quality thin face moves with great pro except for the questionable pro at the last move. The crux is probably the head trip for the last move; if the pro holds, it's PG, if it pulls, it's probably PG-R. Bring Ballnutz and watch out for the acorns when they rain down and pummel you in October.
      START: Directly below the sharp right-facing flake on By The Claw.
      PITCH 1: 5.9 PG Climb up past a tiny right-facing flake and steep white face to horizontal at small pebbly overhang (last bomber pro). Work up face to thin stance (small pocket on left for questionable Alien, a Metolius cam may work better) and make the final committing move up a bit

right and up to large dirt ledge. Finish on By The Claw's 5.8 crack or go left to finish on Nazgul. (50 ft.)

FA 2005: Dick Williams and Annie O'Neill

78   NAZGUL 5.10b/c R

Two good pitches. The first pitch has some really fun climbing; the little white pine can be avoided. Pitch two is exciting for its grade with some good exposure. Pitch three is not recommended because even with the benefit of modern gear it is not any safer.

START: At a small left-facing corner capped by an overhang that's about 15 feet up and about 10 feet left of Nutzville and By The Claw.

PITCH 1: 5.7 G-PG ★ Climb the corner to a stance on the nose and small white pine tree. Move up, step left and work up past bulge (crux-1) and up to dirt ledge (**V1**). Diagonal up right and up boulder till standing on its top. Work straight up thin face (real crux) and up to pine tree belay/rap-station. (80 ft.)

PITCH 2: 5.6 PG ★ Step right of tree and climb slab to the first of the discontinuous left-facing corners. Continue up corners to some clean orange and white rock and old piton and small overhang (about 10 feet left of large, orange left-facing corner). Step left and work up past left-facing flakes to a stance (crux). Step right and climb corner to ceiling and exit right up to small ledges and optional belay (V2). (100 ft.) Move left near lip of ceiling and up past dirty NSGTLedge and up to a white pine tree belay/rap-station. (140 ft.)

Pitch 3: 5.10b/c R The once-tiny pine is now large and constricts one's movement. Thrash up on face behind tree branches to the crux ceiling. Work past ceiling to overhang, move right and up to the top. (50 ft.)

Variation 1: 5.7 PG (Drawn in w/dotted line) Climb straight up about 8 feet to next ledge and step left to nose and sling tree. Climb straight up nose to large ledge and pine tree belay/rap-station.

Variation 2: (**NR**) (Unrated) (Original Route, drawn in w/ dotted line) Climb straight up to large NSGTLedge and then up broken rock past overhang to the obvious crux ceiling.

FA 1971: Richard Goldstone and Dick Williams

78a **COYOTE CRACK 5.4 G ★**

Pitch one is a very nice little one pitch climb. Guess what the first ascent party saw just before doing the climb?

START: 15 feet left of Nazgul, below the obvious crack system.

PITCH 1: 5.4 G Climb the crack system to large ledge and pine tree belay/rap-station. (80 ft.)

FA 2005: Dick Williams and Annie O'Neill

78b **FISHER CRACK 5.4 PG**

Pitch one is pretty good and pitch two has some good climbing, but it leads to a dying tree belay/rap-station. Guess what animal was seen after the climb?

START: 10 feet left of Coyote Crack at the right side of the broken recess area with the hourglass-like feature.

PITCH 1: 5.4 PG Climb crack to alcove, at overhang step up right and then straight up face left of Coyote Crack to ledge and pine tree belay/rap tree. (70 ft.)

Pitch 2: 5.2 PG Step right and move up slab, step back left and up the face left of Nazgul's corners past small over-hangs/bulges to the right side of a dirt ledge. (80 ft.) Traverse left 30 feet to dying oak tree belay/rap-station.

FA 2005: Dick Williams and Annie O'Neill

Immediately left of Fisher Crack is a large, dirty, often wet, broken recess area that contains large boulders.

78c   (**NR**) WHAT? ARE YOU NUTS? 5.7 PG

This dirty, ridiculous climb was only done so as to set up a toprope for a new climb called P/L (78d).

Start: In the gully just up and left of Fisher Crack and just left of the highest block.

Pitch 1: 5.7 PG Climb up and left to laurel bush. Traverse around left and work up past slab at left side of small tree and moss clods (crux). Then continue straight up past small right-facing corner and crack to large pine tree belay/rap-station. (70 ft.)

FA 2005: Dick Williams and Al DeMaria

78d   (**TOPROPE**) P/L 5.10a

Start on the face about 25 feet left of Coyote Crack and just right of a short, white open book capped by an over-hang. Climb up left till standing above the overhang. Then work straight up past small overhang and face (crux) to small dirt ledge at slab below bombay/offwidth chimney. Move up slab to broken rock and then climb back left to crack above the bombay, then climb crack to the rap-tree. (50 ft.) FA 2005: Dick Williams with Al DeMaria

78e   OLD AND MOSSY 5.7 G

I'm recommending this climb even though the very good climbing is only for about 40 feet; from there on it's so-so. Placing pro just above the overhang is strenuous.

START: About 15 feet right of You're In The Wrong Place My Friend at a small right-facing corner immediately right of a mossy open book.

PITCH 1: 5.7 G (V1) Climb short corner and clear overhang at break to a stance (crux). Continue up past a wide crack to two small trees. Step right to small dirt ledge at slab (op-tional belay). Continue up right on slab (V2) to broken rock to join What? Are You Nuts?, and climb straight up fault past oak tree to large pine tree belay/rap-station. (70 ft.)

Variation 1: 5.5 G (Mossy Me) Start 15 feet to the right

and immediately left of (**TOPROPE**) P/L. Step up left to a small ledge. Climb straight up and step up left to another ledge. Continue straight up past small overhang to a stance in open book. Move up to dirt ledge at slab (optional belay). Continue up right on slab to broken rock to join What? Are You Nuts?. (70 ft.)

Variation 2: 5.7 G Move up slab to broken rock and then climb back left to crack above the bombay, then climb crack to the rap tree.

FA 2006: Dick Williams and Annie O'Neill
FA (V1) 2006: Dick Williams and Annie O'Neill

79   WRONG PLACE, RIGHT TIME 5.10d R
(As a Toprope)

Pitch one is quite the lead, maybe best to do on TR. The second and third pitches are not worth doing, dirty with loose rock and a real jungle thrash.

START: On the face about 6-8 feet right of You're In The Wrong Place, My Friend.

PITCH 1: 5.10d R Step up to the "Texas flake," and move up to the right side of the overhang to great holds and first pro. Then up to small ledge and little tree. Work up the intricate crux face to short, small, reddish left-facing flake/corner (being tall really helps). Step left and work up the steep, strenuous corner to the pine tree anchors. Then step left and join YITWPMFriend up lower angle rock past trees to ledge and pine tree belay/rap-station. (90 ft.)

Pitch 2: (**NR**) (Unrated) Continue up and slightly right past dirty rock and huge loose, stacked blocks and up (past ledge on right with dying oak tree with rap-station) past trees to the big NSGTLedge. (130 ft.)

Pitch 3: (**NR**) (Unrated) Go right about 15 feet and climb up right-facing corner through trees and bushes to join the final pitch of You're in the Wrong Place, My Friend.

FA 1986: Todd Swain, Andy Schenkel and John Courtney

80 YOU'RE IN THE WRONG PLACE, MY FRIEND 5.8 PG

Don't bother going beyond the good first pitch. Always a sucker for dirt and loose rock, I tried to figure out where pitches two and three went. Even though I did the first ascent, I always felt I was in the wrong place. Variation one is strenuous and exciting.

START: 60 feet left of Coyote Crack (there is a small jutting block 10 feet up), just right of a ceiling, at a shallow open book with a broken crack that leads up to orange rock and a small right-facing corner capped by a triangular overhang

PITCH 1: 5.8 PG ★ (V1) Move up face and step left to small jutting block. Work past this (crux-1) and up face past short crack (or corner to right) to base of short right-facing corner (V2). Climb corner to a great pointed bucket (crux-2) and up to crack. Follow crack to horizontal and go right to pine tree rap-station or continue straight up lower angle rock past trees to ledge and pine tree belay/rap-station. (90 ft.)

Pitch 2: **(NR)** 5.4 R Climb past ledges, step left, and head straight up the face past loose rock to large NSGTLedge and belay at pine tree just above at arms reach. Same belay as for Elf Stone. (90 ft.)

Pitch 3: **(NR)** 5.4 R Go right on ledge and diagonal up right to block w/oak tree belay/rap-station. (70 ft.)

Pitch 4: **(NR)** 5.4 PG Step up, traverse right on buckets, then up dirty slab to top. (50 ft.)

Variation 1: 5.10b G-PG (Tooth and Nail) (Protection strenuous to place) Start 10 feet left of You're In The Wrong Place My Friend at a short nose formed by an open book/left-facing corner. Move up nose and up on jugs to overhang. Work up right past notch (crux), then up a bit right to join YITWPMFriend's short, right-facing corner.

Variation 2: 5.4 PG (Original Route) Traverse left about 8 feet, step up, then hand traverse back right to sharp nose with great pointed bucket and YITWPMFriend's crack.

FA 1971: Dick Williams and Dave Loeks
FA (V1): 1990 Joe Rommel and Dave Lage

Joe Bridges at crux of
Whet Stone 5.8
(Route 80a)
Photo: Chris Cook 2007

80a   **WHET STONE 5.8 PG ★**

Sharpen your skills in preparation for leading this interesting first pitch. The climb is two star quality if you start on Whet Stone and join Elf Stone at the overhang.

START: At a thin crack/seam about 5-7 feet right of Elfstone direct.

PITCH 1: 5.8 PG Climb seam (Trango Ballnutz helpful) and step up to the overhang (crux). Climb overhang to wide horizontal and up past arching crack to Elfstone's overhang (**V1**). Work up right and up face past short, blocky left-facing corner to low angle ledges. Traverse right about 20 feet to pine tree belay/rap-station. (100 ft.)

Variation 1: 5.6 G ★ Step left and join Elf Stone.

FRA 2005: Dick Williams and Annie O'Neill

81   **ELF STONE DIRECT 5.10b/c PG**

Pitch one with the direct start really adds to the fun and quality, good with continuous moves. Starting on Whetstone makes an excellent variation. No reason to go further than pitch one because of the dirty climbing up to the big ledge. Pitch three is pretty good and the last pitch is wild and is now better protected with modern gear. The first pitch originally began uphill a bit and traversed in to the right.

START: At the left of two thin cracks/seams about 45 feet left of You're in the Wrong Place My Friend, part way up the steepening trail. Someone has tried to make a stone platform at the base of the crack.

PITCH 1: 5.7 PG ★★ Climb the crack/seam and small overhang to a stance. Move up (crux) and climb past notch in overhang to a stance. Then climb straight up face moving a bit right up to broken rock (It's recommended to traverse off left here to Spic And Span's belay tree, rap-station 80 ft.). Continue further up to low angle, broken ledges (**V1**) and traverse off right about 20 feet to pine tree belay/rap tree on YITWPMF (100 ft.) or continue up to make a belay near cedar tree if you're crazy enough to do pitch two.

Dick Williams on
Whet Stone 5.8
(Route 80a)
Photo: Chris Cook 2007

Pitch 2: **(NR)** 5.5 R Move right on small ledge and then climb straight up to small right-facing corner. Move right again and up face past loose rock to large NSGTLedge and belay at pine tree just above at arms reach. (70 ft.)

Pitch 3: 5.5 PG-R Climb straight up to slab and begin the long diagonal up right on nice rock to the base of the huge, imposing left-facing corner capped by right side of the huge, awesome roof. Step down and belay at block with oak tree rap-station. (It's a pain in the butt to rap from here because the ropes can get all tangled up in the trees and bushes below) (70 ft.)

Pitch 4: 5.10b/c PG Climb the corner and hand traverse out right to the roof's lip. Work past roof (crux–scary) and up to the top. (50 ft.)

Variation 1: 5.4 G (Tooth and Nail, drawn in w/ dotted line) Climb the face right of cedar tree and the right-facing corner to a bolt. (This bolt was probably placed by the land owner in 2004) Move up a bit left (crux) and up to ledge and pine tree belay, rap-station. (40 ft.) One can go left from here and join Orc Stone.

FA 1966: Dick Williams and Dave Craft
FFA 1971: Steve Wunsch and Dick Williams
FA (Direct Start) 1990: Dave Lage and Joe Rommel

81a   **SPIC AND SPAN 5.2 G**
An old route done at the time of Orc Stone but was never written up. It is now a nice clean little climb.

START: From Elf Stone Direct, go up trail and up to large oak tree below crack system which is about 10 feet right of Orc Stone.

PITCH 1: 5.2 G Climb up about 15 feet to black birch tree, step right and follow crack system to ledge and belay/rap-tree. (70 ft.)

FA 1966: Dick Williams and Dave Craft

Note: The area between Orc Stone (82) left to Gold Rush (86) stays particularly wet after it rains because of seepage. This is a popular ice climbing area, especially below Lost World (84). One can see all the ice tool scars from Orc Stone, an ugly site indeed.

82   ORC STONE 5.5 PG

Only recommended for those looking for an adventure. The beginning of this climb is dirty and often wet. If it is dry, it's an adventurous and exciting climb, particularly on the last half of pitch one if you don't mind climbing suspicious looking flakes. Most of pitch two is good and all of the final pitch is nice with an interesting crux. Unfortunately, someone recently placed an unnceessary bolt on the last pitch at crux 2, lowering a 41-year-old standard.

START: In the broken corner on the left side of the Elf Stone face, 10 feet left of Spic and Span.

PITCH 1: 5.5 PG Climb the dirty corner past small tree and right-facing flake (crux-1). Continue to top of corner and diagonal up right about 40 feet to overhangs and lots of left-facing flakes above. Climb flakes and large, blocky left-facing corner (crux-2) to small pine tree on left. Then up and right to ledge and pine tree belay/rap-station. (115 ft.)

PITCH 2: 5.4 PG Climb left-facing flakes above to ledge. Step right (optional belay) and climb short crack to a stance on small ledge. Step right again and up face to slab. Then diagonal up left about 30 feet and make a belay at overhang below notch formed by short, narrow open book/corner. (80 ft.)

PITCH 3: 5.5 PG Move up to a stance in corner (crux-1), then work up corner (crux-2) to its top (V1). Step up to horizontal holds and traverse left across slab and up obvious fault to top and oak tree belay/rap-station. (40 ft.)

Variation 1: 5.8 PG-R (Original finish, drawn in w/dotted line) From top of corner, move up to small holds, step right to more small holds (crux), then up to ledge and thicket and on to the top.

One can rappel from oak tree for about 60 feet to a small pine and oak tree with rap-station. It is a 200-foot rappel from here to ground. The rappel takes you down past the impressive overhangs on pitch two of Lost World (5.10b/c R).

FA 1966: Dick Williams and Dave Craft

83 CHERRY'S CLIMB 5.5 PG

There are some rewarding moves on each pitch. Too bad one can't cherry pick the good moves and put them all in one pitch. Unfortunately someone recently placed a bolt on the last pitch at crux 2, completely unnecessary.

START: Same as Orc Stone.

PITCH 1: 5.5 G Follow Orc Stone's corner past a right-facing flake (crux) to it's top. Then climb straight up to make a belay 8-10 feet below large, jutting left-facing flake in corner above. (100 ft.)

PITCH 2: 5.5 PG Climb straight up behind flake and up to top of corner. Exit up right (loose rock) to ledge and shad bush and belay. (60 ft.)

PITCH 3: 5.5 G Climb easy, blocky left-facing corner above up into overhanging left-facing corner (crux) with tree. Once past the tree, continue up past slab to make a belay at overhang below notch formed by short, narrow open book/corner (same as for Orc Stone). (90 ft.)

PITCH 4: 5.5 PG (Same as Orc Stone's) Move up to a stance in corner (crux-1), then work up corner (crux-2) to its top. Step up to horizontal holds and traverse left across slab and up obvious fault to top and oak tree belay/rap-station. (40 ft.) See info for rappel from here that is described in Orc Stone.

FA 1971: Cherry Merritt and Dick Williams

84 LOST WORLD 5.11b/c R

Start: (Same as Phalladio) At large oak tree just 10 feet left of Orc Stone below gully-like open book.

Pitch 1: (Unrated) Climb any way you feel like it to the

large ledge and belay/rap-anchors that the ice climbers put in. (150 ft.)

Pitch 2: 5.10b/c R Step right and climb pretty much straight up to the thin crack that breaks the ceiling and old Bugaboo piton. Work past crack (crux) and some small overhangs to small ledges and small cedar/oak tree belay/rap-station (V1). (50 ft.) It is a 200 foot rappel to the ground from here.

Pitch 3: (Easy/unrated) Go right and up about 20-30 feet to intersect Orc Stone. Continue traversing right, past slab to a pile of large blocks below huge, awesome roof. (70 ft.)

Pitch 4: 5.11b/c R Climb straight up to the roof and pass the first overhang into an inverted right-facing corner. Then traverse left till it's possible to climb to and over/past the lip to a stance (crux). Finish by climbing the small overhang above to the top. (50 ft.)

Variation 1: 5.9+ PG (Tooth and Nail, drawn in w/dotted line) This variation can easily be reached from Orc Stone or Cherry's Climb. From right side of tree, climb tiny overhang and fingertip layback into short, small left-facing corner. At top of corner, step around right onto narrow ledge, then up to finish on Orc Stone/Cherry's climb. (60 ft.)

FA 1978: Don Perry and Mark Robinson
FA (V1) 1990: Joe Rommel and Dave Lage

85   (**NR**) PHALLADIO 5.7 PG-R

The first two pitches really suck, dirty and usually wet till summer. There is only about 15 feet of worthwhile climbing on pitch three and making a belay is not very safe and a pain in the butt to set up. The last pitch is exciting, but you wouldn't want to fall with the lousy belayer stance.

Start: At large oak tree just 10 feet left of Orc Stone below gully-like open book.

Pitch 1: (**NR**) 5.2 PG Scramble to large ash tree, then up slab to large ledge and walk left about 15-20 feet and make a belay. (70 ft.)

Pitch 2: (**NR**) 5.5 PG Move left and climb straight past right-facing flakes/small corners past steepish head wall, staying left of cedar tree on large ledge to fixed belay/rap-station (put there by ice climbers-this is your last chance to get off this climb easily). Walk left about 30 feet on narrow grassy NSGTLedge with lots of loose rock to make a belay at forked cedar tree. (80 ft.)

Pitch 3: (**NR**) 5.7 PG Walk left about 15 feet till below dirty corner capped by tree. At tree, step out left and up to lichen-covered slab (there is a cedar tree to the left with a rap-station). Diagonal up right to the low-angle red rock in huge left-facing corner that leads up left. Climb straight up past short crack w/blueberry bush to a platform-like ledge and make a belay (Trango Ballnutz helpful). (60 ft.)

Pitch 4: (**NR**) 5.7 PG-R Climb up left up short, smooth slab and up to fixed knifeblade/bugaboo pin. Diagonal/traverse right under overhang to break and climb right-facing flake to the top. (60 ft.)

FA 1965: Mike and Sally Westmacott and Paul Ramer

86　　　　　　　GOLD RUSH 5.9 PG

The full adventure is not worth making. If dry, pitch one is quite good with multiple, interesting moves. Pitch two is dirty with loose rock. Pitch three is OK on the red flaky rock section and Pitch four is a struggle with a dirty corner to the top.

START: At left side of the amphitheatre. On the slab at base of low angle right-facing corner 65 feet left of Orc Stone.

PITCH 1: 5.5 G Climb corner to the overhang and step up left to small pine tree (50 ft., optional belay/rap-station). Then up past the chigger-filled grass ledges to make a belay. (70 ft.)

Pitch 2: 5.3 PG Climb pretty much straight up the cleaner rock heading for a reddish, jutting block (about 50 feet up) in blocky right-facing corner. Before the block, move right and up to ledge at small pine tree. Go left about 20 feet and up to a belay in dirty corner below overhang. (90 ft.)

Pitch 3: 5.4 PG Move up, step out left and up to the lichen-covered slab (there is a cedar to the left with a rap-station). Diagonal up right to the low-angle red rock in huge left-facing corner that leads up left. Climb red rock and flakes to a yellow Camalot-size horizontal and make a belay (above you are small bushy oak trees and a pink laurel bush). (60 ft.)

Pitch 4: 5.9 PG Step left and climb to the obvious crack/break in the large overhang. Work past overhang and dirt and grass bog-filled right-facing corner to the top (crux). (40 ft.)

FA 1964: Dick Williams, Pete Geiser and Phil Jacobus
FFA 1973: Bob Anderson and John Stannard

86a **(TOPROPE)** Cam-n-Bearit 5.8

Start on Gold Rush (V1) and move up corner to jutting chockstone. Reach up to triangular overhang and move up to horizontal above overhang. Move left and climb pretty much straight up the face staying right of some trees to the pine tree anchor. Variation 1: 5.5 Start on the unprotectable face left of the corner and climb up to right side of overhang. Move around right and join regular route. FA 2007: Dick Williams, Joe Bridges and Annie O'Neill

86b GOUDA CLIMB 5.8 PG

START: On the face immediately right of Summer Brie, 10 feet left of Gold Rush.

PITCH 1: 5.8 PG Climb straight up face to the V-like open book in the ceiling. Work up past the lip to a stance at the pine tree. Then continue up to the pine tree belay/rap-station. (50 ft.)

FA 2007: Dick Williams and Annie O'Neill

Good footwork gets in the way of strength training
—Eric Murdock

86c   **SUMMER BRIE 5.5 G**
START: 15 feet left of Gold Rush at a short open book.
PITCH 1: 5.5 G Climb open book and low-angle nose and face to the break at left side of the overhang. Step left and work up the face and crack (crux) and up a bit right to the pine tree belay/rap-station. (50 ft.)
FA 2007: Dick Williams and Annie O'Neill

87 (NR)   VULGA-TITS 5.6 PG
Best to stay away from this very dirty climb; there is no supporting evidence or good reason to climb it. There was a massive rockfall just right of pitch two in 1987, very creepy, best to stay far away from it.
Start: 75 feet left of Gold Rush on a dirty nose/outside corner or on the face just to the left. There is a slope full of trees and shrubbery and remains of huge rock fall just to the right.
Pitch 1: **(NR)** 5.4 R Climb the dirty nose or face past ledges to large pine tree with a large block sitting behind it. (50 ft.)
Pitch 2: **(NR)** 5.4 R Continue up the easiest way to ledge and oak tree bushes. Then climb face past more yukky rock to ledge and double-trunked large white pine tree. (100 ft.)
Pitch 3: **(NR)** 5.6 PG Work up into the notch above and exit left onto the steep face. Then climb the face and finish up right to the top. (100 ft.)
FA 1968: Gerd Thuestad, Kaye Arnott and Evy Goldstone

88   **(NR)** THREE GENERATIONS 5.5 PG
A climb between Vulga-Tits and Nowhereland should tell you something; they say one picture is worth a thousand words, well one look at this climb says it all, definitely "gestalt." I could not compel myself to climb it. The route description is from the FA party.
Start: At the base of a short, broken open book, 55 feet uphill to the left of Vulga-Tits.
Pitch 1: 5.5 Climb the open book (or the short crack to

the right) for 20 feet to the large ledge with the oak tree. Continue past the overhang above at a left-facing flake to another ledge with trees. Then climb past another overhang to a grassy ledge with a cedar tree. (90 ft.)

Pitch 2: 5.3 Climb the face to the right of the huge, overhanging right-facing corner, then the obvious chimney, and exit right. Follow a right-facing corner and belay at a tree. (100 ft.)

Pitch 3: 5.5 Follow the corner system past a small overhang to the top. (50 ft.)

FA 1981: Todd Swain, Ira Brant and Kurt Graf

89 NOWHERELAND 5.8 PG

It is recommended to avoid the dirty and long first pitch and to climb the first two pitches of Route Awakening (89a), which takes you to the last two original pitches of Nowhereland.

Start: Same as Three Generations.

Pitch 1: (**NR**) 5.8 PG Follow Three Generations 20 feet to the first ledge, then continue up to a lower-angle grey face to the left of a left-facing flake (or climb the flake itself). Diagonal up left to steep orange rock in the huge, broken right-facing corner. Then weave up the center of the corner and onto the face to a ledge and traverse left to the second pine tree with belay/rap-station. (130 ft.)

PITCH 2: 5.3 PG Step up between cedar and pine tree to base of overhanging, blocky right-facing/leaning corner. Move up (V1) following corner on slab to large block under overhangs and traverse left to beat-up oak tree and threaded-boulder belay/rap-station to the left on the NS-GTLedge. (40 ft.)

PITCH 3: 5.7 PG Climb up right on easy rock to obvious traverse left to the base of imposing bombay chimney. Work up into the chimney (black Camalot helpful), then squeeze your way up the rest of the helmet-clunking chimney till you can step right onto the face and up to an optional belay near top. (60 ft.)

Ivan Rezucha on
Pitch 2 crux of
Zachariah 5.9
(Route 90)
Photo: Rezucha
collection 1975

Variation 1: 5.8 PG (Original Route, drawn in w/dotted line) Exit left and up dirty face to the NSGTLedge and threaded-boulder belay/rap-station.

FA 1984: Mike Steele and John Graul

89a　　　　**ROUTE AWAKENING 5.7 G**

A pretty good, short first pitch. If you decide to continue on and link up with Nowhereland, it's a nice outing. It is a pain to get down unless you have double 60-meter ropes. Pitch two is OK. Pitch three is Nowhereland's; it's short but OK. Nowhereland's last pitch is exciting and worth the trip all the way up there.

START: On face below thin cracks about 6-8 feet right of deep gully that's on the right side of the huge Zachariah detached block.

PITCH 1: 5.7 G Climb cracks to dirt ledges, then up to shady, pine tree belay/rap-station. (60 ft.)

PITCH 2: 5.2 PG Climb straight up past wide crack and diagonal up left till about 5-10 feet from Zachariah's pine tree/rap-station (30 ft. optional belay). Move up face and traverse right under or over small pine tree and climb pretty much straight up face to the long overhang and suspicious rock and shale sill. Move/traverse right and up notch formed by huge boulder at right side of overhang to dirt ledge. Go up left to a shady, pine tree belay/rap-station. (100 ft.)

PITCH 3: 5.3 PG (Nowhereland) Step up between cedar and pine tree to base of overhanging, blocky right-facing/leaning corner. Move up (V1) following corner on slab to large block under overhangs and traverse left past beat-up oak tree to boulder-threaded belay/rap-station on the NSGTLedge. (40 ft.)

PITCH 4: 5.7 PG (Nowhereland) Climb up right on easy rock to the obvious traverse left to base of imposing bombay chimney. Work up into the chimney (black Camalot helpful), then squeeze your way up the rest of the helmet-clunking chimney till you can step right onto the face (optional belay) and up to the top. (60 ft.) To get down, walk left and down about 40 feet to a large oak tree rap-station. Make the 50-foot rappel down Zachariah to the large NS-GTLedge and go left to large pine tree with rap-station. A two-50-meter-rope rappel from here gets you back to cliff base near International Harvesters.

Variation 1: 5.8 PG (Original Route, drawn in w/dotted line) Exit left and up dirty face to the NSGTLedge and threaded-boulder belay/rap-station.

FA 2006: Dick Williams and Annie O'Neill
FA (P 3&4): Mike Steele and John Graul

89b   NOSEY BODIES 5.3 PG-R
Start on face at right side of deep gully below overhang on nose.

Pitch 1: 5.3 PG-R Climb face and short crack to stance on small pedestal at slab (5.3 G). Continue up slab to overhang (crux), step right and up to Route Awakening's pine tree belay/rap-station. (60 ft.)

FA 2006: Dick Williams and Annie O'Neill

One can scramble up the deep gully to an obvious open book with a crack, then climb it (if it's dry, about 5.6 G) to the roof, exit right and up to pine tree belay/rap-station on Route Awakening. (60 ft.)

89c   **(TOPROPE)** Nip & Tuck 5.10b/c
Start on face at right side of Zachariah's detached block, just left of outside corner/arête. Climb to little right-facing flake and jugs. Work up and left on crimpers and dyno for the obvious right-pointing bucket. Then step left and crank up on good holds to ledge and your anchors. To set up anchors, start on Zachariah and stem/bridge outside edge of chimney to ledge and go right to good horizontal. To get down, there is a rap/lowering station on tree in gully to the right. FA 2006: Dick Williams with Annie O'Neill

90 **ZACHARIAH 5.9 G ★★**

The first two pitches are really good. Most people rap after pitch two. Be careful doing pitch three due to some loose rock. The last pitch is fun but short.

START: 75 feet left of Three Generations and 70 feet right of Easter Time Too at a chimney formed by a huge block leaning against the cliff.

PITCH 1: 5.8 G Stem/bridge outside edge of chimney (V1) and step across left to ledge and to crack on International Harvesters. Climb straight up crack past two wide horizontals (crux) to ledge (large pine to the left). Then straight up broken rock to orange rock below overhang. Move right to small pine and diagonal up right around nose and up slab to pine tree belay/rap-station. (90 ft.)

PITCH 2: 5.9 G Climb straight up to notch in overhang (blue Trango Ballnutz and blue Camalot helpful here). Make long reach up right to jugs and swing around and up to stance on small ledge (crux). Then, a straight up easy runout to small ledge and angle piton and make a belay. (60 ft.) It's recommended to go down and right from here to the pine tree rap-station.

Pitch 3: 5.3 PG Move left and up broken orange blocky corner to overhang, step up left to a stance. Then up face past right-facing corner and very loose rock area to large NSGTLedge with lots of bushy oak trees. Go left about 10-15 feet and belay below break in overhangs. (40 ft.)

PITCH 4: 5.6 G Climb face past notch and crack in the overhangs to the top and cedar tree. Traverse left about 15 feet to a cedar tree/rap-station. (40 ft.) Make the short rappel back to large NSGTLedge and pine tree/rap-station where a two-50-meter-rope rappel juuuust makes it back to the ground.

Variation 1: (**NR**) 5.6 PG (Original Route, drawn in w/ dotted line) Continue up to ledge and boulders. Step/move right and climb outside corner (climbing face on left is harder and R protected). Work up corner, step left and up to rounded nose. Climb nose and short slab to ledge and pine tree belay/rap-station.

FA 1971: Dick Williams and Al DeMaria

90a   (LINK-UP) INTERIAH 5.9+ G ★★
INTERNATIONAL HARVESTERS/ZACHARIAH

Wonderful variety of climbing, face, crack and wild overhang. One can also start on Zachariah.

START: In the short open book 15 feet left and uphill from Zachariah and about 50 feet right of Easter Time Too.

PITCH 1: 5.9+ G Move up the open book to ledge, move right and climb thin cracks past two wide horizontals (5.8 G) to ledge and large pine tree. Continue up to and climb the next crack system (crux: harder if short) to Zachariah's ledge and pine tree belay/rap-station. (90 ft.)

PITCH 2: 5.9 G Climb straight up to notch in overhang (blue Trango Ballnutz and blue Camalot helpful here). Make long reach up right to jugs and swing around and up to stance on small ledge (crux). Then, a straight up easy runout to small ledge and angle piton and make a belay. (60 ft.) There is a rap station down and to the right on a pine tree.

91   INTERNATIONAL HARVESTERS 5.10a PG-R

The first pitch has good moves, well protected. Pitch two is strenuous with long reaches (harder if short) and the pro is strenuous to place.

START: In the short open book 15 feet left and uphill from Zachariah and about 50 feet right of Easter Time Too.

PITCH 1: 5.9+ G ★ Move up the open book to ledge, move right and climb thin cracks (5.8 G) (V1) to large pine tree. Continue to and climb the next crack system (crux) to Zachariah's ledge and pine tree belay/rap-station. (90 ft.)

Pitch 2: 5.10a PG-R From left side of tree, climb up, then left under hanging blocks and up past ledge into left-facing corner (5.6 PG, optional belay, 40 ft.). Climb corner and work up past overhang at left-facing corner to a stance (crux, long reach, pro strenuous to place). Then climb pretty much straight up onto NSGTLedge and pine tree belay/rap-station. (100 ft.) Two-50-meter-rope rappel back to packs.

PITCH 3: 5.6 PG Finish on Zachariah. (40 ft.)

Variation 1: **Toprope**: 5.9 Start on face at base of Zachariah's chimney. Climb face straight up to 5.8 thin crack.

FA 1981: Todd Swain, Ed Grindley and Mike Lovatt

92   BETWEEN A ROCK AND A HARD PLACE 5.8 R

Pitch one and two have some good climbing (can be combined), although it's a little dirty. Hopefully, these pitches will be cleaner in time as they are climbed more often. **Pitch three is Not Recommend**, because it has loose rock and a monster-suicide block that may guillotine the leader before crashing down on the belayer and all the climbers below Easter Time Too area. On the first ascent, the belayer refused to follow this pitch due to loose rocks being pitched off and the ominous, direct threat imposed by the block.

START: Uphill and 20 feet left of International Harvesters at a short chimney with off-width crack in its back.

PITCH 1: 5.8 G Climb chimney/off-width (crux, black Camalot helpful but not necessary) to a stance, step left and up to dirt ledge. Climb pretty much straight up nice face till just below wide overhang. Diagonal up left on grassy ramp to belay at short, blocky left-facing corner capped by overhang. (60 ft.)

PITCH 2: 5.6 PG Step up corner to overhang, step right and climb face to a stance about 15-20 feet below and right of cedar tree on ledge above. Step/move right and climb past bulge to the large ledge, then traverse left to cedar tree belay/rap-station. (60 ft.)

Pitch 3: (**NR**) 5.8 (R- if the block doesn't kill you) Follow the broken corner or rib to the dangerously tilted loose, finger/projectile-like block. Climb between the block and the ceiling, then up dirty rock to the big NSGTLedge pine tree belay. (100 ft.)

Pitch 4: Finish on Zachariah.

FA 1984: Mike Steele with John Graul

It takes about 15 minutes of moderate-pace walking to reach this section of the cliff. There is a nice group of climbs here. Easter Time Too is a very popular, and a good warm up for some of its more difficult neighbors.

93   GOOD FRIDAY CLIMB 5.9+ PG

Enjoy this good first pitch to the bolt anchors; there are technical moves with some intricate, critical gear placements. Pitch two is dirty with loose rock. Pitch three is better than it looks, good pro with long reaches, but not quite recommendable, maybe in time.

START: At the thin crack 65 feet left of Zachariah and just 5 feet right of Easter Time Too.

PITCH 1: 5.9 PG ★ Climb face and crack up right (crux), then pretty much straight up steep face till it's obvious to go left to the bolt anchors (70 ft.) **or** (original route) continue up and right to join pitch one belay of Between A Rock And A Hard Place at short, blocky left-facing corner capped by overhang. (90 ft.)

Pitch 2: **(NR)** 5.6 PG Clear overhang and climb pretty much straight up passing loose rock to cedar tree. (60 ft.) (Better to climb pitch two of Between a Rock And a Hard Place)

PITCH 3: 5.9+ PG Climb the 20 foot-high, right-facing corner and face past overhang at right-pointing flake to horizontal at next overhang. Step right and climb straight past overhang (crux: long reach) past some blueberry bushes and dirty face with small overhangs to the final and nasty move onto the NSGTLedge and pine tree belay/rap-station. (60 ft.) Two-50-meter-rope rappel back to base of cliff.

PITCH 4: **5.6 G** Walk right and finish on Zachariah.

FA (P1) 1980: Mike Freeman

FA (P2 & P3) 1981: Dana Bartlett, Todd Swain

94   **EASTER TIME TOO 5.8 G ★★**

Classic hand and finger jams make this a wonderful one-pitch climb. I went back to re-climb Pitch two twice and finally decided–yuk!–I'm not going to bother, way too dirty; loose rock and all that stuff.

START: About 70 feet left of Zachariah's chimney and 20 feet right of Day-Tripper at the very obvious crack that diagonals up right.

PITCH 1: 5.8 G Climb the crack to the bolt anchors (80 ft.), **–or– (NR**, Original Route) continue straight up broken right-facing corner and go left to make a belay near cedar tree. (100 ft.)

Pitch 2: (**NR**) (Unrated) Continue pretty much straight up on dirty, loose rock past ledge and up steep non descript dirty rock to the NSGTLedge. (70 ft.)

Pitch 3: (**NR**) (Unrated) Climb dirty rock to top. (40 ft.)

FA 1966: Dick Williams, Jim McCarthy and John Hudson

94a   **WOOLLY CLAM TACO 5.10c PG ★**

The name doesn't evoke thoughts of a tasty, yummy-like climb. Good moves, tricky pro, a bit height-related, harder if you're short.

START: Same as Easter Time Too.

PITCH 1: 5.10c PG Step left and move up to a very small, short, left-facing corner and small pebbly overhang (5.9 R). Work past the thin crack (crux) to another small, short left-facing corner caped by a very small overhang. Work up to some orange rock, move left and up to some small bushy trees and traverse left to the Day-Tripper oak tree belay/rap-station. (80-foot rappel)

FA 1989: Gary Terpening and Joe Bridges

It ain't what they call you, it's what you answer to.
        — W.C. Fields

95 **BOSTON TREE PARTY 5.8 G ★**

A bit run out to the first pro in the corner and then technical and multi-cruxed steep face above.

START: About 15 feet left of Easter Time Too, below the orange-ish, concave-like open book that's immediately right of Day-Tripper's nose.

PITCH 1: 5.8 G (V1) Climb the open book and face to the right side of the ceiling (5.7 PG), move up to a stance, then continue past a thin crack and steep face to a horizontal and small overhang (one can step left here and join Day-Tripper). Keep climbing straight up the steep face, then move up left and up to the Day-Tripper oak tree belay/rap-station. (80 ft.)

Variation 1: (**NR**) 5.9 G Climb the nose that is immediately to the right. The crux is well protected but then there is a 5.7 X runout to the right side of the ceiling.

FA 1981: Ed and Cynthia Grindley and Todd Swain

96 **DAY-TRIPPER 5.8 PG ★★**

A unique first pitch, good moves, a bit atypical up to the ceiling. The direct variation finish is great; it's a piece of cake if you are either tall or really good at dyno's. I went back to re-climb Pitch two twice and finally decided–to hell with it–way too dirty, loose rock and all that crap.

START: About 8 feet left of Boston Tree Party below a prominent nose formed by a left-facing corner with a laurel bush half way up the corner.

PITCH 1: 5.8 PG Climb the nose and chimney to the face (**V1**), then up to right side of the roof. Work up and then a bit left past overhang to a stance (crux), then up to oak tree belay/rap-station. (80 ft.)

Pitch 2: (**NR**) (Unrated) Climb dirty face past cedar tree and loose rock up to dirt ledge. Work up the dirty face to the left edge of the overhang and climb a corner with loose rock to the face above. Then head up to the large NSGT-Ledge. (140 ft.)

Pitch 3: **(NR)** (Unrated) Continue to the top. (40 ft.)

Variation 1: 5.10c G (Direct Finish) Climb straight out the crack to the lip (crux: long reach) and crank up to a stance, then to oak tree belay/rap-station.

FA 1966: Dick Williams, Dave Craft and Larry Roberts

FA (V1) 1984: Mike Dimitri and Mike Avery

97 AS THE CLIFF TURNS 5.9 G ★★

This climb is especially good with this newer direct finish. There are short, sustained, interesting cruxes.

START: At the short, thin crack just about midway between Day-Tripper and Scuttlebutt.

PITCH 1: 5.9 G (V1) Climb the thin crack to the wide horizontal. Continue straight up to left side of first overhang. Climb up left into a short left-facing corner and overhang with crack. Work straight up crack (crux-1) to good horizontal (V2). Move up to the overhang, step right and up to the ceiling, step up left to crack and work up it to a stance (crux-2), then up to Day-Tripper's rap-station. (80 ft.)

Variation 1: 5.4 PG Start on Day-Tripper. Step up to ledge and corner. Step left and climb to left side of first overhang.

Variation 2: 5.6 PG (Original Route) Escape left to good stance and then either diagonal up right on lower-angle rock (past sticker bushes) to the Day-Tripper oak tree belay/rap-station or move left and join Scuttlebutt to the pine tree belay/rap-station.

FA 1986: Todd Swain and Kathy Beuttler

Guy Waterman, walking along the carriage road in the early 70s met Fritz Wiessner and Jim McCarthy.

Guy: "Fritz, I understand you did High Exposure."

Fritz: "No, I didn't do it, Jim led it."

98   **SCUTTLEBUTT 5.7 R**

Pitch one is a quality pitch with nice moves on good rock. Pitch two has some exciting climbing; however, it's too bad its crux isn't protected better. Pitch three is short but fun all the same.

START: On the face 15 left of Day-Tripper, just right of a short outside corner.

PITCH 1: 5.5 G ★ (V1 & V2) Climb face (crux-1) to the highest horizontal. Step left around nose and move up a bit right on to nose (crux-2) to a stance. Continue up a bit left and up slab (blue Camalot helpful) the easiest way to the pine tree belay/rap-station at a short left-facing corner. (90 ft.)

Pitch 2: 5.7 R From the pine, climb the left-facing corner, then the face (staying left of the corner) to overhangs and move right to ledge with cedar tree. Step up to good holds above overhang, then work up to a bucket (crux), move left to old, fixed angle piton near base of left-facing corner. Climb corner and face up left to finish on left-jutting, flaky left-facing corner to the large NSGTLedge and pines. (100 ft.)

PITCH 3: 5.5 PG Step right and climb low overhang and short lichen face to clean white rock. Work up (crux) and left to the top and pine tree belay/rap-station. (50 ft.) Two-50-meter-rope rappel will get you back to pitch one belay/rap-station.

Variation 1: 5.4 G Climb the short, thin crack 6-8 feet right of Scuttlebutt (same as for As The Cliff Turns) to the wide horizontal. Make a move or two up and diagonal left to join Scuttlebutt.

Variation 2: 5.9+ G (Peyton Paltz, drawn in w/dotted line) Only "G" if you're tall enough to place the pro in the undercling pocket at ceiling, otherwise it's R. Be careful not to get rope jammed in crack at lip. Start 8 feet left of Scuttlebutt below a short open book capped by ceiling. Crank up to the undercling and work left on slab (crux) following crack to lip of overhang and up to a stance. Then straight up to finish on Here's The Scoop's open book/crack **or** go up right to finish on Scuttlebutt.

FA 1973: Dick Williams and Tom Bridges

FA (V1) 1985: Todd Swain and John Goobic

98a   (**TOPROPE**) Here's the Scoop 5.10b

This could be led, but it'd be a ground fall if all didn't go well. Same thing for variation one. At the time, it didn't seem like it was worth leading.

Start about 25 feet left of Scuttlebutt below a whiteish concave face with a vertical fracture that is a bit right of center. Move (V1) up face till feet are at lip of low overhang, then work right to bucket (crux: long reach) and swing around to a stance. Then up the nice open book and join Halfbeak.

Variation 1: 5.11b/c Start just right of the concave face and diagonal up right to first bucket on nose, then strenuously work up to a stance. FA 2004: Dick Williams with Annie O'Neill

98b   **HALFBEAK 5.8 G**

Some very nice climbing on this one. Named in memory of the submarine U.S.S. Halfbeak (SS352) on which I served for four years (1957-1961) while in the U.S. Naval Submarine Service. An amazing experience which I shall never forget.

START: Below and immediately right of Gunks Burghers.

PITCH 1: 5.8 G Step up onto short slab (hard to not use little tree) and climb past small pocket/waco to horizontal at overhang. Hand traverse around right along black-Camalot-size horizontal (V1) and move up to a stance on nose (crux), then up to small black birch tree. Move straight up to ledge or go right to open book. Continue up past right side of overhang to next overhang, step up left and up short crack to final bulge/overhang. Continue straight up to slab and to Scuttlebutt's pine tree belay/rap-station. (80 ft.)

Variation 1: 5.4 G Traverse right and climb open book to join Halfbeak.

FA 2007: Dick Williams and Annie O'Neill

98c   **GUNKS BURGHERS 5.5 PG**
START: Several feet right of Summer Breeze.
PITCH 1: 5.5 PG Climb nose (pink and red Tri-Cams) and face to overhang, step right a few feet and up face past undercling flake and shallow horizontal to a stance (there is a pine tree to the left). Traverse right about 5 feet and climb face and short slab to overhang (V1), step up into short left-facing corner to short gold Camalot-size horizontal. Move right around nose and up face and slab to ledge, go right to Scuttlebutt's pine tree belay/rap-station. (80 ft.)
Variation 1: 5.4 PG Move left to tree, and finish up obvious fault and low angle face on right to ledge to join regular route.
FA 2007: Dick Williams and Annie O'Neill

98d   **SUMMER BREEZE 5.5 G**
A fun little climb. If you do **V1** wear a helmet.
START: At a right-facing corner 10 feet left and uphill from the **toprope** climb, Here's The Scoop.
PITCH 1: 5.5 G Step up to a horizontal on the outside corner/arête, then move left and up (V1) to small overhangs. Step up left and work up face (crux) and then up right to low angle white nose. Climb straight up to ledge to birch tree belay/rap-station. (70 ft.)
Variation 1: 5.9+ PG (Breezy Fall-Arête) Climb short arête then steep face and outside corner till just below the triangular overhang. Work left and up (crux) to join Summer Breeze.
FA 2005: Dick Williams and Annie O'Neill
FA (**V1**) 2007: Elaine Mathews, Dick Williams and Larry Randall

98e   SPRING REIGNS 5.5 G
Not bad, short and simple with a couple of nice moves. Be careful of loose rock on way up to and on ledge at rap-station. Variation one is good, protection strenuous to place, plus it's best to use double ropes.
START: On the nose immediately right of the Mud, Sweat and Beers corner.

PITCH 1: 5.5 G Step up right to nose and horizontal (**V1**). Work straight up to handholds on grassy ledge (crux), diagonal up right past rounded nose and up slab past dirt ledge and broken crack to birch tree rap-station. (70 ft.)

Variation 1: 5.8 G From horizontal, hand traverse right 15 feet to a good stance (V2 joins here). Climb straight up face to rap-station.

Variation 2: 5.11a PG (Summer Storm) Start about 15 feet right and boulder straight up to right side of horizontal to meet Variation 1. Have a good spotter.

FA 2006: Dick Williams and Annie O'Neill

98f   (**NR**) MUD, SWEAT AND BEERS 5.7 G

One look at the climb and one understands immediately how it got its name and why it's not worth doing. However, if someone with nothing else to do were to clean it up, it would probably be a good little climb when dry.

Start: 40 feet left of Summer Breeze at a short, wide right-facing corner capped by a ceiling.

Pitch 1: 5.7 G Move up to ceiling, exit right and up past jungle to an escape. (50 ft.)

FA 1995: Tejvir Singh Khurana and Andrew Robinson

99   GOLD FLAKES 5.8 PG

Adventurous climbing, quite a good climb to the Not So Grand Traverse Ledge, but not traveled enough to recommend. Double ropes best and needed for the rappels. The climb was named for all the gold rock flakes on pitch-two belay ledge.

Start: From Mud, Sweat and Beers, scramble left, up hill to the base of slab and a comfortable belay seat on the chair-like rock.

PITCH 1: 5.4 PG Climb straight up passing short left-facing corner to dirt and tree-filled ledge. (40 ft.)

PITCH 2: 5.8 PG Walk right and climb up aiming for a bushy tree. Climb past tree on right side to base of left-facing corner. Move up into corner and then traverse left 5-10 feet and climb face to huge blocky corner and overhangs. Work past overhangs (crux) and follow corner to large NS-GTLedge, then go left about 20 feet to a belay at bushy oak tree below short, broken right-facing corner with crack. (140 ft.) If you don't want to do the last pitch, you can traverse right from the top of the corner about 50 feet and rappel to pitch one's rap-tree on Scuttlebutt.

PITCH 3: 5.7 PG Climb the steep fault above past right-pointing flakes/block (crux-1) and small tree. Then climb up to ceiling (crux-2) and traverse right about 10 feet to a good stance. Continue up face easiest way to the top. (60 ft.) Walk right about 50 feet to pine tree with rap-station where Scuttlebutt tops out. Two-60-meter-rope rappel down to pitch one pine tree rap-station on Scuttlebutt.

FA 1965: Dick Williams and Dave Craft

100 **(NR)** ENERGY CRUNCH 5.8 R
Some very good reasons to stay away from this one: poor protection, rotten rock and just plain dirty.

Start: At a broken area 30 feet left of Gold Flakes.

Pitch 1: **(NR)** 5.8 R Climb past a couple of grassy ledges and continue up the jagged left-facing corner to the NSGT-Ledge. (150 ft.)

Pitch 2: **(NR)** 5.8 R Climb the face just right of Deception to a ledge. Follow Deception to the ceiling (**extremely rotten rock**), go left a few feet, and clear the overhang at a thin crack. Then to the top. (100 ft.)

FA 1981: Todd Swain and Brett Wolf

101 **(NR)** DECEPTION 5.7 PG
This route looked quite serious when it was first spotted while refreshing on cold beers from Emile's parking lot below. I hadn't climbed this in 41 years and turns out for good reason. It is a serious climb and **not recommended**. The main section of pitch two has lots of good climbing

with good gear to the belay/rap-tree. The problem is the dirty climbing on pitch one and the chigger-filled grass belay ledge. Pitch three is a hellish nightmare of very dangerous, rotten loose rock up to the overhangs.

Start: At the base of a low-angle open book, just left of a low-angle arête, 50 feet left of Gold Flakes.

Pitch 1: (**NR**) 5.4 G Climb face and open book past a broken, dirty area to a grassy ledge. Just above ledge is a wide crack at small overhang (large cams for belay). (50 ft.)

Pitch 2: 5.6 PG Diagonal up right and climb straight up the clean face to a small ledge on the left with a pine tree belay/rap-station. (70 ft.)

Pitch 3: (**NR**) 5.7 PG Step right and move up very cautiously to a horribly rotten loose band of red rock on the NSGTLedge. Move up again (you must be crazy if you continue on from here) to and up a blocky corner past more horrible loose rock. If you make it this far you don't need any more info other than to continue past overhang and up the face to the top. (70 ft.)

FA 1964: Dick Williams and Pete Geiser

Note: The huge white pine that's in the route photo page that was used for pitch one rappels for Animal Farm and other climbs died and fell down in 2002, sad to say.

101a   ANTSY OH! 5.5 PG
Good climbing with a couple of exciting moves for the grade.

START: On the face about 8-10 feet left of Deception's low angle open book.

PITCH 1: 5.5 PG Climb face past horizontals to a small pointed overhang. Step up left to small dirt ledge, then straight up and right to a stance (crux). Climb face up and left to a short crack below grassy ledge. Step right and move up past right-pointing flake to grassy ledge. Go up left and finish on the short right-facing corner and up left to oak tree belay/rap-station. (90 ft.)

FA 2005: Dick Williams and Annie O'Neill

101b   SNAIL'S FACE 5.4 G

Very nice slab/crack climbing. The variation is good, but there is no pro in the little corner unless you have red and blue Trango Ballnutz.

START: 10 feet left of Antsy Oh! at a crack that diagonals up right.

PITCH 1: 5.4 G (V1) Climb crack to small tree, then diagonal up left on slab to undulating crack. Follow crack (crux) and up short, shallow left-facing corner to grassy ledge and short, steep headwall. Go right about 5 feet and climb Antsy Oh!'s short right-facing corner and go up left to oak tree belay/rap-station. (90 ft.)

Variation 1: 5.6+ G Begin 8 feet left, below a small right-facing corner that arches right. Work up face and corner (crux) to join the regular route.

FA 2005: Dick Williams and Annie O'Neill
FA (V1) 2005: Dick Williams and Annie O'Neill

102   WOLF AND THE SWINE 5.9 PG-R

The first pitch is fun with an exciting slab move and short headwall crux. The second pitch is new and a lot better than it looks, if it is dry, with neat holds. The third pitch is pretty wild and exciting with OK pro and has a long reach crux, harder for shorter climbers. It's just amazing that it goes at 5.9 PG.

START: About 15-20 feet left of Snail's Face at a shallow open book that looks a bit like a scoop below two stepped overhangs 15 feet up.

PITCH 1: 5.9 PG-R Climb past overhangs to a stance. Step right, then diagonal up and left on slab (5.6 PG-R) to a stance at a short crack. Continue straight up past faults to grassy ledge and short, steep headwall (V1). Climb straight up (black Alien) headwall (crux) and mantel up onto ledge and oak tree belay/rap-station. (90 ft.)

PITCH 2: 5.5 PG The original route climbed the dirty unappealing face just right of the huge scary-looking right-facing corner (directly behind where the huge old pine used to be) and finished near top of corner. Described here is a much nicer line to climb, if it is dry. Starting above the belay go right about ten feet to where there are signs of some rock fall (V2). Climb straight up the face aiming for the cedar tree on the NSGTLedge about 70 feet up. The crux is just below ledge, 5-8 feet left of cedar tree. (70 ft.)

PITCH 3: 5.9 PG From cedar belay/rap-tree, you will see a laurel bush about 30 feet up and a bit left, just above the first roof. Climb straight up past stepped overhangs that form a left-facing corner to the roof. Step right (at hanging dead cedar) and reach above overhang to good holds and fixed pin. Then work past next overhang (crux, long reach) up to slice-of-pie shaped roof. Step right and move up to the next roof. Then diagonal right about 30 feet and make a belay just right of "the house of cards" stacked blocks. (70 ft.)

PITCH 4: 5.4 PG Continue up lichen face to the top. (60 ft.)

Variation 1: 5.4 PG Traverse/go right about 5 feet and climb Antsy Oh's short right-facing corner to oak tree belay/rap-tree.

Variation 2: (**NR**) 5.6 PG-R (Original pitch two of Animal Farm) Diagonal up right, wandering the best way to finish on face left of the broken left-facing corner to the NS-GTL. (70 ft.) Then cautiously traverse left about 40 feet to a large oak tree below notch in overhang that is about 20 feet below a roof.

FA (P1 & P2) 1981: Brett Wolf and Todd Swain
FA (P3, pre 1981): Ivan Rezucha
FA (New P2) 2006: Brian McGillicuddy and Dick Williams

102a   DOUBLE QUACKS 5.7 PG

START: About 12-14 feet left of Wolf and The Swine below two parallel cracks that diagonal up right.

PITCH 1: 5.7 PG Begin at seam and move up to the base of the left crack. Layback up to a stance or climb face on right to same stance (crux). Then follow low-angle open book and nose to small ledges. Either finish on Animal

Farm Link-Up **or** diagonal up right to bushy oak tree rap-station. (60 ft.)

FA 2005: Dick Williams and Annie O'Neill

102b **(TOPROPE)** Frau's Prow 5.7

Start on face immediately left of Double Quacks (one can begin a bit further left but it's at least a grade harder). Climb straight up to small overhang w/short crack above. Continue straight up to a stance on prow. Then step up right and up face and prow to your anchors. FA 2007: Annie O'Neill, Keith La Budde and Dick Williams

102c BEAUTY AND THE SKINK 5.6 PG ★

Short, but really nice face climbing.

START: 15 feet left of Double Quacks and 10 feet right of Animal Farm, directly below a short left-facing flake/crack.

PITCH 1: 5.6 PG Climb straight up to short crack/left-facing flake. Continue straight up face to horizontal, then work up face (crux) till near Animal Farm's corner. Stay right and diagonal up right to bushy oak tree rap-station. (70 ft.)

FA 2005: Dick Williams and Annie O'Neill

102d SLAB HAPPY 5.4 R

Only fun climbing if you are comfortable on the 15 foot crux runout.

START: On the face 5 feet right of Animal Farm's pointy block start.

PITCH 1: 5.4 R Climb to small, short right-facing corner. Then climb straight up face (crux: runout) till near Animal Farm's corner. Stay right and diagonal up right to bushy oak tree rap-station. (70 ft.)

FA 2005: Dick Williams and Annie O'Neill

The best thing about the future is that it comes only one day at a time.
— Abraham Lincoln

103 **(NR)** ANIMAL FARM 5.6 PG

Most of this route is described and drawn in with a dotted line for historical purposes only and is not recommended. I am recommending instead, Animal Farm link-up (103a), which combines the best of Animal Farm with other climbs and some new variations.

Start: On the right side of a pointed block below huge overhanging, orange right-facing corner that diagonals up right, 80 feet left of Deception.

Pitch 1: 5.3 PG Climb the corner all the way up right to a short, flared chimney and roof. Move to right side of roof, then scramble up right to the center of ledge with belay/rap-tree. The huge old white pine rap tree that was on this big ledge died and fell down in 2002 but it can be seen in the old cliff photo.

Pitch 2: 5.6 PG **(NR)** (Original Route, drawn in w/dotted line) This pitch would have been more direct but everything was wet, so the driest line was taken. Diagonal up right easiest way and up past corner to the NSGTLedge. Then traverse/walk about 40 feet left (V1) to pines. (120 ft.)

Pitch 3: **(NR)** 5.8 PG-R (Drawn in w/dotted line) Start 10 feet right of BM, below right-leaning flake. Climb past flakes to ledge with lots of loose rock. Then up to overhang and work up right (crux) around overhang and up left (5.6 R) to make a belay on/from blocky ledge below short shallow open book with crack. (60 ft.)

PITCH 4: 5.6-5.8 Climb straight up open book to small overhang with fixed pitons. Traverse immediately right and then diagonal up right on easy ground about 35- 40 feet till below thin, white, hollow left-facing flake. Climb straight up past flake to the top (Trango Ballnutz) 5.7 PG-R. **Or**, from flake, step left a few feet and climb past vertical seam to the top 5.6 PG. **Or**, from flake, move left about 6 feet and work straight up face past thin horizontal to the top, 5.8 G.

Variation 1: **(NR)** 5.6 PG-R (Original pitch three of Cherokee, drawn in w/dotted line) Climb a fault just right of a short, blocky right-facing corner with right-facing flake to first overhang and then diagonal up right past right side of overhang up to the next overhang (loose rock, poor pro). Traverse left about 20 feet to join Animal Farm at blocky ledge below short, shallow open book with crack. (60 ft.)

FA 1964: Dick Williams and Brian Carey
FA (V1) 1981: Ivan Rezucha and Uwe Bischoff

103a　　(LINK-UP)　ANIMAL FARM　5.7 PG

Pitch one is pretty good, two ropes best to minimize rope drag. Although pitch two has loose rock and is not recommended, it's still the best way to get to the NSGTLedge. Pitch three is good with a couple of nice moves. Pitch four is a great exhilarating finale.

START: On Animal Farm, at the right side of a pointed block below huge overhanging, orange right-facing corner that diagonals up right, 80 feet left of Deception.

PITCH 1: 5.3 PG (Animal Farm) Climb the corner all the way up right to a short, flared chimney and roof (V1). Move to right side of roof, then diagonal up left passing two small trees and a short right-facing corner to Cherokee's pine tree belay/rap-station. (100 ft.)

Pitch 2: (NR) 5.6 PG (Cherokee) From right side of tree, climb up right following a fault (loose rock about 15 feet up), then continue up the face and up through a jungle of trees and dirt to the NSGTLedge and large oak tree. Go left to belay at pine tree that's closest to large block where BM starts. (70 ft.)

PITCH 3: 5.5 PG From BM's large block, climb the corner-like weakness to a stance about 15 feet up on ledge with loose rock and two pointy triangular projections (looks like a "W" from the belay ledge). Pass this overhang to a stance, then diagonal up right on slab to blocky ledge below short shallow open book with crack to join Cherokee. (60 ft.)

PITCH 4: 5.7 G ★ (Cherokee) Climb straight up short, shallow open book with crack past fixed pins (V2) up into the overhang. Make the airy/exhilarating step up left (crux),

Peter Darmi on
the wild traverse of
B M 5.8 (Route 106)
Photo: Robert Schehr 1981

Thom Campbell on
the wild traverse of
B M 5.8 (Route 106)
Photo: Dick WIlliams 2006

then climb the face past a smooth right-rising ramp to the top. (60 ft.)

Variation 1: 5.7 PG Stem up flared chimney to the roof and exit up left to small ledge and tree (crux). Continue straight up short right-facing corner to Cherokee's pine tree belay/rap-station.

Variation 2: 5.6-5.8 (Animal Farm) Traverse immediately right and then diagonal up right on easy ground about 35-40 feet till below thin, white, hollow left-facing flake (V2a). Climb straight up past flake to the top (Trango Ballnutz) 5.7 PG-R. **Or**, from flake, step left a few feet and climb past vertical seam to the top 5.6 PG. **Or**, from flake, move left about 6 feet and work straight up face past thin horizontal to the top, 5.8 G.

Variation 2a: 5.1 PG (Escape Right) Continue traversing right another 40 feet past small pine to exit onto grass ledges and scramble to the top.

104   RAVEN AND THE CAT 5.11a R
(As a Toprope)

START: From the top of Animal Farm's narrow block and at a crack that diagonals up right with thin slab to short prow/nose.

PITCH 1: 5.11a R Follow crack and short, low-angle left-facing corner to a stance. Then, either avoiding Animal Farm or using it, move up and around past a short right-facing corner/prow/nose to the reddish face below vertical seam. Climb face past seam (fixed pin) to a horizontal at the overhang near blueberry bush. Finish by climbing past the right side of the ceilings to pine tree belay/rap-station. (100 ft.)

FA 1984: Paul Craven and Felix Modugno

Success is not final, failure is not fatal: It is the courage to continue that counts.
— Winston Churchill

105   **CHEROKEE 5.9 G ★★**

A technical pitch one crux, great pro, lots of good moves. Although pitch two has loose rock and not recommended, it's still the best way to get to the NSGTLedge. Pitch three now starts on BM to join Animal Farm. The last pitch is a great exhilarating finale.

START: At the left side of the huge Animal Farm block, 15 feet left of Animal Farm's start.

PITCH 1: 5.9 G Climb up right past broken right-facing corner with crack about 15 feet to a short, shallow open book. Work up this (crux, harder if short) to a good stance at some loose blocks. Step right and follow the fault/slight left-facing corner to overhang. Step right and climb straight up (V1) past red rock to large wedged block. Continue straight up to the ledge and pine tree, belay/rap-station. (100 ft.)

Pitch 2: (**NR**) 5.6 PG From right side of tree, climb up right following a fault (loose rock about 15 feet up), then continue up the face and up through a jungle of trees and dirt to the NSGTLedge and large oak tree. Go left to belay at pine tree closest to a large block where BM starts. (70 ft.)

PITCH 3: 5.5 PG From BM's large block, climb the corner-like weakness to a stance about 15 feet up on ledge with loose rock and two pointy triangular projections (looks like a "W" from the belay ledge). Pass this overhang to a stance, then diagonal up right on slab to blocky ledge below short shallow open book with crack. (60 ft.)

PITCH 4: 5.7 G ★ This is the original last pitch of Cherokee. Climb straight up short, shallow open book with crack past fixed pins up into the overhang. Make the airy step up left (crux), then climb the face past a smooth right-rising ramp up to the top. (60 ft.)

Variation 1: 5.5 PG Move left and up slab past right side of small pine tree and up right to pine tree belay.

FA 1981: Ivan Rezucha and Uwe Bischoff

105a   ANNIE DOTES 5.6 PG

Contrivance was the antidote for some fun and a new climb; surprisingly, it has some good moves.

START: Same as Cherokee

PITCH 1: 5.6 PG From block, step up left and move left of short corner onto face with hands at dirt ledge that diagonals up left. Move/traverse left till about 5 feet from BM's right-facing corner. Climb straight up face and angle up left crossing BM just above its crux to the right-facing corner with crack. Climb corner past crack to oak tree belay/rap-station. (70 ft.)

FA 2006: Dick Williams and Annie O'Neill

106   **BM 5.8 PG**

Quite the adventure to do the entire climb. Surprisingly, pitch one has one good move after another. The last two pitches getting past the roofs are quite exciting, just an amazing area with these giant roofs.

START: On the face just right of the first right-facing corner 40 feet left of Animal Farm.

PITCH 1: 5.7 G Move up face to first laurel bush in corner. Work up corner to its top (crux: long reach) to a stance. Continue up a bit right following grooves/faults to small overhang with short, thin crack. Move up crack to a stance and then go left 6-8 feet to oak tree belay/rap-station. (70 ft.)

Pitch 2: 5.8 PG Step back right and climb straight up on to slab and diagonal up right to very blocky left-facing corner capped by overhang. Move up corner and work past overhang to a stance (crux). Then continue up easiest way and up past ledges and trees to a belay on the NSGTLedge at pine tree nearest a large block. (120 ft.)

PITCH 3: 5.8 PG From the large block, climb the obvious corner-like weakness to a stance about 15 feet up on a ledge with some loose rock and two pointy triangular projections (looks like a "W" from the belay ledge). Traverse left about 10 feet or so till below a whitish flared corner with a fern bush in it. Meander up left and right past it to the jagged/right-pointing flake under the overhang (Trango Ballnutz helpful). Climb past overhang (crux) and move up right to make a belay under the roof (old angle pin). (60 ft.)

PITCH 4: 5.8 PG (V1) Make the all-too-obvious hand traverse left to a stance (crux). Move up and right and make a belay near lip because you are thinking of your partner's mental state. (40 ft.)

Pitch 5: (Unrated) Scramble up slabs to top. (40 ft.)

Go south to rap-tree on Highway 51 (109) or go north to rap-tree on Scuttlebutt (98).

Variation 1: 5.6 G (Escape Right) Traverse right about 20 feet to join Animal Farm and Cherokee.

FA 1964: Dick Williams, Brian Carey and Jim McCarthy

106a   **(TOPROPE)** In The Nick Of Time 5.9
Start on BM, move up 8-10 feet to small black birch tree. Work up left and climb groove/shallow right-facing corner and face to finish on the right-facing corner of Annie Dotes. FA 2007: Joe Bridges, Elaine Mathews and Dick Williams

106b   **(TOPROPE)** Nickel and Timing 5.8
Start on Gardiner's Delight. Move up into corner and then step up right to the protruding block that forms a small overhang. Climb straight up and up past groove and face above to Gardiner's Delight's oak tree belay/rap-station. FA 2005 Dick Williams and Annie O'Neill

106c   GARDINER'S DELIGHT 5.5 G
The climbing is better than it looks because almost all the vegetation can be avoided, making for an interesting climb for its grade.
START: 14 feet left of BM, at a short, tapering right-facing corner.

PITCH 1: 5.5 G Climb corner, step left into short chimney. Climb straight up past small overhang to white pine and oak tree. Work up right on nose (crux) and up to oak tree belay/rap-station. (70 ft.)

FA 2005: Dick Williams and Annie O'Neill

106d   SERFS' UP 5.7 PG

Some good moves, should be cleaner in time.

START: 12 feet right of Slab Shtick at a short, shallow right-facing flake with a small tree about 10 feet up (same start as Slab Shtick's V1).

PITCH 1: 5.7 PG Move up to the ledge just above the tree, then up to grassy ledge and small tree (V1). Step left and climb up to highest right-facing flake and great holds. Move/step right and work up to good stance below small, short crack (crux 1, PG). Climb crack (crux 2, G) to small ledge. Climb straight up to Slab Shtick's pine tree belay/rap-station. (70 ft.)

Variation 1: (**Toprope**) 5.10c/d Climb just right of tree straight up past small break/crack.

FA 2006: Dick Williams, Elaine Mathews and Annie O'Neill

FA (V1) 2007: Andrew Reed

Wine comes in at the mouth
And love comes in at the eye;
That's all we know for truth
Before we grow old and die.
I lift my glass to my mouth,
I look at you and I sigh.
     — W.B. Yeats

107   SLAB SHTICK 5.8 PG

Pitch one is excellent, with many good moves and a new direct start. Double up on small wires for the beginning seam/crack. Pitch two is not worth doing; it's dirty and there is enough loose rock on it to build a small stone wall. Pitch three is exciting and strenuous. Pitch four has a nice slab; best to use double ropes.

START: About 40 feet left of BM, below a thin seam/crack that's directly below the main right-facing corner system.

PITCH 1: 5.7 G ★★ (V1) Climb straight up the face past right side of thin seam/crack to good horizontal at small overhang. Step right and climb corner and crack to ledge with trees, then up another 20 feet to pine tree belay/rap-station. (70 ft.)

Pitch 2: (**NR**) 5.4 PG Scramble up to loose ledge, move left and then climb the obvious broken left-facing corner to the NSGTLedge and large oak tree rap-station; go 15 feet further left and belay at bushy oak tree. (100 ft.)

PITCH 3: 5.8 PG Walk left about 5 feet till below right side of huge block/flake that's stuck on face about 15 feet up. Move up and climb crack to overhang, step right to small grassy ledge below overhangs. Step up and hand traverse left at/on lip past wide horizontal (blue Camalot) and up left (watch out for loose flakes which are completely avoidable) to pine tree and belay. (50 ft.)

PITCH 4: 5.3 PG-R Climb straight up using tree to gain a stance. Then diagonal up right and up slab finishing right of long overhang and just left of large pine on top. (60 ft.)

Variation 1: 5.4 PG (Original Route) Start 12 feet to the right at a short, shallow right-facing flake with a small tree about 10 feet up. Move up to the block just above tree, then move/traverse left to the right-facing corner.

FA 1980: Ivan Rezucha and Annie O'Neill

FA (Direct Start) 2005: Dick Williams and Annie O' Neill

107a   **(TOPROPE)** Shtick It 5.10c/d
Start immediately left of Slab Shtick. Climb straight up short, steep right-facing corner and up face to Ambien Knights and up to Slab's rap-station. FA 2007: Elaine Mathews and Dick Williams

107b   AMBIEN KNIGHTS 5.9 G-PG ★
Really good moves, long reach crux, dyno-friendly.
START: About 20 feet left of Slab Shtick below the first overhang with a short, thin crack that begins on its right side about 12-14 feet up.
PITCH 1: 5.9 G-PG Climb straight up to the right side of the overhang and crack. Work past crack to jug (crux), then crank up one more move to a good stance. Continue straight up the face to small pine with fixed directional and dirt ledge. Diagonal up right to Slab Shtick's pine tree belay/rap-tree. (70 ft.)
FA 2005: Dick Williams and Annie O'Neill

107c   **(TOPROPE)** Pump Ethyl 5.11d
Start about 15 feet left of Ambien Knights and work past short, incipient crack/seam that begins about 15 feet up. (As of 10/2007 there was a small wired nut near base of seam) FA 1987: Todd Swain

107d   ONE WAY OR ANOTHER 5.8 PG-R
START: 40 feet left of Ambien Knights and 20 feet right of Eat Here and Get Gas, below a crack with shallow open book that leads to left side of left-pointing, jagged overhang that's about 20 feet up.
PITCH 1: 5.8 PG-R Reach way out right to jugs and crank up to a stance (crux). Step left and move up to buckets at overhang (5.6 R). Then up short left-facing corner and easy rock to oak tree rap-station. (50 ft.)
FA 2005: Dick Williams and Annie O'Neill

108 EAT HERE AND GET GAS 5.6+ PG

START: 20 feet left of One Way Or Another and 20 feet right of Highway 51, at a crack that diagonals up right for about 15 feet to a block and laurel bush.

PITCH 1: 5.6+ PG Follow crack to horizontal just below block. (Original route thrashed up past laurel and block.) Diagonal up left to jugs and up to a stance. Go up right to dirt ledge and short corner. Work up short corner (crux) to bushy left-facing corner. Step right and up to a cluster of bushy trees, then diagonal right to oak tree belay/rap-station. (60 ft.)

FA 1986: Todd Swain, Randy and Andy Schenkel

108a BENADRYL DAZE 5.6 PG

Interesting crux, fun slab climbing if dry.

START: On face 12 feet left of Eat Here and Get Gas and 8 feet right of Highway 51, below arching flake/crack system.

PITCH 1: 5.6 PG Climb face/slab to the right-facing flakes and move up to the overhang. Traverse to right side of overhang (crux) and up easy face right of short nose to bushy trees. Diagonal right to oak tree belay/rap-station. (60 ft.)

FA 2005: Dick Williams and Annie O'Neill

109 HIGHWAY 51 5.7 PG

There is some good climbing on each pitch but also some not-so-good climbing. Overall I think it's a worthwhile climb/adventure, but doesn't quite meet the recommended status level. Stay off if wet.

START: On the face 8 feet left of Benadryl Daze and 30 feet right of 3,4,5,6 Over and Out Porkypine's huge right-facing corner. Below a short right-facing corner that forms a nose that has a huge block on its top that's about 20 feet above the ground.

PITCH 1: 5.4 PG Climb face past the block and then diagonal up right following a ramp-like left-facing corner that leads up right to dirt ledges. Traverse right about 20 feet to an oak tree belay/rap-station. (70 ft.)

PITCH 2: 5.7 PG Go back left and climb the dark face on holds you can't see from below, straight up to the overhang and short wide crack below the short right-facing corner (purple Camalot). Climb straight up (crux) to corner (great holds) and up face passing a sharp left-facing flake to small ledge. Continue up right to belay at large pine just below the NSGTLedge. (80 ft.)

PITCH 3: 5.6 PG Step up to ledge, go left and climb face and right-facing corner that juts right at its top to mossy ledge (Trango Ballnutz). Step left and climb overhang to a stance (crux), then work your way up slabby face passing bulges to final ceiling (best pro to the left in and near corner). Hand traverse left to ledge with small trees and the top. (100 ft.) To rappel, bushwack up and right to an oak tree rap-station and rappel back to last pine tree belay. Then, a two-60-meter-rope rappel will get you back to the trail at base of One Way Or Another.

FA 1973: Dick Williams and Claude Suhl

109a   TWO FEATHER FLAKE 5.3 PG

START: About 15 feet left of Highway 51, at an obvious right-facing, blocky flake with wide crack.

PITCH 1: 5.3 PG Climb to top of flake (crux) (V1), step right and climb slab to left side of overhang. Move up into short left-facing corner, step right and up low-angle rock to small grass covered ledge (10 feet further up is large grass covered ledge). Make the easy, but long traverse right about 60 feet to an oak tree belay/rap-station. (160 ft.)

Variation 1: Traverse right and join Benadryl Daze.

FA 2005: Dick Williams and Annie O'Neill

The dread of loneliness is greater than the fear of bondage. So we got married.
— Cyril Connolly

110   3, 4, 5, 6, OVER AND OUT PORKYPINE 5.9 G

I re-visited this climb after a 43-year absence. Pitch one now starts on Two Feather Flake because it has a nicer start and a more direct line. The upper part of pitch one is multi-cruxed and takes good route-finding judgement. Pitch two is short but with a nice overhang. Pitch three is wild and exposed, especially for whoever follows. Bring double ropes.

START: About 15 feet left of Highway 51, at an obvious right-facing, blocky flake with wide crack. There is a huge right-facing corner 15 feet further left that has a large, wedged hanging block in it.

PITCH 1: 5.7 PG (V1) Climb to top of flake, step right and climb slab to left side of overhang. Move up into short left-facing corner, step right and up low-angle rock to highest grassy ledge (optional belay). Continue pretty much straight up using flaky right-facing corner to small bushy tree. Work up past overhang that has a horizontal crack in it up to small overhang. Move up left, then right and up to small tree on the chossy NSGTLedge. Don't go up on to the ledge, traverse left to pine tree and right-jutting blocks just below NSGTLedge below oak bushes. (200 ft.)

PITCH 2: 5.6 PG Diagonal up right (avoiding bushes) to the very chossy NSGTLedge till below white overhangs with V-notch. Carefully climb to overhang and then work past it (long reach) to a ledge. Traverse right about 15 feet and make a belay at base of huge open book. (40 ft.)

PITCH 3: 5.9 G Diagonal up right on slab till below right side of ceiling with jutting flake. Move up past its right side to the roof (V2). Begin the spectacular and exposed traverse left (about 40 feet, 5.8 PG) to the corner and notch. Work up the finger crack (crux) to the top. (100 ft.) There is a rap-tree about 100 feet to the left and about 15 feet from cliff's edge. It's a 100-foot rappel to NSGTLedge and a large pine tree with rap-station. From here it's a 200-foot rap to the trail at the base of Bush League.

Variation 1: 5.6 PG-R (Original Start) This should only

be climbed if very dry. Start 15 feet left of Two Feather Flake directly below large right-facing corner with hanging wedged block. Climb corner past block to the overhang, then diagonal up right to join the regular route.

Variation 2: 5.6 PG (Chicken Shit Escape) Traverse right to join Highway 51 to the finish.

FA 1964: Dick Williams and Brian Carey

FFA 1973: Henry Barber, John Stannard and E. Marshall

111   (**TOPROPE**) Mighty White Of Us 5.11d

Start in the laurel bushes below a large, pointed, beautifully sculptured right-facing flake directly below a bulging white face, just left of 3, 4, 5, 6, Over and Out Porkypine. Climb straight up past the flake (or traverse left to it from the corner) and continue up the bulging face above. FA 1987: Darrow Kirkpatrick

111a   BUSH LEAGUE TOO 5.7 PG

Start: Just left of the slab below Mighty White.

Pitch 1: 5.7 PG   Climb past overhanging right-facing corner (crux) and up arête left of slab and dirty corner to blocky overhangs. Continue up left till one can traverse left on huge block to large Bush League's pine tree belay/rap-station. (50 ft.)

FA 2005: Dick Williams and Annie O'Neill

111b   (**TOPROPE**) Raven's Run 5.10a

Start on the face immediately to the left of where a large boulder sits on the trail, almost touching the cliff midway between Bush League Too and Bush League. Climb straight up face past small, two-foot wide overhang and bulge (crux), then on up to the pine tree. FA 2005: Dick Williams and Annie O'Neill

112 BUSH LEAGUE 5.8 PG

Star quality climbing on pitch one. Pitch two is not recommended because of the laurel bush thrash, a bit run out and difficult pro. Pitch three is pretty good and the last pitch is quite good with high exposure.

START: At the right-facing corner that leads to the left side of an overhang about 30 feet up, 70 feet left of Over and Out Porkypine and 15 feet right of Drohascadamfubast 1's right-facing corner.

PITCH 1: 5.8 PG * Climb corner to the overhang and wide horizontal (V1). Traverse to the right side of the overhang. Then work up and right to a stance on a small ledge (crux) (V2). Continue straight up broken rock and a bit left to large pine tree belay/rap-station. (60 ft.)

Pitch 2: (**NR**) 5.8 PG-R Go up left to the laurel bush and climb/struggle past bush and notch to the lip of the left edge of the ceiling. Traverse right delicately for 8 feet to a short, shallow left-facing corner and then up a bit right to a big ledge and belay at first pine to the left. There are pines directly above and below belay pine. (70 ft.)

PITCH 3: 5.8 PG Go left till midway between pine and oak bushes and climb straight up to a two-foot high right-facing corner capped by small overhang. Move up left, then diagonal up right passing the first overhang on the left, then up passing the second overhang in the center; step right to final overhang and base of right-facing corner. Step right and climb the face about five feet right of corner to the NSGTLedge and oak tree belay. (80 ft.)

PITCH 4: 5.6 PG (V3) Walk right about 20 feet till below a blocky right-facing corner with a small pine about 20 feet up. Climb corner to tree, then move up left to ledge. Move up till near white streak and traverse right, squeezing behind pine tree onto white face and some right-facing flakes. Climb straight up, then up a bit left and finish straight up least licheny part of face (crux) to the top. (90 ft.)

Variation 1: 5.7 G Traverse left about 6 feet to join Bush

Lite and climb past a small overhang at crack (crux) and up slab to ceiling. Traverse right about 20 feet under huge laurel bush to pine tree belay/rap-station.

Variation 2: 5.7 G Step left and climb straight up to pine tree.

Variation 3: **(NR)** 5.8 PG (Original Route) From oak tree, step right to pine tree that leans against the face. Climb straight up (reachy-much easier if you use the tree) to small overhang. Work up past dirt/grass bogs to ledge (crux).

FA 1980: Ivan Rezucha and Annie O'Neill

112a   BUSH LITE 5.7 G

Short, fun climb with good moves.

START: 5 feet right of Drohascadamfubast 1's, right-facing corner.

PITCH 1: 5.7 G Climb face/crack/fault system to right-facing flake that arches right. Climb flake, then work straight past overhang at crack (crux) and up slab to ceiling. Traverse right about 20 feet under huge laurel bush to pine tree belay/rap-station. (90 ft.)

FA 2005: Dick Williams and Annie O'Neill

112b   DROHASCADAM 1 5.5 PG

This corner is where Drohascadamcubast's first pitch originally started. At the top of the corner the route went left (dirty); now there is a more direct start to Drohascadamcubast's first pitch crux.

START: At the first left-facing corner, 15 feet left of Bush League.

PITCH 1: 5.5 PG Climb corner to its top, step right and work up bulge and slab to ceiling. Traverse about 20 feet right under huge laurel bush to pine tree belay/rap-station. (90 ft.)

112c   **(TOPROPE)** Liddle Lamzy Divey 5.9

Start 6 feet left of Drohascadam 1. Climb up into short right-facing corner to the overhang. Step around left and climb to first horizontal that takes pro. Then work up steep

Annie O'Neill on
Pitch one of
Bush League 5.8
(Route 112) Photo: Dick Williams 2007

face (crux) to the anchors. The easiest way to get off this is to go right to Bush League's pine tree rap-station. FA 2007: Dick Williams and Annie O'Neill

112d DOZY DOATS 5.3 G-PG

Fun climbing up to the long traverse. Blue and gold Trango Ballnutz helpful.

START: About 5 feet right of Drohascadamfubast below a short right-facing corner capped by an overhang 6-8 feet up.

PITCH 1: 5.3 G-PG Step up to overhang, move right and up short right-facing corner to the next overhang. Move right again (crux) and climb notch to small ledge and short left-facing corner. Step up right and climb short face and slab to big overhangs. Put in directionals, then diagonal up right to large laurel bush on Bush League. Traverse right to pine tree belay/rap-station. (100 ft.)

FA 2007: Dick Williams and Annie O'Neill

112e WHATAYAMACALLIT 5.9 PG

START: Do the first two pitches of Drohascadamfubast (113).

PITCH 3: 5.6 PG Go right on ledge about 15 feet till below right-facing flake in V-shaped notch with triangular overhang about 20 feet up. Climb to loose rock and flake below overhang, step left, work up face till possible to then move back right above overhang and flake. Continue straight up face passing short right-facing corner and up past loose rock and sloping dirt ledges to large white pine tree belay/rap-station that's a body length above the NSGT-Ledge. (80 ft.)

PITCH 4: 5.9 PG Climb up left of pine on right and left-facing flakes to the overhang. Move right around overhang and up face past very short left-facing corner and small overhang (looks like a notch from below). Continue up face past short crack to large ledge with large pine to the right. It is about 5.4 PG to this point and one can escape here by walking off left about 100 feet if you don't want to do the 5.9 finish on the final short headwall. Walk and step up onto short rounded nose (V1) to overhang, step right and work up following the overhanging right-leaning corner and face to the top. (100 ft.)

Variation 1: 5.7 PG Step up left and up fault to the top.

FA 2005: Dick Williams and Annie O'Neill

113　　　　DROHASCADAMFUBAST 5.9 G

Good climbing on the first pitch crux. Pitch two and three are not recommended: dirty, loose rock, etc. Pitch four is good, with a nice open book finale.

START: 30 feet left of Drohascadam1 and 35 feet right of Moxie. At the base of a corner that leads to an arching right-facing corner/flake that forms a wide crack.

PITCH 1: 5.9 G Climb corner and squeeze under the laurel bush, then up flake/crack to good stance below a very small, short right-facing corner, 5.4 PG (V1). Move up corner to jug and thin horizontal that leads left. Finger traverse left about 6 feet (crux) and up slab to large pine tree belay/rap-station. (80 ft.)

Pitch 2: (**NR**) 5.5 PG Diagonal up right past shallow horizontal to dirt ledges with boulders and trees. Continue up and climb blocky arête formed by left-facing corner to more dirt ledges and pine tree belay/rap-station. (50 ft.)

Pitch 3: (**NR**) 5.8 R Go left about 10 feet and climb a steep dirty face past a bulge and red rock and then follow a steep left-facing corner to the large dirt NSGTLedge covered with thickets; go right to oak tree belay. (75 ft.)

PITCH 4: 5.6 PG Walk back left and climb up into flared right-facing corner with right pointing flake/block on top. At top of corner, step left and climb straight up to a ledge on top of block (one can climb face right of pointy block and step left to ledge). Continue straight up face (some 5.4 run-out) to ledge and open book. Work up the open book (crux) to the top. (90 ft.)

Variation 1: (Escape Right) Traverse right onto Dozy Doats to Bush League's rap-tree.

FA 1971: Dick Williams and Claude Suhl

113a   SAVING FACE 5.8- PG

The first ascent party protected the move off the dirt ledge with a large cam on Saving Grace's flake.

START: On Drohascadamfubast.

PITCH 1: 5.8- PG Climb the steep, pointed right-facing corner on the left to a dirt ledge (V1). Work your way up the steep face to a small, short left-facing corner (crux), then up to large pine tree belay/rap-station (70 ft.).

Variation 1: 5.7 PG Go left and join Saving Grace.

FA 2005: Dick Williams and Annie O'Neill

113b   SAVING GRACE 5.7+ G-PG

Being graceful at the crux makes it a cinch. Very important to get in good pro at small crux flake.

START: About 8 feet left of Drohascadamfubast at left side of stacked blocks, 25 feet right of Moxie.

PITCH 1: 5.7+ G-PG Climb to thin stance at a very small, sharp left-facing flake. Work up onto slab (crux) and up to dirt ledge. Step right and climb right-facing flake and thin crack to large pine tree belay/rap-station. (70 ft.)

FA 2005: Dick Williams and Annie O'Neill

113c   GRACELAND 5.10a PG

Challenging face moves worth the effort, a bit strenuous to place pro at first horizontal break, Trango Ballnutz very helpful.

START: Midway between Saving Grace and Moxie (about 10 feet) at a 6-foot-high shallow left-facing corner/open book.

PITCH 1: 5.10a PG Move up corner (with a good spotter) to the horizontal break. Finger traverse right 5 feet and work up groove/fault (crux) to shallow horizontal (V1). Continue straight up on better holds and up a bit right to the overhang. Climb straight past break in overhang to small ledge between blueberry bushes, then up past bulge to wide horizontal and go right to Saving Grace's pine tree belay/rap-station. (70 ft.)

Variation 1: Move right and up to dirt ledge and up to overhang.

FA 2005: Dick Williams and Annie O'Neill

114   **MOXIE 5.9 G-PG ★**

Pitch one has a really good corner crux move, thin and technical. Pitch two takes good route finding and has some scary loose rock, an adventure for sure. Not much to say about Pitch three. Partly named for an old 1940s soda pop company.

START: On the face 15 feet right of Giddah (at left side of large oak tree) below a short left-facing corner that's about 25 feet up and 35 feet left of Drohascadamfubast.

PITCH 1: 5.9 G-PG Diagonal right, then up to the corner. Climb corner (crux) to the pine tree belay/rap-station. (60 ft.)

Pitch 2: 5.7- PG-R Continue straight up past rounded nose and up nice grey rock face moving from side to side, passing the left side of a rock sitting on small ledge up to dirt ledge (V1). Move left a bit and climb steep rock pretty much straight up to base of slab just below overhangs. Work up onto slab and diagonal left till below right-facing corner. Climb corner past loose rock and up right to the NSGTLedge. (150 ft.)

Pitch 3: 5.4 PG Climb up a bit right following obvious fault to roof and trees. Fight your way past the tree and diagonal up right, and then head for the top. (70 ft.)

Variation 1: 5.7- PG-R (Drawn in w/dotted line) Go right about 10-15 feet and climb up, wandering a bit, to grass hummocks at base of slab. Move left and up onto slab (crux) and diagonal left till below right-facing corner.

FA 1973: Dick Williams, Bob Anderson and Steve Lessin

114a   **AMAZING GRACE 5.8 PG ★**

Pray to be elegant and smooth at the crux because pure strength may not save the day. There is a fairly strenuous small wired nut placement in the corner near the crux and a 5.6 R move above the crux stance.

START: Midway between Moxie and Giddah (about 10 feet) at small notch in small overhang that forms a flake.

PITCH 1: 5.8 PG Under-cling flake, then straight up face till about 6 feet below overhang. Move up left to overhang and great under-cling holds. Work straight up past next over-hang and outside edge of small right-facing corner to a thin stance (crux). Then one thin move (5.6 R) before finishing up and left to Giddah's birch tree belay/rap-station. (60 ft.)

FA 2005: Dick Williams and Annie O'Neill

115 GIDDAH 5.6 R

Delightful first pitch climbing. Pitch two is not recommended; it starts out nicely but leads to dirty rock that makes it one of those "scary, hard to figure out where to go situations" kinda climbs.

START: 20 feet left of Moxie, on top of some boulders beneath a blocky right-facing corner. If you look straight up at the top of the cliffs, you'll see a Z-shaped skyline formed by a giant roof.

PITCH 1: 5.6 G ★ (V1) Climb the corner to the crack in the overhanging white rock. Follow crack/flake (crux) and go up left to black birch tree belay/rap-station. (60 ft.)

Pitch 2: (**NR**) 5.6 R Move right and climb the nice but poorly protected face to a ledge below overhangs. Diagonal first up right and then up left and up the scary, dirty face to the NSGTLedge. (90 ft.)

Pitch 3: 5.5 PG Step right and climb up left passing flaky overhang (crux). Diagonal left (there is a big, hanging dead cedar, and above it is a huge multi-forked tree that was just a small sapling at the time of the first ascent; the original route climbed past tree to ceiling and exited left, drawn in w/dotted line) passing under tree and up to the top. (70 ft.)

Variation 1: 5.6 PG Diagonal up to right side of short ramp. Climb straight up to join Giddah or step right to join Amazing Grace.

FA 1965: Dave Craft and Dick Williams

115a (**TOPROPE**) Git-Git Giddah 5.10a

Climb up to and past the break in the overhang immediately left of Giddah. FA 1994: Joe Bridges and Dick Williams

Annie O'Neill about to follow
Amazing Grace 5.8
(Route 114a)
Photo: Dick Williams 2005

NOTE: There was a huge rockfall in this area in the Winter/Spring 2007 that came from Rock Around The Clock and Flake Rattle And Roll area. There is still lots of loose rock up there and it is highly recommended NOT TO CLIMB these two climbs that were kind of scary to climb even before the rockfall.

116 (**NR**) ROCK AROUND THE CLOCK 5.6 R
Start: On a slab below two short cracks that almost converge 25 feet up (the left crack is formed by a right-facing flake), directly below the base of an obvious fault/crack system that diagonals up right, 50 feet left of Giddah and 15 feet right of Flake, Rattle and Roll.

Pitch 1: (**NR**) 5.6 R Climb straight up to the base of the fault/crack system and follow it for about 30 feet. Continue up right to a shallow left-facing corner, work up the corner, and step right onto the face. Then belay above a bulge in a short right-facing corner. (120 ft.)

Pitch 2: (**NR**) 5.6 R Continue up and left to the orange flake in the overhang, and move straight up to a NSGT-Ledge. (90 ft.)

Pitch 3: 5.2 PG Climb up left and thrash past twin-forked tree, then up right-facing corner to overhang. Exit left and up to the top where there is a memorial plaque dedicated to the memory of Kenicihi Shimizu. (70 ft.)

FA 1973: Dave Loeks and Claude Suhl

117 (**NR**) FLAKE, RATTLE AND ROLL 5.7 R
Many loose flakes and rocks were removed during the first ascent, one of those "trust but verify" kinda climbs.

Start: At a very thin 15-foot high crack, 15 feet left of Rock Around the Clock and 7 feet from the right side of two huge boulders that are directly below a very broken right-facing corner.

Pitch 1: 5.6 G Climb crack and face to a short right-facing corner that begins at the lip of an overhang. Pass this and diagonal up right to some right-facing flakes that form a shallow open book. Follow flakes to a small overhang, step left, and move up to a belay. (60 ft.)

Pitch 2: **(NR)** 5.7 R Diagonal up right and traverse right under the overhang to a small ledge that has loose rock. From right side of the ledge, climb up a move or two and then diagonal up left to the top of a right-facing flake system that leans right. Move up to a long ledge (loose rock) below the long band of overhangs and traverse left about 25 feet to make a crunched-up belay at small pine tree. (70 ft.)

Pitch 3: 5.5 G-PG From right side of tree climb overhang, step left, and work up the face till 10-15 feet below the overhangs. Then diagonal up right around them and up to a belay on the NSGTLedge with a pine tree and tons of loose rock. (70 ft.)

Pitch 4: Finish on Rock Around The Clock.

FA 1988: Dick Williams, Dave Craft and Joe Bridges

117a   BIRCH BEER CRACK 5.6 G
START: At the obvious right-facing corner system that's about 10 feet left of the left side of two huge blocks at base of the cliff. These blocks are about 12-15 feet left of Flake, Rattle And Roll.

PITCH 1: 5.6 G Step up corner to the overhang, step right and follow corner to the pine tree belay/rap-tree. (60 ft.)

FA 2005: Dick Williams and Annie O'Neill

117b   ROOT BEER CRACK 5.6 G
START: 13 feet left of Birch Beer Crack at a short right-facing corner.

PITCH 1: 5.6 G Move up corner and step right to finger/hand crack. Climb crack to birch tree (crux), then diagonal up left and up low angle rock to pine tree belay/rap-station. (60 ft.)

FA 2005: Dick Williams and Annie O'Neill

117c (**TOPROPE**) TurtleFly 5.7

Start immediately left of Root Beer Crack and climb the thin face to the center of the wave-like bulge/overhang. Continue straight up passing the overhang just left of center and up to pine tree anchors. FA 2005: Annie O'Neill and Dick Williams

118 JUST ALLOW ME ONE MORE CHANCE 5.6 PG

NOT recommended to go beyond pitch one which is OK. The main reason is the dangerous loose rock getting up to the slopey grass ledge at the end of pitch two, and to add to that, there is no place to get in pro once you are on the ledge. The FA party used a tree for a belay; it is not there anymore. The ledge is about 100 feet wide with **NO** place for any pro. The best choice is to belay to the right at a small bushy tree. There is a pine tree belay, rap-station another 15-20 right of the bushy tree which is the same belay as for pitch two of Flake, Rattle and Roll.

START: 12-14 feet left of Root Beer Crack and about 20 feet right of Honky Tonk Woman, below short right-facing corner.

PITCH 1: 5.5 PG Climb corner or face to the left, up past right side of fern/grassy ledge (crux) to slab. Diagonal up right to pine tree belay rap-station. (60 ft.)

Pitch 2: (**NR**) 5.6 PG Move up and right to the large right-facing corner. Move up and make the obvious traverse left around nose onto the face. Move up (blue Camalot) to a good stance. Step left, move up the face, step left above short broken right-facing corner. Then work up dirty face to a grassy ledge (crux), and carefully traverse right about 15 feet to a bushy oak tree belay. The original belay was at a tree to the left that is no longer there. (80 ft.)

Pitch 3: (**NR**) 5.6 PG Traverse back left about 15 feet and climb the steep face, past an overhang, to lower-angle rock just below a large orange overhang. Exit left, work up the steep face for a few feet and climb past the final overhang to easier rock that leads to the NSGTLedge and oak tree belay. (80 ft.)

Pitch 4: **(NR)** 5.3 PG Diagonal up left and climb past overhang at notch and up to the top. (50 ft.)

FA 1971: Dick Williams, Cherry Merritt and Al DeMaria

119   **SHE'S THE BOSS 5.9+ X**
                    (As a Toprope)

START: On the slab immediately right of Honky Tonk Woman below the short nose on the left edge of the fern-covered ledge.

PITCH 1: 5.9+ X Climb slab and nose, then move up right to a sloping corner/groove. Exit up left and then straight up to join Honky Tonk Woman.

FA (Toprope) 1985: Todd Swain

FA (Lead) 1985: Todd Swain and Iza Koponicka

120   **HONKY TONK WOMAN 5.9 R ★**

You could really go for a ride if you screw up at the crux; even though modern gear now allows one to get in a little wired nut, it may or may not be reliable. No need to go beyond pitch two; it's dirty and scary.

START: On the face just right of the White Pillar (directly below bolt 25 feet up), about 130 feet left of Giddah.

PITCH 1: 5.9 R Climb to the bolt, step right and work up past the overhang (crux), then straight up to the right side of the long overhang and wide crack (blue Camalot). (60 ft.) Traverse left here **or** step back down a few feet and follow a thin horizontal (small cams) about 20 feet left to the big ledge atop The White Pillar (there are two pine tree belay/rap-stations) or (original route), continue up the groove-fault system to the second overhang, hand traverse left about 10 feet and up to a grassy ledge. (125 ft.)

Pitch 2: **(NR)** 5.7 R Walk right about 10 feet, climb to overhangs, and skirt around them by stepping right. Continue up the face and pass an overhang. Then climb another 10 feet, move left, and work up to a small, loose rock NSGTLedge. (120 ft.)

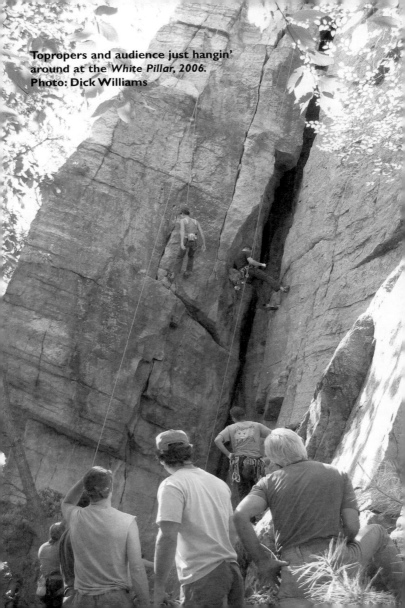

Topropers and audience just hangin' around at the *White Pillar*, 2006.
Photo: Dick Williams

Pitch 3: **(NR)** 5.2 PG From very small pine tree, climb up to orange left-facing corner. Diagonal up left past slabs to the top. (40 ft.)

FA 1971: Dick Williams and Dave Loeks

121   THE WHITE PILLAR 5.7 PG-R

Fritz Wiessner put up this route in 1940, very impressive. The quality of the rock on the last pitch is poor and takes good route finding judgement. Most people rappel from atop the pillar. This huge corner is a major feature of the cliff that can be seen from the intersection of route 44-55 and route 299.

START: About 130 feet left of Giddah, in the chimney at the back of the huge pillar's corner.

PITCH 1: 5.7 PG Work up the chimney to the top of the pillar and rappel from pine tree, or continue past ledges, blocks and face to a large ledge, then traverse left about 25 feet to a tree beneath a right-facing corner. (130 ft.)

Pitch 2: **(NR)** 5.7 PG-R Climb corner to an area of loose rock, traverse right carefully (as the loose rock dictates) and diagonal up right to the ceilings. Continue up left, climb straight up a bit, then move left again and straight to the top. (150 ft.)

FA 1940: Fritz Wiessner and Mary Millar

122   HARVEST MOON 5.11a G ★★

This climb will have you howling with pain if you don't tape up. A wonderful lead with great protection.

START: Same as White Pillar.

PITCH 1: 5.11a G (V1) Follow White Pillar's chimney till it's possible to reach left to the finger/hand crack on the pillar's face. Climb crack to pine tree/rap-station. (60 ft.)

Variation 1: 5.11b/c G Start on The Mincer and move right to Harvest Moon's crack at first opportunity.

FA 1980: Alex Lowe

123   THE MINCER 5.12a PG-R

Strenuously hard to protect, a pump fest.

START: At the thin parallel cracks that begin at the ground, just left of White Pillar's chimney.

PITCH 1: 5.12a PG-R Climb cracks to the top of pillar, staying left of Harvest Moon's crack. (60 ft.)

FA 1984: Jim Damon

123a   **SHOOTIN' THE CURL 5.10b/c PG**

Bring little wires and Trango Ballnutz. The crux ceiling is height-related, long reach. A very quick dyno for the shorter people works.

START: Immediately left of The White Pillar's outside corner at a 6-foot high block.

PITCH 1: 5.10b/c PG From the top of block, climb past a short right-facing corner (5.7 R) to the ceiling. Work past ceiling (crux) to another short right-facing corner and small tree, step left and up to the rap-station. (80 ft.)

FA 1989: Dick Williams with Dave Craft

124   **HANG TEN 5.10a PG ★**

Good overhang crux that can be done with finesse if you use your feet thoughtfully.

START: On the face, 10 feet right of Tree Filled Chimney, which is 30 feet left of Shootin' The Curl.

PITCH 1: 5.10a PG Climb straight past overlaps in the overhang to short, left-facing corner and ceiling. Move right on good holds and clear the overhang to a stance (crux). Continue straight up the face to top of pillar (5.6 PG-R) **or** move up and left at bushy tree past small left-facing corner to pine tree belay/rap-station. (80 ft.)

FA 1985: Todd Swain, Andy and Randy Schenkel

124a   **TFC Nein 5.6 PG-R** (Variation)

This may be the most pleasant and moderate way to get to the top of the White Pillar.

START: Same as for Hang Ten.

PITCH 1: 5.6 PG-R Climb straight past overlaps in the overhang to short, left-facing corner and ceiling (crux). Step left and move up into the chimney. Then, step around right on to face and rejoin Hang Ten. Continue straight up the face to top of pillar (5.5 PG-R) **or** move up and left at bushy tree past small left-facing corner to top. (80 ft.)

FRA 2004: Dick Williams and Annie O'Neill

125   **(NR) TREE-FILLED CHIMNEY**

It's the chimney with two big trees in it just up and left of Hang Ten, TFC for short. The nicest way to get to the top of the White Pillar is to climb Hang Ten's 5.6 variation, TFC Nein. It is **Not Recommended** to go up the chimney beyond the second tree because it has some very dangerously-loose rocks that could crash down if disturbed. If you decide to go up it, climb past the two big trees into chimney and loose rock, then step around right to join Hang Ten. Then straight up face (crux) to top of pillar or move up and left at bushy tree past small left-facing corner to top (5.6 PG-R). (80 ft.)

125a   BOOGY BORED 5.11b/c R

Start: 12 feet left of Tree Filled Chimney.

Pitch 1: 5.11b/c R   Climb the steep face past the overhang to the first opportunity to get lowered.

FA 1986: Todd Swain

126   **THE NEAR SIDE OF FAR 5.9 G**

This climb was written up incorrectly as Far Trapps 5.4 PG in my 1991 Black Dick guide; how it ever got written up as such is a mystery. I apologize to those climbers who over the years have had erroneous beta. This new climb has some good, interesting moves up to the slab which may be covered with pine needles.

START: Behind a tree and below blocky right-facing corner, 25 feet left of Tree-Filled Chimney.

PITCH 1: 5.9 G Climb past clunky flake and short right-facing corner to the top overhang. Step around left to a small stance and good holds, then work up past crack system (crux) till it's obvious to diagonal up left on low angle rock to a pine tree belay/rap-station. (60 ft.)

FA 2006: Dick Williams and Annie O'Neill

127   JUST FOR THE RECORD 5.8 PG

Very awkward first moves should keep you focused; the slab is usually covered with pine needles. Pitch two is quite exciting.

START: At the second right-facing corner, which is capped by an overhang, 20 feet left of The Near Side of Far, and 45 feet left of Tree Filled Chimney.

PITCH 1: 5.5 G (V1) Make an awkward move up left to a stance and creaky block, then up low-angle rock to a pine tree (optional belay/rap-station, 50 ft.). Then up past some pine trees to a small belay ledge below overhang. (130 ft.)

PITCH 2: 5.8 PG Climb the orange-colored rock, move left, and weave up to the overhang formed by the large left-facing flake. Step left and work up past the flake. Then go up and slightly left past some small overhangs (5.6 PG) to a large ledge. (One can exit here by scrambling off to the left or right). Climb the bulge (crux) a few feet left of the broken left-facing corner and reach an overhang. Then step right and continue to the top. (120 ft.)

Variation 1: 5.8 PG (Swells Good) Start 10 feet left of the corner and move up to pointed bucket. Work up the face to a stance (crux) and up to small overhang, step right and join Just For The Record.

FA 1972: Dick Williams, Joe Bridges and Dick DuMais
FA (V1) 2006: Dick Williams and Annie O'Neill

127a   UP ROOT 5.6 PG

Despite the initial grunge, some people might find this a fun climb.

START: 20 feet left of Just For The Record at a dirty open book.

PITCH 1: 5.6 PG Climb the open book, avoiding as much of the grunge as possible, to the overhang. Move to the right side of overhang and then climb the broken arête (upper part is the crux) straight up to pine tree belay/rap-station. (80 ft.)

FA 2006: Dick Williams and Annie O'Neill

127b   LIKE A BOX OF CHOCOLATES 5.8 PG

Like the proverbial box of chocolates, you never know what you're going to get (from the *Forrest Gump* movie). The initial committing move is awkward and a bit reachy; the first pro is a Blue Trango Ballnutz (strenuous to place unless you have a long reach) in a thin horizontal just above and left of a little corner.

START: 8 feet left of Up Root at a short, small left-facing corner which is just above the right side of blueberry-covered ledge.

PITCH 1: 5.8 PG Work up corner and face on good edges to jugs and lower angle rock. Continue up crack/fault and left-facing corner to dirt ledge. Then up a bit left to pine tree belay/rap-station. (90 ft.)

FA 2006: Dick Williams and Annie O'Neill

127c   WHATEVER 5.10a PG ★

Good climbing, exciting crux. Exiting left at crux seam turns this into a very nice 5.7. When you get to the final short headwall and seam, work straight up or go left or go right–whatever!

START: 15 feet left of Like A Box Of Chocolates and 12 feet right of Across From The Fruitstand.

PITCH 1: 5.10a PG Move up 5 feet to a stance on small ledge, then work past bulge to a stance (5.7 G). Climb straight up slab following crack to short headwall and seam at pebbly horizontal (V1 & V2) (can get yellow Alien in pocket on right). Work straight past seam (crux) to large ledge with pine tree belay/rap-station. (50 ft.)

Variation 1: 5.7 G-PG Traverse left about 6 feet and finish up a short crack to ledge and pine tree belay/rap-station.

Variation 2: 5.4 G Traverse right to join Like A Box Of Chocolates.

FA 2004: Dick Williams and Annie O'Neill

After heavy rains, Across From The Fruitstand to Inter-lewd remain wet for several days.

128   ACROSS FROM THE FRUITSTAND 5.4 PG

A fun climb with fantastic holds on pitch two. No need to do the last pitch; one can retain the 5.4 grade by walking off left to the top as the first ascent party did **or** going left about 50-60 feet to the rappel tree.

START: Almost 60 feet left of Just for the Record at a short, right-leaning, right-facing corner below a white, right-facing/jutting flake that's 25 feet up.

PITCH 1: 5.3 PG Climb short corner, then up face past the flake and up left to end of ramp. Then up short slab (crux) to a big ledge with pine tree rap-station. (50 ft.) Walk right about 10 feet and go up short face with crack to ledge with pine trees. (70 ft.)

PITCH 2: 5.4 PG Climb straight up to the ramp (about 40 feet up) that rises up left, and move up left to white rock. Step left and work past overhang to a stance up to the right (crux). Continue straight up right past the huge NSGTLedge to the left side of the monster block. (120 ft.)

PITCH 3: 5.7 PG (V1) Climb short face directly behind be-lay at a short, left-facing corner to the top. (20 ft.) **Or** don't do the 5.7 and go left about 60 feet to a pine tree rap-sta-tion. Two-50-meter-rope rappel gets you back to the pine tree belay/rap-station on pitch one.

Variation 1: 5.9 PG-R (On monster block, drawn in w/ dotted line) Work up broken crack that leads up right to the top of block. (Scramble down back side)

FA 1958: Dave Craft and Jim Andress

129   TO COME OR BECOME 5.6 PG

It is not recommended to venture on the final one third (40 feet) of the second pitch. There is a very large jammed, loose-looking block (6 feet wide), plus some loose rock on small ledges. To add to these poor qualities, the final slabs before the large ledge w/rap-tree is full of moss and is usually wet.

START: Same as Across from the Fruitstand.

PITCH 1: 5.3 PG Climb the short corner, then up face past the flake to a big ledge with pine tree belay/rap-station. (50 ft.)

Pitch 2: **(NR)** 5.6 PG Climb corner and slab to right side of 15-foot long/wide ceiling. Continue up face (good moves) and up past grassy ledges to some overhangs. Step left and follow the weakness in light-colored rock to an overhang (V1). Continue past some left-facing flakes to the left side of a large 6-foot-wide block jammed on a ledge. Finish by stepping up onto the block, moving to its right side, and up to NSGTLedge and rap-tree. (120 ft.)

Variation 1: Instead of going up past flakes, move right and up to right side of 6-foot-wide block.

FA 1987: Dick Williams and Burt Angrist

129a   **MISS MANTLE 5.9 PG**

Don't miss this thoughtful and exciting crux.

START: On the slab about 15-18 feet left of Across From The Fruitstand.

PITCH 1: 5.9 PG Climb the nice face to the final horizontal and short headwall. Step straight up till both hands are on the sloping ledge, then mantle up to a stance (crux). Go up right to the ledge and pine tree belay/rap-station. (50 ft.)

FA 2004: Dick Williams and Annie O'Neill

130   ROMAN'S CLIMB NEXT TO ACROSS FROM
THE FRUITSTAND 5.5 PG

Now there is a new and more direct start to the first ledge; the original route started in the huge, dirty right-facing corner about 60 feet to the left.

Start: About 8 feet left of Miss Mantle at a thin crack that breaks the face.

Pitch 1: 5.5 PG Climb crack to lower-angle rock and large ledge below a broken left-facing corner that begins at the left end of a 15-foot long/wide ceiling (5.3 PG, optional belay at tree on the right) (50 ft.) Climb broken left-facing corner till below the obvious vertical fault system first formed by left-facing corners. Follow fault to the highest corner, which is short and right-facing. At top of the corner (V1 & V2), either traverse left along the ledge system past tons of loose rock to better ground (the original route) **or** finish on Parsifal and Potato Chips. (180 ft.)

Variation 1: 5.8+ PG-R Climb to the overhang, traverse right about 10 feet, and continue up past an overhang at a 2-foot-high right-facing corner to a ledge with an oak tree belay/rap-station.

Variation 2: 5.4 PG-R Climb to the overhang, traverse right about 20 feet and work up to the ledge near the oak tree belay/rap-station.

FA 1965: Roman Sadowy and friends

131   PARSIFAL AND POTATO CHIPS 5.7 PG-R

This climb also has a new and more direct start.

Start: At the thin seam immediately left of Roman's Climb Next To Across From The Fruitstand.

Pitch 1: 5.7 PG-R Climb the seam past grass hummocks and low-angle rock to ledge and go left 5-10 feet to pine tree optional belay (5.4 PG) (50 ft.). Climb the corner above, step right and continue up the face past a grassy ledge to a higher ledge. Angle up right and then back left and up to a short slab. Continue straight up to the Roman's Climb ledge, which has an oak tree (optional belay here to avoid rope drag). Climb up right a few feet and then continue up and left in a zig-zag fashion to a small pine tree. From the tree, exit up right through wicked oak tree bushes to a ledge and rappel tree. (170 ft.)

FA 1987: Dick Williams and Ed and Karen Clark

132   INTERPLANETARY AGENTS 5.9+ PG

START: At huge, blocky right-facing corner, 90 feet to the left of Across from the Fruitstand.

PITCH 1: 5.9+ PG Climb past the short open book/groove with a seam to the pebbly overhang. Work past the overhang (crux) to a finger pocket and a marginal stance (if you use this welcomed pocket hold for protection (tri-cam), the next move will be harder, but safer, 5.9 G; otherwise it's 5.8 but you have to trust an old fixed bashie for pro–bad idea). Move left and up right a bit to easier rock (the corner to the left can be used for protection to avoid the otherwise 5.6 X runout) and the final 5.6 move to the fixed anchor/rap-station. (70 ft.)

FA 1985: Todd Swain and Iza Koponicka

133   INTERLEWD 5.6 PG ★

Lots of good climbing on this route described here which incorporates a new start and finish via new variations named Lady and The Tramp. The original route is drawn in w/dotted line as variation two. Two ropes best and also convenient for the rappel.

START: Three feet right of Eowyn.

PITCH 1: 5.6 PG (V1) Climb past the right side of the overhang and go straight up slab (pro to left on Eowyn) to the orange right-facing corner and crack that arches up right. Follow corner and crack to ledge. Move up corner to small tree below large overhang (V2). Move left and up into stacked blocks in corner near arête, then climb up to large right-facing corner with slab on right. Stem/work up to top of corner (crux), then up on jugs to small ledge and make a belay on arête (blue Camalot helpful). (110 ft.)

PITCH 2: 5.2 PG Step left and climb straight up to pine tree belay/rap-station. (40 ft.)

Variation 1: (Original Start) At the beginning of a small, vegetated ramp that leads up left from the base of the huge Roman's Climb corner. Scramble up left on ramp to the right-facing corner and crack. (25 ft.)

Variation 2: 5.5 PG (Original Route, drawn in w/dotted line) Then work up past vertical fault in orange overhang (crux). Continue up final stacked overhangs and exit/traverse left to pine tree on nose. Then step left and up about 20 feet to pine tree belay/rap-station.

FA 1967: Dick Williams, Burt Angrist and Kaye Arnott

FA (Variations) Lady and The Tramp, 2004: Dick Williams and Annie O'Neill

134   EOWYN 5.4 PG ★★

START: On the face below a notch in the overhang 15 feet up, 45 feet downhill and left of Interplanetary Agents' huge right-facing corner, and 40 feet right of I'm OK-You're OK.

PITCH 1: 5.4 PG Climb past notch (crux) and diagonal up left on the slab (run-out) to a large ledge and pine tree belay/rap-station. (50 ft.)

PITCH 2: 5.4 PG Climb the corner to its top, step left and move up to the overhangs. Move right a few feet and climb the white rock to low angle slab. Continue straight up past overhangs till about 10-15 feet from the top. Go right to pine tree belay/rap-station and rappel, (need two 60-meter ropes) or continue to the top. (140 ft.)

FA 1971: Dick Williams, Cherry Merritt and Herb Cahn

Beer is proof that God loves us and wants us to be happy.
— Benjamin Franklin

135　　　　　LIVE AND LET DIE　5.10b/c PG-R

One can avoid the steep, hard to protect (Trango Ball-nutz) initial face moves and start on Eowyn and then traverse left to the little flake. A hold broke off on variation two, so it's now harder.

Start: On the face about 10 feet left of Eowyn.

Pitch 1: 5.10b/c PG-R (V1 & V2) Climb thin face to the overhang and then work past the break/small pointy flake (long reach) up to a stance, then up left to the pine tree belay/rap-station. (50 ft.)

Pitch 2: (**NR**) 5.7 X Continue up and right on the unprotected face to the overhangs at the outside corner and up to the top. (120 ft.)

Variation 1: (**Toprope**) 5.11a Work up past the overhang 10 feet left of Live And Let Die. Crux: long reach.

Variation 2: (**Toprope**) 5.10d Climb the left side of the long overhang at short right-facing corner.

FA 1985: Dave Saball and Todd Swain

136　　　　　I'M OK-YOU'RE OK　5.9 PG ★

Pitch one's face has thin and sustained climbing, blue Trango Ballnutz helpful. Pitch two is committing and scary.

START: On the face 40 feet left of Eowyn, at two short offset thin cracks.

PITCH 1: 5.9 PG Climb up and left past the second short crack and up to the small overhang that's about 20 feet up. Continue straight up and work past the vertical seam (crux) to a stance, then up to the pine tree belay/rap-station. (50 ft.)

Pitch 2: 5.8 R Step left from tree and climb straight up the unprotected face to a stance below the break/notch (V1). With good pro at your feet, work up right (long reach) and make the committing crux move up to a stance. Then climb straight up the unprotected slab (40 feet, 5.3) and up past overhang to optional pine tree belay/rap-station. (100 ft.) Continue up another 40 feet to the top.

Variation 1: 5.9 R Climb straight up past the break in overhang.

FA 1975: Dick Williams and Roy Kligfield

136a R2-OK? 5.8 PG

START: 5 feet right of Akidlleativytoowouldn'tyou?

PITCH 1: 5.8 PG Climb the shallow, broken left-facing corner that's about 15 feet high (Trango Ballnutz helpful). Continue up the unprotected (5.5) slab to horizontal directly below the vertical seam (last pro till top of seam). Work up seam (crux) to ledge and go right about 15 feet to I'm OK's pine tree belay/rap-station. (80 ft.)

FA 2004: Dick Williams and Annie O'Neill

137 AKIDLLEATIVYTOOWOULDN'TYOU? 5.7 G ★★

Interesting climbing, named after a popular song from the 1940s.

START: At the obvious 20 foot high thin crack that's about 25 feet left of I'm Ok-You're Ok.

PITCH 1: 5.7 G Climb crack, then straight up past a bulge (V1) to the small overhang at a vertical seam (a bit runout). Climb straight up past seam to ledge (crux) and pine tree belay/rap-station. (80 ft.)

PITCH 2: 5.5 PG Climb up left to top of block, then up to the overhang, move left and finish on the steep vertical fault to the top. (80 ft.)

Variation 1: (Original Route, drawn in w/dotted line) Go up right and up past the small right-facing corner to ledge, walk left about 15 feet to the pine tree belay/rap-station.

FA 1971: Dick Williams and Dave Loeks

138 FAR FROM THE MADDING CROWD 5.8 PG ★

Pitch one has good, sustained moves all the way; it has PG protection if you use Trango Ballnutz. It was way run out in the old piton days.

START: On the face 10 feet left of Akidlleativytoo's crack, below a tree and block/flake sitting on a ledge about 20 feet up.

PITCH 1: 5.8 PG Step up to small ledge 4 feet above ground (or climb the face on left), step left and then climb face past crack to top of block. Follow vertical seam straight up to smooth face just below short, left-facing corner (V1) (red Trango Ballnutz in horizontal seam). Climb to top of corner (black Alien or gold Trango Ballnutz helpful), then work up steep face (crux) to pine tree belay/rap-station. (80 ft.)

PITCH 2: 5.5 PG Walk left of block and move up short open book, step left, and diagonal up left to intersect LP at the obvious fault that diagonals up right. Follow fault and then climb straight up past right side of small tree under overhang to the top. Go right about 20 feet to pine belay/rap-station. (80 ft.)

Variation 1: One can escape left here to join Punch and Judy's 5.5 crux.

FA 1975: Roy Kligfield and Ivan Rezucha

139 PUNCH AND JUDY 5.5 PG ★

Good first pitch face climbing and an amazing example of easy climbing past intimidating overhangs on pitch two.

START: 35 feet left of Akidlleativytoo, at base of left-facing corner.

PITCH 1: 5.5 PG Carefully climb the face just right of corner for about 25 feet (no pro). Continue up a bit right and up white rock to left side of triangular overhang. Then up face (crux) to ledge; go right to pine tree belay/rap-station. (100 ft.)

PITCH 2: 5.4 PG Go back left and move up short open book (V1) and continue up slightly right following the obvious fault line past intimidating overhangs to the top and oak tree belay/rap-station. (100 ft.)

Variation 1: (**NR**) 5.2 PG (Original Route, drawn in w/dotted line for historical purposes) Diagonal up right under the overhangs (loose rock all over the place) to I'm OK's pine tree belay/rap-station or continue up more rotten rock to the top. (100 ft.)

FA 1965: Mike and Judy Yates and Al DeMaria

139a FOSSIL FOOLS 5.6 G ★

Very nice, fun 5.3 climbing till you get to V1, then it's still fun but with a thin and balancy 5.6 crux.

START: 10 feet left of Punch and Judy at beginning of ramp that diagonal's up left (same as for Variation 1 of LP).

PITCH 1: 5.6 G Climb straight up about 15 feet (first pro at small horizontal pocket) to short, small right-facing corner that leans right. Move up right till standing atop large flake sitting on ledge. Continue straight up to crack in right-facing corner. At corner's top, move up to small ledge below cedar tree. Step right a few feet and move up to grassy ledge, then step back left to wide horizontal. Move up left to short right-facing corner/flake. Climb straight up (one can exit left here and join LP) and follow short seam (crux) (V1) and face just left of steep head wall straight up to pine tree belay/rap-station. (100 ft.) Either rappel or finish on L.P.

Variation 1: 5.9 R-X Move right about 6-7 feet and work up steep face to finish at small, short right-facing corner to jugs.

FA 2006: Dick Williams and Annie O'Neill

140 L P 5.9 R

Pitch one has good climbing but has a 15-foot, unprotected bouldery start. Pitch two's variation weaves its way past the overhangs with some loose rock. Pitch one variation is good climbing but way run out (there is sketchy pro at crux). Two ropes recommended for last pitch and the rappel.

Start: 30 feet left of Punch and Judy, directly below an arching right-facing corner that begins 15 feet up.

Pitch 1: 5.9 R (V1) Work up the short steep face (crux) to good holds, then run it out to the corner. Climb corner and up low-angle rock to top of short, wide crack formed by big block. Climb the low-angle face pretty much straight up (pocket on left for gold Camalot) to left side of small ledge and pine tree belay/rap-station. (100 ft.)

Pitch 2: 5.3 PG (V2) Climb straight up to top of left-jutting flake. Then, one will notice an obvious ramp/fault system that diagonals up right. Follow this for about 30 feet and then climb straight up past right side of small tree under overhang to the top. Go right about 20 feet to pine belay/rap-station. (60 ft.)

Variation 1: 5.6 R Start 20 feet to the right and climb the ramp that leads up left. At its top, from good holds and sketchy pro, step left and move up slab (crux) to LP's right-facing corner.

Variation 2: 5.6 PG Continue almost straight up to notch in overhangs. Move up (crux) then up and right under overhangs to small tree. From right side of tree, move up left and up to the top.

FA 1965: Dave Craft and Dick Williams
FA (V1) 1965: Dick Williams and Dave Craft
FRA (V2) 2004: Dick Williams and Annie O'Neill

140a   KING OF P 5.6 PG ★

The first pitch is really good for beginners; it was an old route most likely done in the early 60s that needed a name. The new second pitch is exciting and fun for the grade.

START: 5 feet left of LP at a nice crack that goes straight up to large white pine tree.

PITCH 1: 5.3 G Climb crack to pine. (45 ft.)

PITCH 2: 5.6 PG Go up past left side of pitch pine to top of boulder sitting on ledge 10 feet up. Climb straight up bulging face to overhang below nose in arching right-facing corner. Step up corner and step left to a stance on the nose, then straight up to broken ledges just right of easy, vegetated corner that goes up left to the top. Climb straight up past overhang to larger overhangs. Move up left a bit, then up passing final overhang at left side of small tree to the top. (100 ft.) Go left to pine tree rap-station for Little White Mushroom and Gil-Galad.

FA (P1) Back in the 1960s
FA (P2) 2004: Dick Williams and Annie O'Neill

141   LITTLE WHITE MUSHROOM 5.6 PG

Some fun climbing, two ropes best for pitch two.

START: About 30 feet left of LP, on a grassy ledge behind a double-trunked tree and below a flaky right-facing corner with a small overhang 15 feet up.

PITCH 1: 5.3 PG Climb to top of corner, then up left to pine tree belay/rap-station. (50 ft.)

PITCH 2: 5.6 PG Step right and up (V1) slab past break at right side of a small overhang. Diagonal up right to follow right-facing corners till about 5-10 feet from grassy top (V2). Traverse left about 20 feet (blue Camalot helpful) and up (crux) passing left side of small pine tree to a large pine tree belay/rap-station on top. (80 ft.)

Variation 1: 5.3 PG (Original Route, drawn in w/dotted line) Diagonal right under overhang, then up left on low-angle ramp and vegetated corner to the top.

Variation 2: Up to here it's 5.3 PG; you avoid the traverse and just go straight up to the top.

FA 1970: Art Gran, Toni Wilson and Dottie Baker
FA (P2) 2004: Dick Williams and Annie O'Neill

Science without religion is lame, religion without science is blind.
— Albert Einstein

142   GIL-GALAD   5.6 PG

If the slabby, unprotected first moves do not bother you, then you're in for a very fun, clean first pitch.

START: Just left of Little White Mushroom.

PITCH 1: 5.6 G-PG Diagonal up left on slab to left side of overhang 10 feet up (blue Trango Ballnutz helpful). Step left and climb face (crux) to left side of second small overhang. Continue straight up face to pine tree belay/rap-station. (50 ft.)

PITCH 2: 5.6 PG Climb face straight up to the short, blocky (loose looking), right-facing corner capped by overhangs. Move up, step left and up past overhang to low-angle ramp-like system. Then move up right (crux, awkward crouched move) up to the right side of a short pillar. Then diagonal up left past the overhangs (crux) to a low-angle ramp-like system that's followed up right under the ceilings to the top. (80 ft.)

FA 1967: Joe Kelsey and Roman Laba

142a   **(TOPROPE)** Barely Memorable   5.8

Start: At the rounded nose immediately below and left of Gil-Galad. Climb smooth/thin nose/face straight up to the left side of overhang to meet Gil-Galad. Move up and then right and up face past right side of small but long overhang. Then finish up face near rounded nose to the pine tree anchors. FA (Memorial Day) 2007: Joe Bridges, Dick Williams and Patty Matteson

143   KEYSTONE KOP   5.7 PG

Pitch one is nice; pitch two is exciting and interesting for its grade. The loose-looking, jutting block at the top of the climb has been rigorously tested for stability and seems OK, but it's probably best to be safe and avoid it.

START: 20 feet left of Little White Mushroom, on top of the left side of a boulder, below right-facing flakes with overhang 20 feet up.

PITCH 1: 5.4 PG Climb short face (crux) and up past the right-facing flakes to the overhang. Climb pretty much straight up face, and once on slab, diagonal up left to pine tree. Climb straight up face or step up left onto slab, then straight up to cedar tree belay/rap-station and ant's nest at the base of right-facing corner. (100 ft.)

PITCH 2: 5.7 PG Climb the fault line on face just right of corner till below scary looking block. Step left and climb past block (crux) to the top. (50 ft.)

FA 1965: Dick Williams and Dave Craft

144   DE COLORES 5.6 PG

Pitch one has three good moves and is fun; it can be used as an alternate pitch to Keystone Kop. Pitch two is not recommended, way too much loose rock.

START: Almost 20 feet left of Keystone Kop, at a short crack formed by left-facing flakes with a tree at its top 10 feet up.

PITCH 1: 5.6 PG (V1) Climb crack and face straight up past small left-facing corner that pinches off at its top. Then straight up short face to low angle slab and pine tree belay to the left to meet Keystone Kop. (80 ft.)

Pitch 2: (**NR**) 5.5 PG Traverse left and climb straight up past the easy overhang. Move up right past a lot of loose rock and just right of a block split by a crack. Continue up and slightly left, following the obvious weakness to the top. (50 ft.)

Variation 1: (**NR**) 5.6 PG (Original Route, drawn in w/dotted line, starts about 15 feet further left) Climb the unprotected face/slab to a crack and a small pine tree about 25 feet up. Move left a few feet and work up the clean face past a grassy ledge to lower-angle rock below an overhang. Either set up a belay here **or** move left about 15 feet to a more comfortable stance, hopefully out of the way of any loose rock.

FA 1987: Dick Williams and Burt Angrist

145   **TRICK OR TREAT 5.7 PG**

Except for the first-20-foot 5.6 runout, it's fun climbing. Pitch two has some loose rock that takes away from the fun factor, but has an exciting crux.

START: 25 feet left of De Colores and 15 feet right of Roman's Climb Next to Keystone Kop. On the thin face that leads up to a left-facing corner that arches up left with lots of little overhangs in it.

PITCH 1: 5.6 R Climb the face 5 feet left of the tree and bush-filled corner (crux is the runout), and follow the arching corner (5.5 PG) above for about 60 feet. Then step right and continue up the face to a belay at a short crack in some orange rock. (85 ft.)

PITCH 2: 5.7 PG Climb past the crack, move up and right through an area of loose rock to old pin. Then work straight up past overhangs to a stance (crux) and another fixed pin. Either climb straight up past overhangs (Original route) or (easier) diagonal right on lip of overhangs and up to the top. (50 ft.)

FA 1973: Dick Williams and Tom Bridges

146   **D. S. B. 5.8+ PG ★**

Some exciting climbing on the whole route.

START: Just left of Trick or Treat. Scramble up the dirt ramp (same as Roman's dirt ramp) till below a large right-facing, pointy triangular block/flake.

PITCH 1: 5.6 PG Climb to top of flake, step left and then straight up past a small overhang and slab (easy but run-out) to meet the top of arching left-facing corner. Then up slab to small ledge under right-facing corner. (80 ft.)

PITCH 2: 5.8+ PG Climb straight up past two overhangs to the right side of a large pointed block (staying about 5 feet right of the corner), step right, work up past the final overhang (crux) at a notch to the top. (50 ft.)

FA 1987: Dick Williams and Joe Bridges

147 ROMAN'S CLIMB NEXT TO KEYSTONE KOP 5.4 G-PG

Pitch one is unpleasant; its only redeeming value is that it leads to an easy, airy, and exciting pitch two. Pitch one also affords easy access for setting up a **toprope** on Omega 12 Clausthaler.

START: At the dirt ramp that leads up left, immediately left of Trick or Treat.

Pitch 1: 5.1 PG Follow the dirt ramp past trees to a right-facing corner. Climb corner past blocks and up past hanging cedar tree into huge, right-facing corner capped by jagged, formidable-looking blocky overhangs. (100 ft.)

PITCH 2: 5.4 G-PG Climb straight up into corner, move left (crux) and up past overhangs to the top. Go left to Main Line's pine tree belay/rap-station. (50 ft.)

FA 1965: Roman Sadowy and friends

148 AFTERMATH 5.6 PG

Fun climbing from Pitch one belay to the top. Variation 1 (Pitch three of Omega 12 Clausthaler) is particularly exciting, airy and lots of fun for its grade.

START: About 30 feet left of Trick or Treat, at a flaky crack just right of short nose and about 25 feet right of Omega 12 Clausthaler.

PITCH 1: 5.1 PG Climb flaky crack about 25 feet to dirt ramp and large tree. Move up to slab and next tree and make a belay. (45 ft.)

PITCH 2: 5.6 PG Move up left to follow thin crack and slab above, passing to the left of a cedar tree with a rap-station (optional Pitch one belay) to a short, fat right-facing corner. Step up right (**V1**) and then up left past overhangs (5.5 PG) to a stance (blue Camalot helpful). Move left (Original route went straight up to top from here) and up to finish on an awkward crux (5.6) of Positively 4th Street's phallic, protruding block to the top and bush belay. (80 ft.) Go left to Main Line's pine tree belay/rap-station.

Variation 1: 5.6 PG ★ (Pitch three of Omega 12 Clausthaler) Traverse right on good holds below overhang for about 15 feet till both feet are on the pointed arête. Climb straight up or a bit right on arête's jugs (crux) to the top. (50 ft.)

FA 1972: Dick Williams, Dick DuMais and Dave Craft

149   OMEGA 12 CLAUSTHALER 5.7 X
(As a Toprope)

The face climbing on Pitches one and two is really nice, too bad they can't be protected. Pitch one can be easily set up with a **toprope** via Roman's Climb's dirt ramp that's starts about 50 feet to the right. Pitch three is best reached from Aftermath (148).

START: From atop grassy ledge 10 feet up, formed by a left-facing block directly below an undulating, shallow right-facing corner which is about 20 feet left of Aftermath and about 35 feet right of Positively 4th Street.

PITCH 1: 5.7 X (As a Toprope) Climb to a small pedestal above the undulating corners about 20 feet up (last pro). Work up the thin face to the tree belay. (50 ft.)

Pitch 2: 5.6 X Step left (staying right of Aftermath's crack) and climb directly up the steep slab (crux) to a cedar tree belay/rap-station. (50 ft.)

PITCH 3: 5.6 PG ★ From the left side of tree, climb up to the Aftermath corner, step up right and then traverse right on good holds below overhang for about 15 feet till both feet are on the pointed arête. Climb straight up or a bit right on arête's jugs (crux) to the top. (50 ft.)

FA 1988: Dick Williams, Joe Bridges and Dave Craft

150   GRIM AND TONIC 5.8+ R

Start: 5 feet left of Omega 12 Clausthaler and about 30 feet right of Positively 4th Street. Behind a small tree below small double-tiered overhangs about 12 feet up.

Pitch 1: 5.8+ R Climb straight up past the overhangs (no protection, crux) to a small left-facing corner. Continue up till about 10 feet below the obvious overhang (V1), traverse left and move up to white rock on the left side of the overhang. Then work up the face (5.6 R) to a belay at the same level as the Aftermath tree off to the right. (70 ft.)

Pitch 2: 5.8 PG Diagonal up right to the overhang, step right, climb past a notch and continue to the top. (40 ft.)

Variation 1: 5.11b/c G (Computer Blue) Continue up the corner and past the overhang and follow Aftermath to a belay.

FA 1980: Ivan Rezucha and Annie O'Neill

FA (V1) 1984: Felix Modugno

151   SHIRLEY TUMBLE 5.10c R

The protection grade has changed from PG to R due to holds breaking off just above the lip of the first overhang. This crux move is easier if you're tall.

Start: On top of a detached block that projects right, about 25 feet left of Grim and Tonic and 8 feet right of Positively 4th Street.

Pitch 1: 5.10c R Climb past the widest part of the overhang at the break (crux). Continue up the face (passing between a tree and some bushes), cross Positively 4th Street variation, and then rejoin Positively at its belay. (60 ft.)

Pitch 2: 5.7 R Follow Positively 4th Street for about 15 feet before swinging out left and continuing to the top. (40 ft.)

FA (P1) 1986: Todd Swain and John Thackray

FA (P2) 1979: Ivan Rezucha and friends

After heavy rains, climbs from Positively 4th Street left to Main Line usually remain wet for 2-3 days.

152　　　POSITIVELY 4th STREET　5.6- PG ★

Pitch one is fun and better than it looks. Pitch one's original route (drawn in w/dotted line) has clean rock and is also fun. Pitch two is good but not if it's wet.

START: From atop a pile of boulders with some laurel bushes 10 feet right of Ground Control and about 65 feet left of Aftermath, below a large right-facing corner that starts about 20 feet up.

PITCH 1: 5.5 PG Follow the corner and at the first overhang and obvious horizontal (**V1**) step left around the nose and up clean face to a small, short left-facing corner and make a belay. (75 ft.)

PITCH 2: 5.6- PG Climb to overhangs, then (V2) diagonal up way right under the overhangs heading for a huge protruding block. Move up left before the huge block to finish up past a notch formed by a jutting, phallic-like block (crux). (60 ft.)

Variation 1: 5.6- G (**Original Route**, drawn in w/dotted line) Move right (crux) and follow crack another 15 feet, then up face past a small overhang and slab to make a belay at a wide horizontal or to the left in a small, short left-facing corner.

Variation 2: 5.9 PG (Direct finish, Shirley Tumble) Climb out left and up past a series of overhangs, finishing past a notch to the top (loose rock).

FA 1965: Dick Williams and Dave Craft

FA (V1) 1991: Ivan Rezucha and Bill Ravitch

153　　　GROUND CONTROL　5.9 PG ★★

Good climb, good moves on clean rock, two ropes recommended.

START: Immediately left of Positively 4th Street's boulder pile, at a small, short right-facing corner just above the overhang.

PITCH 1: 5.8 PG Diagonal up a bit left to a very shallow right-facing corner and climb to the overhang (5.7 PG)

(V1). Traverse to left side of the overhang and work up to a stance on the face (crux-1) (**V2**), then go straight up into the short left-facing corner. Move around right onto face (crux-2), and up to the bolt-anchors. (100 ft.)

PITCH 2: 5.9 PG Climb up left to the short right-facing corner (that's about 10 feet left of Main Line's notch). Move up to the ceiling and exit left (crux) to a stance, then up past overhangs to the top. (60 ft.)

Variation 1: 5.10d PG Climb straight past the overhang. Height related, long reach.

Variation 2: 5.7 PG (Original Route) Diagonal up right to a fault/break, then climb straight up face (crux) to the bolt anchor belay.

FA (P1) 1979: Paul Clark, Lotus Steele, Ivan Rezucha and Laura Chaiten

FA (P2) 1973: Richard Goldstone, Barbara Thatcher, Joe Bridges and Hans Hartmen

FA (V1) 1984: Felix Modugno and Paul Boissonneault

154   STRANGE CUSTOMS 5.11d R

Start: From a stack of blocks 12 feet right of the right-facing corner that is directly below the upper Main Line corner.

Pitch 1: 5.11d R Climb the ceiling (past a piton in a thin horizontal) and then move up left past small, scalloped right-facing corners to another piton below an overhang. Exit left and go up the face to the top of the short, wide left-facing corner capped by a ceiling. Then exit right immediately and climb to the bolt anchors. (60 ft.)

FA 1987: Ed Webster and Todd Swain

FFA 1987: Todd Swain and Paul Trapani

Well in my opinion there are no hard rules for climbing a route, only for talking about it later.
  — Peter Boyle

155   **MAIN LINE 5.8 PG ★★★**

One of this area's best climbs, lots of variety and variation options.

START: On the face, 30 feet left of Ground Control, below the large, left-facing corner capped by an overhang.

PITCH 1: 5.7 PG Climb the corner (**V1**) to its top (**V2**) and exit right onto face. Then up face past the final, short left-facing corner (crux) to a small ledge. Traverse right about 20 feet to the bolt-anchor belay/rap-station placed in 2000. (100 ft.)

PITCH 2: 5.8 PG (V3) Climb straight past the notch in the overhang above, then up right to the top and pine tree belay/rap-station. (60 ft.)

Variation 1: (Original Route) At flake about 12 feet below the overhang, move right around the corner and up face.

Variation 2: 5.9 G At top of corner step left to High Anxiety's flake in the overhang, work past it to a stance (crux), then step right to join Main Line or diagonal up left to join MacReppy.

Variation 3: 5.9 PG (Ground Control) Climb up left to the base of the short right-facing corner (that's about 10 feet left of Main Line's notch), move up to the ceiling, exit left (crux) to the face and up past overhangs to the top. (60 ft.)

FA 1965: Dick Williams, Dave Craft and Claude Suhl

155a (LINK-UP) MAIN LINE/MAC-REPPY 5.8 G-PG ★

A good, fun link-up that combines the fine qualities of two hugely different climbs that have equal quality. Try not to use the tree on pitch two to help keep it alive.

PITCH 1: 5.7 PG Climb pitch one of Main Line to where you'd normally go right 20 feet to the bolt anchors. Foot traverse left about 20 feet to meet Mac-Reppy at a short wide crack and make a belay (blue Camalot helpful). (100 ft.)

PITCH 2: 5.8 G-PG Climb straight up into the deep right-facing corner with small but tall tree (V1). Stem up (not using tree) and pass huge overhang to the top. (50 ft.)

Variation 1: 5.7 R Step left around the corner onto face and up to the top.

156   **HIGH ANXIETY 5.9 R**
               (As a Toprope)

Good climbing but scary to lead, best to do Main Line/Mac-Reppy Link-up or do pitch one on **toprope**.

START: On the face midway between Main Line and Mac-Reppy. Directly below a short incipient crack that leads to another.

PITCH 1: 5.9 R Follow the cracks past smooth, bulging, whitish rock (crux) to a stance below the horizontal that divides the face. Continue up to a point about 8 feet below the overhang and traverse right and up to the obvious flake immediately left of Main Line's corner. Work past overhang to a stance (5.9 G), then diagonal up left to small ledge to join Mac-Reppy at a short wide crack and make a belay (blue Camalot helpful.) (100 ft.)

Pitch 2: 5.7 PG Follow Mac-Reppy past the notch. Then diagonal up right, clear the overhang, and up to the top. (50 ft.)

FA (P1) 1980: Paul Rezucha and friends
FA (P2) 1981: Ivan Rezucha and Annie O'Neill

157   **MAC-REPPY 5.11c G ★**

This used to be one of the nicest 5.8's until 1987 when the flake broke off, making it a "no excuse not to lead" 5.11c G climb.

START: At a left-facing corner 30 feet left of Main Line.

PITCH 1: 5.11c G Climb corner and crack to the overhang. Crank your butt past the overhang (crux) to easier climbing up to the left side of narrow ledge and short wide crack for an optional belay (blue Camalot helpful). Climb straight up into the deep right-facing corner with small but tall tree (V1). Stem up (not using tree) and pass huge overhang (5.8 G-PG) to the top. (130 ft.)

Variation 1: 5.7 R Step left around the corner onto face and up to the top.

FA 1965: Jim McCarthy and John Reppy
FA (V1) 2004: Dick Williams and Annie O'Neill

158   **INSIDE OUT 5.9 G ★**

Cool climbing whether or not it's a hot day. Not your normal climb, lots of variety, body and hand jamming, strenuous overhanging crack and some steep face climbing. How this climb was first rated 5.7 is a mystery. If you don't want to chimney, start on variation one, at right side of flake.

START: In the chimney 45 feet left of Main Line at the left side of 20-foot-high, detached right-facing flake.

PITCH 1: 5.9 G (V1) Chimney to top of flake (V2), work up jam crack (crux) and up to top of large, wedged boulder. Stem up into cave and make a belay near base of obvious zig-zag crack that's on the back side of the huge block. (50 ft.)

PITCH 2: 5.9 G Climb the crack (crux) and exit up through obvious hole to top of huge block and a threaded-cable belay/rap-station. (30 ft.)

PITCH 3: 5.6 PG Step onto main face and move up to the overhang, step right and climb past notch, passing a jutting flake (crux) to ledge and belay tree/rap-station. (50 ft.)

Variation 1: 5.5 PG Climb the right side of the flake to its top and walk left to the jam crack.

Variation 2: Go into cave formed by huge block and scramble up inside to base of zig-zag crack that is in the back side of huge block.

FA 1965: Dick Williams, Dave Craft and John Weischel

159   **OUTSIDER 5.7 G ★★**

Excellent, fun climbing

START: From the trail directly below the base of the nose/outside corner of the huge Inside Out block, 45 feet left of Main Line and 12 feet right of Avoid Where Inhibited.

PITCH 1: 5.7 G Move up and climb to the top of crack (V1), move up slab and then step around right and follow the exposed, low-angle, right-leaning corner to the top of the block and a threaded-cable belay/rap-station. (60 ft.)

PITCH 2: 5.6 PG (Inside Out's last pitch) Step onto main face and move up to overhang, step right and climb past notch, passing a jutting flake (crux) to ledge and belay tree/ rap-station. (50 ft.)

Variation 1: (Original Route) Step left and diagonal up left to the Void's pine tree belay/rap-station.

FA 1981: Ivan Rezucha and Annie O'Neill

160   AVOID WHERE INHIBITED 5.11a G ★★

A strenuous layback crux, with some very nice face climbing above. Somehow the "A" in Avoid got lost and this climb became known as Void Where Inhibited by mistake.

START: 12 feet left of Outsider, below a short left-facing corner that begins at the ceiling 10 feet up.

PITCH 1: 5.11a G Crank up and layback the corner (crux) to a stance, traverse left 10 feet, then up the thin face to the pine tree belay/rap-station. (80 ft.)

FA 1977: Rich Romano

161   VOID WHERE PROHIBITED 5.11d G ★★

Looks sure can deceive; this is the "easiest-looking 5.11" I know of.

START: On the face below an open book, 8 feet from the left side of the block, 30 feet left of Avoid Where Inhibited.

PITCH 1: 5.11d G Move up to and work past the concave open book (crux), then up the face to the blocky overhang (V1) then diagonal up right to the pine tree belay/rap-station (70 ft.) or continue to top of the block. (80 ft.)

Pitch 2: 5.8 PG (This pitch stays wet for many days after heavy rains) Step across onto main face below roof and traverse left past a small nose. Move up to the roof, and follow thin horizontal out right to the lip and up to the top. (70 ft.)

Variation 1: Climb past overhang to top of block.

FA 1975: Rich Romano, Ivan Rezucha and Ajax Greene

161a   NOT TO AVOID 5.4 G

This chimney affords the easiest access to the top of the huge Inside Out block.

START: Immediately left and around the corner from Void Where Prohibited at the chimney.

PITCH 1: 5.4 G Climb chimney to black birch tree belay/rap-station. (40 ft.)

162   FRIGHT TO THE FINISH 5.9+ PG

Not your straight-forward kind of climb, but there are lots of good moves. It's a bit complicated with rope management, so best done with double ropes and bring along two blue and one black Camalot.

START: Same as for Muriel's Nose. Scramble up right till atop block at base of the right-arching flake.

PITCH 1: 5.9+ PG Follow the crack/flake to its top, hand traverse left a few feet and move up to left side of small oak tree and cramped ledge under triangular roof. Finger traverse left till past left side of overhang and crank up to horizontal at base of ceiling (crux, long reach). Traverse right around nose to overhang (big cams). Climb straight up past right-pointing flake to jugs, stem back right and pass overhang on the right (5.8+ PG-R), then up to the final roof. Traverse left to the notch in overhang, then pass overhang and up short left-facing corner to the top and oak-tree thicket. (100 ft.)

FA 1980: Ivan Rezucha and Harvey Arnold

162a   SPLIT ROCK TRAVERSE 5.2 G

A fun little climb, two blue Camalots helpful in the horizontal.

START: Same as Muriel's Nose. Scramble up right and belay at large oak tree.

PITCH 1: 5.2 G Scramble up right to laurel bushes, then climb short face and left arching crack to wide horizontal that leads right for about 20 feet. Follow the horizontal (crux) to the slab and right-facing flake. Continue right till it's possible to step down to large blocks and black birch tree belay/rap-station at top of chimney. (100 ft.)

FA 2007: Dick Williams and Annie O'Neill

162b SPINAL EXAM 5.10b/c PG ★★

If Muriel's Nose ever needed a face-lift, this is it. This new route is a three-star beauty if you link-up with Muriel's Nose prow finish.

START: Same as for Muriel's Nose. Scramble up to the glacier-polished, fat right-facing corner just right of where one ropes up/belays for Muriel's Nose.

PITCH 1: 5.10b/c PG Climb the corner past overhangs to the ceiling. Work up past it and the notch above and short thin crack (crux) to blocky ledge below corner to meet Muriel's Nose. Follow corner to the top **or** finish by making the traverse left to climb the 5.9 G prow on Muriel's Nose. (100 ft.)

FA 2007: Brian McGillicuddy and Dick Williams

163 MURIEL'S NOSE 5.10b/c R

It is recommended to climb Spinal Exam and finish on Muriel's exposed prow.

START: 60 feet left of the left side of the huge Inside-Out block below an overhang with a rounded nose above it. If you look at the top of the cliffs you'll see the huge prow of Muriel's Nose.

PITCH 1: 5.10b/c R Scramble up left side of nose (**or** left-facing flakes to the right of the nose) to a laurel bush at the base of a glacier polished, fat right-facing corner. Climb up left to the thin crack that breaks the roof, then work past it (crux) to fixed pin. Then up the (5.8 R) face to the right face of the prow to blocky ledge below corner (V1). Make the traverse left to the prow and up it (5.9 G) to the top. (110 ft.)

Variation 1: Escape up corner to the top.

FA 1966: Bill Goldner and Ants Leemets

FFA 1975: John Bragg and Rich Hatch

Climber on final 5.9 moves
of *Muriel's Nose* 5.10b/c
(Route 163)
Photo: Dick Williams 2007

164   HOLD THE MAYO 5.9 G
Start: Same as Muriel's Nose.
Pitch 1: 5.9 G Follow Muriel's Nose to the crack in the roof, traverse left and continue up low-angle rock to a fault in steeper rock below a triangular overhang. Climb left of overhang to the next overhang, traverse right onto the face, and up to the top. (100 ft.)
FA 1985: Todd Swain and Sue Rogers

165   SCRAMBLED LEGS 5.10d G
START: Below a crack/flake that leads up left above a ledge and a broken area, around and left of a blocky nose, 20 feet left of Muriel's Nose and 60 feet right of Spinal Traction.
PITCH 1: 5.10d G Climb the crack/flake and follow a ramp up left to the roof. Hand traverse along crack to the lip and then up to the top. (80 ft.)
FA 1981: Ivan Rezucha

166   SPINAL TRACTION 5.6 A3 PG
Will this one ever go free?! At present (11/07), there is an effort to climb it free with fixed pro along the aid crack. It has been said "it should go at 14a." Some climbers still do it the way Ivan did on the FA.
Start: At a large right-facing corner capped by a 20-foot roof split by a diagonal crack 30 feet above the ground, 80 feet left of Muriel's Nose.
Pitch 1: 5.6 A3 PG Climb corner and follow the diagonal crack out the roof and to the top. (100 ft.)
FA 1978: Ivan Rezucha (self belayed)

Overheard: Of course it's only a Gunks 5.7,
there's no move on it tougher than 5.9

167   DARK SIDE OF THE MOON 5.12b PG ★★
Great moves, a real grunter with no rest spots, every move seems like the crux.
START: At the crack in the huge right-facing corner below the left side of Spinal Traction's roof.
PITCH 1: 5.12b PG Climb cracks about 10 feet, then diagonal up left to follow some cracks that lead up right to the short, overhanging right-facing corner capped by a roof. Work up to the roof then undercling out past it and up past the final overhang to the top. (100 ft.)
FA 1984: Felix Modugno, Kevin Bein and Don Lauber

168   LEAN AND MEAN 5.8 PG
Some thin face climbing on pitch one. Pitch two is awkward and pretty wild, but often wet.
START: On the face just right of the nose/outside corner about 40 feet downhill from Dark Side Of The Moon.
PITCH 1: 5.7 PG Climb the face just right of the lower nose (crux). Continue up the short face to a slab and go up left passing the right side of a pine tree belay/rap-station and make a belay at the backside of the block opposite the obvious open book below the imposing corner. (70 ft.)
PITCH 2: 5.8 PG Climb crack in the open book and step left at the overhang and move up into the corner. Then work up past another overhang (crux) and up wild corner to the top. (50 ft.)
FA 1980: Ivan Rezucha with Annie O'Neill

169   FAT AND FLABBY 5.11a PG
The ceiling crux is height-related, long reach, much harder if you're short. Often done on **toprope**.
Start: About 10 feet left (around the nose) from Lean and Mean.
Pitch 1: 5.11a PG Climb straight past a three-tiered overhang and up a bit right on a slab to another set of larger three-tiered overhangs forming a roof. Step left (V1), move

to lip of roof at a small break (3-4 feet left of nose), then work up to good holds at horizontal (crux). Then up to pine tree belay/rap-station. (50 ft.)

Variation 1: 5.10a PG Move left about 5 feet and pass the overhang just right of a small tree.

FA 1985: Todd Swain

170   SHORT AND SASSY 5.5 PG
START: On the nose 30 feet left of Lean And Mean's outside corner/nose.

PITCH 1: 5.5 PG Climb up slightly right and follow the thin zig-zag crack (crux) to the overhang about 5 feet left of a wide crack in the overhang. Either climb straight up **or** move right and climb overhang at wide crack to a tree. Climb slab to pine tree belay/rap-station. (50 ft.)

FA 1985: Todd Swain

170a   SENIORS IN MOTION 5.8 G
START: Same as Up In Arms.

PITCH 1: 5.8 G (V1) Move up crack and exit right at first opportunity along short horizontal and step around the nose to a good stance Move up to the overhang, step right, and up past left side of small pine and follow white nose before moving right to Short And Sassy's pine tree belay/rap-station. (60 ft.)

Variation 1: **(Toprope)** 5.9+ (Hump n' Pump) Start directly below nose and climb straight past overhang on nose to a stance to join regular route.

FA 2007: Dick Williams, Al Limone, Elaine Mathews (all seniors) and Ethan Ladof (the kid)

FA (V1) 2007: Joe Bridges and Dick Williams

There was a time when I felt that the rock was alive. But the fact of the matter was —at that time— I wasn't really alive without the rock.
— Dick Williams

171   **UP IN ARMS 5.9 G ★**

Great hand jamming, the more gear you put in the more endurance you will need; it's a good idea to tape up. Pitch two is exciting for its grade and takes some route finding abilities.

START: At the crack in the overhanging left face of the huge block, just left and around the corner from Short and Sassy.

PITCH 1: 5.9 G Climb the finger crack to the overhang (crux), then step left and go up chimney (V1), exit out right onto the nose and up to the pine tree at the top of the block. (60 ft.)

PITCH 2: 5.8 PG Walk left and step up onto top of block, then step across chimney onto nose and up to the largest overhang at the crack that breaks the ceiling. Move right and work past overhang (crux) and easier rock to the top. (40 ft.)

Variation 1: 5.12a G Step over and up on slab till under overhanging right-leaning corner with thin crack. Work up crack and corner to join Up In Arms.

FA 1981: Frank Valendo and Maury Jaffe

FA (V1) 2001: Christopher Lawrence

172   **THE SHADOW NOSE 5.7 PG**

An interesting, fun climb, including its variations. Variation one has an awkward move getting up onto huge boulder ledge after the first move. The senior citizens who first climbed variation two's offwidth thought it was quite burly for a 5.9; a blue Camalot to a #6 Friend makes it "G," the smaller the cam the more strenuous it is to place. If one wants to do this climb in one pitch, best to use double ropes.

START: At a short nose about 30 feet left of the boulders at the base of the Up In Arms chimney.

PITCH 1: 5.7 PG (V1) Climb short nose to ledge below roof. Step right and undercling up past overhang to small tree that is used for pro. Move right around nose and climb straight up short outside corner to a good stance (crux). Continue past a short crack in overhang to buckets. Traverse right about 5 feet and move up to stance on the slab. Move immediately left a few feet and follow a small ledge to make a belay at a short horizontal **or** use the black birch tree just above with a rap-station for a belay anchor. (60 ft.)

PITCH 2: 5.6 PG Continue up past left-facing corner to a laurel bush below the obvious offwidth and overhang. Move up to the overhang (**V2**) and hand traverse left along flake 6-8 feet (crux), then move up and right onto face above overhang. Continue up to the top and shadbush belay/rap-station. (50 ft.) One-60-meter-rope rappel down past the offwidth gets you back to your packs, **or** walk back into woods and down Smede's cove gully.

Variation 1: 5.7 PG Start about 15 feet to the right. Climb the short crack and awkwardly gain a stance on the huge block and short nose formed by a triangular overhang on the left and sling the small tree.

Variation 2: 5.9+ G (Huffin & Puffin) Reach above overhang to lip buckets and work past offwidth and overhang to a welcomed rest on small ledge.

FA 2007: Dick Williams and Annie O'Neill

FA (V1) 2007: Dick Williams, Joe Bridges, Annie O'Neill and Burt Angrist

FA (V2) 2007: Dick Williams, Joe Bridges and Larry Randall

173   HERE A BUCKET, THERE A BUCKET,
               EVERYWHERE... 5.6 G

START: About 50 feet left of The Shadow Nose, atop a huge fern-covered boulder. There is a natural spring under the boulder.

PITCH 1: 5.6 G Climb up right past a short, right-leaning, right-facing corner (crux) and up to a roof. Exit right and climb short right-facing corner to large pine tree rap-station. (50 ft.)

FA 2007: Dick Williams and Annie O'Neill

Annie O'Neill following
on first ascent of
Split Rock Traverse 5.2
(Route 162a)
Photo: Dick Williams 2007

174   HERE A QUACK, THERE A QUACK,
EVERYWHERE... 5.5 G

START: Same as Here A Bucket...

PITCH 1: 5.5 G   Climb up left past glacier-polished rock and overhang at crack to a ledge. Continue up left following an offwidth and fault to ledge and pine tree belay/rap-station. (50 ft.) One can exit/scramble left to Smede's Cove from here.

FA 2007: Dick Williams and Annie O'Neill

If, at the end of the day you don't feel like walking all the way back along the base of the cliff, try going left and up the first gully to what is known as Smede's Cove to meet the Millbrook Ridge blue trail (which goes north and south) where it intersects the (Bayard) red trail. It's a bit of a bushwack since it isn't traveled much. Either follow blue trail north over the Near Trapps with great views of the Wallkill valley or go (west) down the red trail to Trapps road, then go right (north) to the steel bridge. Smede's Cove property–and the southern-most part of the Near Trapps–was first contracted for sale by the Friends of the Shawangunks and then purchased by The Mohonk Preserve and The Access Fund in 1993.

NEAR TRAPPS
ROUTE
PHOTOGRAPHS

D Rt Wichita 5.3 PG

C Rt Saint Louis 5.5 G

B Rt Independence 5.4 G

A A1 Topeka 5.10a G ★

B 1 Kansas City 5.12b G ★★

C 2 Outer Space 5.8 PG ★

- 3 Easy Rider 5.9- G ★★ (Not Shown)

D 4 Le Plie 5.7- PG ★

E 5 (Link-Up) Crass/Outer Space-
Direct Finish 5.10b PG ★

E 5a Crass 5.10b PG

- 5b Infinite Space 5.12a PG ★★ (Not Shown)

F 6 Iron Cross 5.12d PG

G 8 Criss Cross 5.10a PG

Aa 2 **Outer Space 5.8 PG ★**

A 4 **Le Plie 5.7- PG ★**

B 5a **Crass 5.10b PG**

- 5b **Infinite Space 5.12a PG ★★** (Not Shown)

C 6 **Iron Cross 5.12d PG**

D 7 **Criss 5.11a PG**

E 8 Criss Cross 5.10a PG

F 9 **Criss Cross Direct 5.10a PG ★★★**

G 10 Between The Lines 5.11a/b R

H 12 **Broken Sling 5.8 PG ★★★**

I 13 Squat Thrust 5.12a PG

J 14 **Disneyland 5.6 PG ★★★**

K 15 **Sling TIme 5.11d G**

L 16 **Swing Time 5.11a PG ★★**

M 17 **Leftovers 5.7 PG**

N 18 **Te Dum 5.7 G ★★**

O 19 **Inverted Layback 5.9 PG ★★★**

A 18 Te Dum 5.7 G ★★
B 19 Inverted Layback 5.9 PG ★★★
C 20 Burning Babies 5.1 lb/c PG
D 21 Layback 5.5 PG ★★
E 21a Ba-Ba Moran 5.11a PG ★
F 22 Grand Central 5.9 PG ★★★
– 23 Penn Station 5.10b/c PG (Not Shown)
G 24 Alphonse 5.8 G ★★★
H 25 Sissy Boys 5.10d R
I 26 No Slings Attached 5.10b/c R
– 27 Bongos and Beached.. 5.10a R (Not Shown)
J 28 Yellow Belly 5.8 PG ★★
K 29 Yellow Ridge 5.7 PG ★★★

L 30 Fat Stick Direct 5.10b PG ★★★
M 31 Fat Stick 5.8 G-PG ★
N 32 Generation Gap 5.1 lb/c PG
O 32a (Link-Up) 5.8 PG ★★★
      Dog-Stick Ridge
O 32b The Hounds 5.10b PG
P 33 Requiem for a Heavyweight 5.12d PG-R
Q 34 Baskerville Terrace 5.7 PG ★★
Q 34a (Link Up) 5.7 PG ★★★
      Basking Ridge

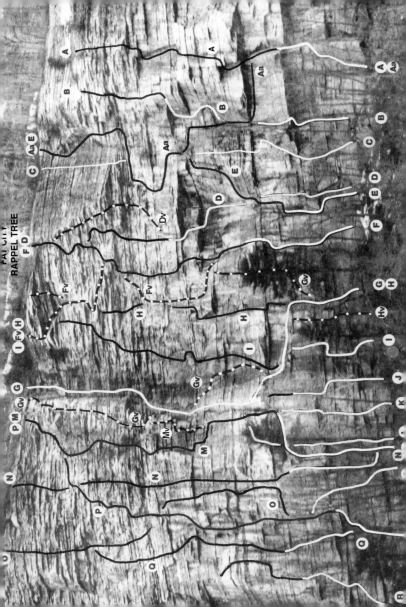

FALCON
RAPPEL TREE

A   30   Fat Stick Direct 5.10b PG ★★★
Aa 31   Fat Stick 5.8 G-PG ★
B   32   Generation Gap 5.11b/c PG
C   32a (Link-Up) 5.8 PG ★★★
         Dog-Stick Ridge
C   32b The Hounds 5.10b PG
D   33   Requiem for a Heavyweight 5.12d PG-R
E   34   Baskerville Terrace 5.7 PG ★★
E   34a (Link Up) 5.7 PG ★★★
         Basking Ridge
F   35   Fat City Direct 5.10d G-PG ★★★
G   36   Gelsa 5.4 PG ★★★
H   37   Land of the Giants 5.10a/b PG

I   37a (Link Up) 5.8 G ★★
         G-String Giants
I   38   G-String 5.9 PG
J   39   Pain Strain 5.11a/b PG
–   41   Eraserhead 5.11d/12a R (Not Shown)
K   42   Shitface 5.10c PG ★★
L   43   Revolving Eyeballs 5.10b/c R
M   44   Roseland 5.9 PG ★★★
N   45   Bogeyman 5.11d R ◆
O   46   El Camino Real 5.11b PG ★★
–   47   El Kabong 5.12b/c R (Not Shown)
P   48   Transcon... Nailway 5.10b PG ★★★
Q   49   Road Warrior 5.11d R ◆
R   51   Bird Brain 5.11d X ◆

A   **52   Birdland 5.8 PG ★★★**
B   **53   Birdcage 5.10b PG**
C   **54   Farewell to Arms 5.8 PG ★★**
D   **55   To Be or Not To Be 5.12a PG ★★★** ◆
E   56   To Have or Have Not 5.12a/b R
-   57   Son of Stem 5.11d R (Not Shown)
-   58   Soylent Green 5.11a R (Not Shown)
F   **59   Grease Gun Groove 5.6 PG ★★**
G   **59a   Tulip Mussel Garden 5.10d G ★**
H   59b   Broken Spring 5.11a PG-R
I   60   Corporate Conglomerate 5.9+ R

J   60b   Fat and Weak 5.7 PG-R
-   **60c   Grey Hair Arête 5.6 PG** (Not Shown)
K   **61**   Grey Gully 5.8 PG-R
-   **61a   Back to the Future 5.8 G ★** (Not Shown)
L   **61b**   Princess Leia 5.9 PG-R
M   **62   Lonely Challenge 5.6 PG**
N   **63   Horney 5.7 PG**
O   **64   Wildmere 5.10a PG-R**
P   **65   Elder Cleavage Direct 5.10b PG ★★★**
Q   **64a   Bee Bite 5.7 G-PG ★★**
R   **64b   Born Again 5.10b/c G-PG**
Ra **66a   Boob Job 5.10a PG ★**
S   **66   Up Yours 5.7 PG ★**

A **60b** Fat and Weak 5.7 PG-R

– **60c** **Grey Hair Arête 5.6 PG** (Not Shown)

B **61** Grey Gully 5.8 PG-R

– **61a** **Back to the Future 5.8 G ★** (Not Shown)

C **61b** Princess Leia 5.9 PG-R

D **62** **Lonely Challenge 5.6 PG**

E **63** **Horney 5.7 PG**

F **64** **Wildmere 5.10a PG-R**

G **64a** **Bee Bite 5.7 G-PG ★★**

H **64b** **Born Again 5.10b/c G-PG**

I **65** **Elder Cleavage Direct 5.10b PG ★★★**

J **66** **Up Yours 5.7 PG ★**

Ja **66a** **Boob Job 5.10b PG ★**

K **67** **Loose Goose 5.6 PG ★★**

L **67a** **5.8 Crack Climb 5.8 G ★**

M **68** Swissair 5.8 PG

N **69** Ain't Dis Yab Yum? 5.5 PG

O **70** Where the Wild Things Are 5.10d PG

Oa **70a** **Preying Mantle 5.10a PG**

P **70b** **Predator 5.10a PG-R**

Q **71** Vultures Know 5.10b/c R-X

R **72** **After You 5.7 PG-R**

S **73** **Yum Yum Yab Yum 5.3 PG ★★★**

T **73a** **Silver Bullet 5.7 G**

U **74** B.Warewolf 5.8 PG

– **74a** Curley 5.4 G-PG (Not Shown)

– **74c** Moe 5.8 G (Not Shown)

V **75** **Eenie Meenie 5.7 PG**

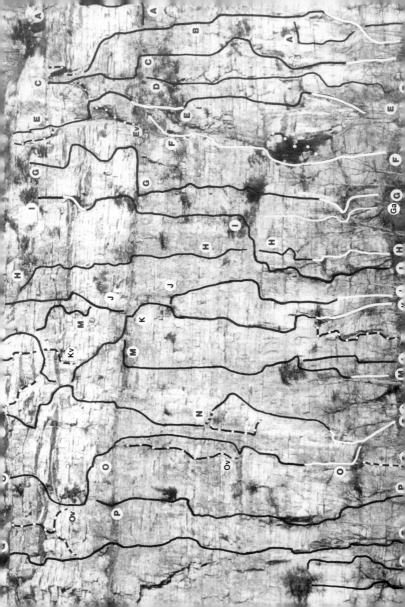

A 65 Elder Cleavage Direct 5.10b **PG** ★★★

B 66 Up Yours 5.7 **PG** ★

C 67 Loose Goose 5.6 **PG** ★★

D 67a 5.8 Crack Climb 5.8 **G** ★

E 68 Swissair 5.8 PG

F 69 Ain't Dis Yab Yum? 5.5 PG

G 70 Where the Wild Things Are 5.10d PG

Ga 70a Preying Mantle 5.10a **PG**

H 70b Predator 5.10a **PG-R**

I 71 Vultures Know 5.10b/c R-X

J 72 After You 5.7 **PG-R**

K 73 Yum Yum Yab Yum 5.3 **PG** ★★★

L 73a Silver Bullet 5.7 **G**

M 74 B.Warewolf 5.8 PG

- 74a Curley 5.4 G-PG (Not Shown)

- 74c Moe 5.8 G (Not Shown)

N 75 Eenie Meenie 5.7 **PG**

O 76 My-Knee Moe 5.9 **PG** ★

P 76a Catch a Tiger 5.5 PG

- **76b** Left Meets Right 5.8 **G** (Not Shown)

Q 77 By the Toe 5.9+ PG

R 77a Catnip 5.6 **G** ★★

S 77c By the Claw 5.10b **G**

- **77d** Nutzville 5.9 **PG** (Not Shown)

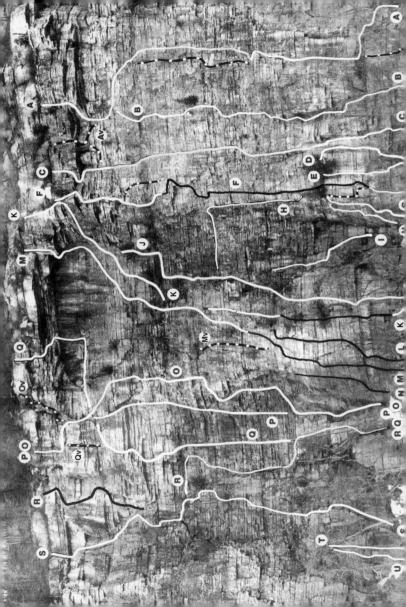

THE NEAR TRAPPS ◆ 211

A 76 **My-Knee Moe 5.9 G-PG ★**

B **76a** **Catch a Tiger 5.5 PG**

- **76b** **Left Meets Right 5.8 G** (Not Shown)

C 77 By the Toe 5.9+ PG

D **77a** **Catnip 5.6 G ★★**

E **77c** **By the Claw 5.10b G**

- **77d** **Nutzville 5.9 PG** (Not Shown)

F 78 Nazgul 5.10b/c R

G **78a** **Coyote Crack 5.4 G ★**

H **78b** **Fisher Crack 5.4 PG**

I 78c What? Are You Nuts? 5.7 PG

- **78e** **Old and Mossy 5.7 G** (Not Shown)

J **79** **Wrong Place, Right Time 5.10d R ◆**

K 80 **You're in the Wrong Place... 5.8 PG**

L **80a** **Whet Stone 5.8 PG ★**

M 81 Elf Stone Direrct 5.10b/c PG

N **81a** **Spic and Span 5.2 G**

O **82** **Orc Stone 5.5 PG**

P **83** **Cherry's Climb 5.5 PG**

Q 84 Lost World 5.11b/c R

R 85 Phalladio 5.7 PG-R

S **86** Gold Rush 5.9 PG

T **86b** **Gouda Climb 5.8 PG**

U **86c** **Summer Brie 5.5 G**

MAJOR ROCKFALL 1987

A 86 Gold Rush 5.9 PG
Aa 86b Gouda Climb 5.8 PG
Ab 86c Summer Brie 5.5 G
B 87 Vulga Tits 5.6 PG
C 88 Three Generations 5.5 PG
D 89 Nowhereland 5.8 PG
E 89a Route Awakening 5.7 G
- 89b Nosey Bodies 5.3 PG-R (Not Shown)
F 90 Zachariah 5.9 G ★★
G 90a (Link-Up) 5.9+ G ★★
        Interiah
G 91 International Harvesters 5.10a PG-R

H 92 Between a Rock and a Hard Place 5.8 R
I 93 Good Friday Climb 5.9+ PG
J 94 Easter TIme Too 5.8 G ★★
- 94a Woolly Clam...5.10c PG ★ (Not Shown)
K 95 Boston Tree Party 5.8 G ★
L 96 Day-Tripper 5.8 PG ★★
M 97 As The Cliff Turns 5.9 G ★★
N 98 Scuttlebutt 5.7 R
O 98b Halfbeak 5.8 G
P 98c Gunks Burghers 5.5 PG
Q 98d Summer Breeze 5.5 G

A 94 Easter Time Too 5.8 G ★★
- 94a Woolly Clam...5.10c PG ★ (Not Shown)
B 95 Boston Tree Party 5.8 G ★
C 96 Day-Tripper 5.8 PG ★★
D 97 As The Cliff Turns 5.9 G ★★
E 98 Scuttlebutt 5.7 R
Ea 98b Halfbeak 5.8 G
Eb 98c Gunks Burghers 5.5 PG
F 98d Summer Breeze 5.5 G
G 98e Spring Reigns 5.5 G
H 98f Mud, Sewat and Beers 5.7 G
I 99 Gold Flakes 5.8 PG
J 100 Energy Crunch 5.8 R
K 101 Deception 5.7 PG
L 101a Antsy Oh! 5.5 PG

M 101b Snail's Face 5.4 G
N 102 Wolf and the Swine 5.9 PG-R
O 102a Double Quacks 5.7 PG
P 102c Beauty and the Skink 5.6 PG ★
Q 102d Slab Happy 5.4 R
R 103 Animal Farm 5.6 PG
R 103a (Link-Up) 5.7 PG Animal Farm
- 104 The Raven and...5.11a R (Not Shown) ◆
S 105 Cherokee 5.9 G ★★
- 105a Annie Dotes 5.6 PG (Not Shown)
T 106 BM 5.8 PG
U 106c Gardiner's Delight 5.5 G
- 106d Serfs' Up 5.7 PG (Not Shown)
V 107 Slab Shtick 5.8 PG
W 107b Ambien Knights 5.9 G-PG ★

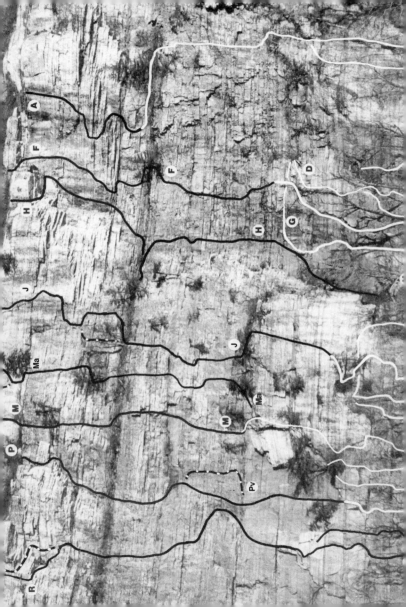

A 107 Slab Shtick 5.8 PG

B 107b **Ambien Knights 5.9 G-PG ★**

C 107d One Way or Another 5.8 PG-R

D 108 Eat Here and Get Gas 5.6+ PG

E 108a Benadryl Daze 5.6 PG

F 109 Highway 51 5.7 PG

G 109a **Two Feather FLake 5.3 PG**

H 110 **3, 4, 5, 6, Over and Out... 5.9 G**

I 111a Bush League Too 5.7 PG

J 112 **Bush League 5.8 PG**

K 112a **Bush Lite 5.7 G**

L 112b Drohascadam 1 5.5 PG

– 112d Dozy Doats 5.3 G-PG (Not Shown)

Ma 112e Whatayamacallit 5.9 PG

M 113 Drohascadafmubast 5.9 G

– 113a **Saving Face 5.8- PG** (Not Shown)

N 113b **Saving Grace 5.7+ G-PG**

O 113c **Graceland 5.10a PG**

P 114 **Moxie 5.9 G-PG ★**

Q 114a **Amazing Grace 5.8 PG ★**

R 115 Giddah 5.6 R

- **A** 115 Giddah 5.6 R
- B 116 Rock Around the CLock 5.6 R
- C 117 Flake, Rattle and Roll 5.7 R
- **Ca** 117a Birch Beer Crack 5.6 G
- **Cb** 117b Root Beer Crack 5.6 G
- D 118 Just Allow Me One More Chance 5.6 PG ◆
- - 119 **She's the Boss 5.9+ X** (Not Shown)
- **E** 120 **Honky Tonk Woman 5.9 R** ★
- **F** 121 **The White Pillar 5.6 PG-R**
- - 122 **Harvest Moon 5.11a G** ★★ (Not Shown)
- - 123 The Mincer 5.12a PG-R (Not Shown)
- **G** 123a **Shootin' the Curl 5.10b/c PG**
- **H** 124 **Hang Ten 5.10a PG** ★

- - 124a **TFC Nein 5.6 PG-R** (Not Shown)
- I 125 Tree Filled Chimney
- - 125a Boogy Bored 5.11b/c R (Not Shown)
- **J** 126 **The Near Side of Far 5.9 G**
- **K** 127 **Just for the Record 5.8 PG**
- **L** 127a Up Root 5.6 PG
- **M** 127b **Like a Box of Chocolates 5.8 PG**
- **N** 127c **Whatever 5.10a PG** ★
- **O** 128 **Across from the Fruitstand 5.4 PG**
- **P** 129 To Come or Become 5.6 PG
- **Q** 129a **Miss Mantle 5.9 PG**
- R 130 Roman's Climb Next to... 5.5 PG
- S 131 Parsifal and Potato Chips 5.7 PG-R

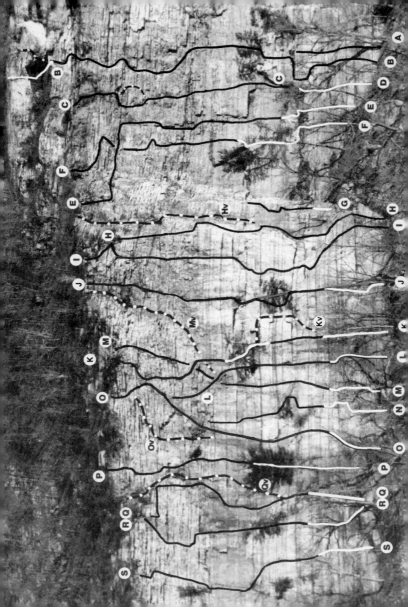

A 127c Whatever 5.10a PG ★
B 128 Across from the Fruitstand 5.4 PG
C 129 To Come or Become 5.6 PG
D 129a Miss Mantle 5.9 PG
E 130 Roman's Climb Next to... 5.5 PG
F 131 Parsifal and Potato Chips 5.7 PG-R
G 132 Interplanetary Agents 5.9+ PG
H 133 Interlewd 5.6 PG ★
I 134 Eowyn 5.4 PG ★★
– 135 Live and Let Die 5.10b/c PG-R (Not Shown)
J 136 I'm OK-You're OK 5.9 PG ★

– 136a R2-OK? 5.8 PG (Not Shown)
K 137 Akidlleativytoo... 5.7 G ★★
L 138 Far From the Madding... 5.8 PG ★
M 139 Punch and Judy 5.5 PG ★
N 139a Fossil Fools 5.6 G ★
O 140 LP 5.9 R
P 140a King of P 5.6 PG ★
Q 141 Little White Mushroom 5.6 PG
R 142 Gil-Galad 5.6 PG
S 143 Keystone Kop 5.7 PG

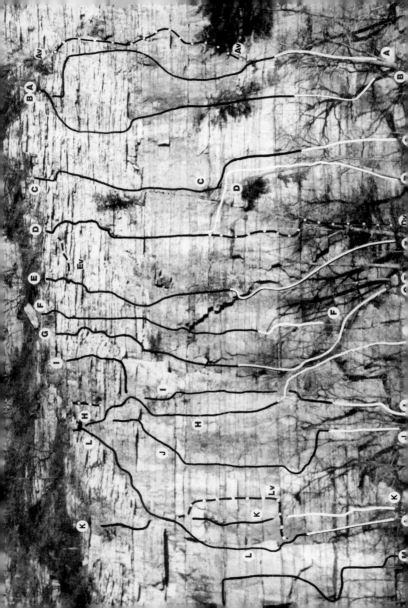

A   141   Little White Mushroom 5.6 PG
B   142   Gil-Galad 5.6 PG
C   143   Keystone Kop 5.7 PG
D   144   De Colores 5.6 PG
E   145   Trick or Treat 5.7 PG
F   146   D.S.B. 5.8+ PG ★
G   147   Roman's Climb Next... 5.4 G-PG

H   148   Aftermath 5.6 PG
I   149   Omega 12 Clausthaler 5.7 X ◆
J   150   Grim and Tonic 5.8+ R
K   151   Shirley Tumble 5.10c R
L   152   Positivly 4th Street 5.6- PG ★
M   153   Ground Control 5.9 PG ★★

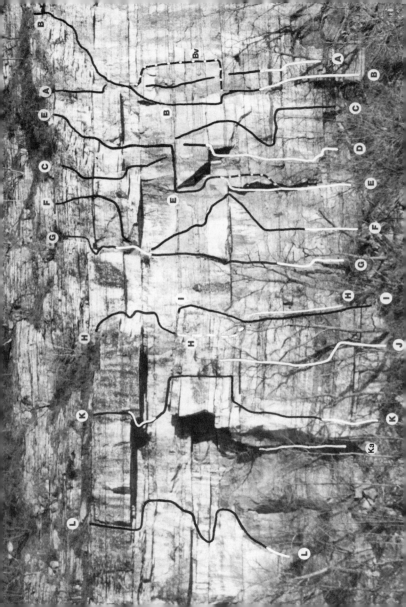

A   151   Shirley Tumble 5.10c R
B   152   Positivly 4th Street 5.6- PG ★
C   153   Ground Control 5.9 PG ★★
D   154   Strange Customs 5.11d R
E   155   Main Line 5.8 PG ★★★
E   155a (Link-Up) 5.8 G-PG ★
          Main Line/Mac-Reppy
F   156   High Anxiety 5.9 R ◆

G   157   Mac-Reppy 5.11c G ★
H   158   Inside Out 5.9 G ★
I   159   Outsider 5.7 G ★★
J   160   Avoid Where Inhibited 5.11a G ★★
K   161   Void Where Prohibited 5.11d G ★★
Ka 161a Not to Avoid 5.4 G
L   162   Fright to the Finish 5.9+ PG
-   162a Split Rock Traverse 5.2 G (Not Shown)

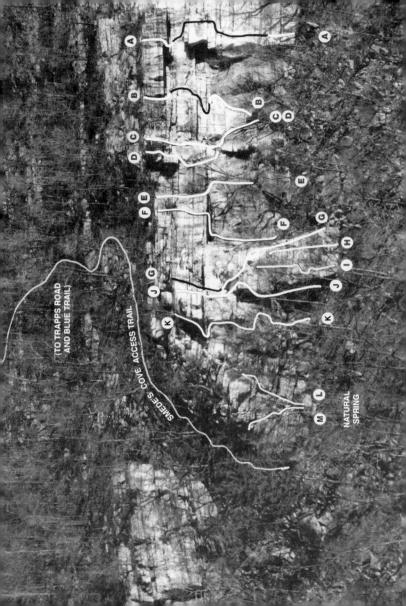

(TO TRAPPS ROAD AND BLUE TRAIL)

SMEDES COVE ACCESS TRAIL

NATURAL SPRING

A B C D E F G H J K L M

A 161 **Void Where Prohibited 5.11d G ★★**
- 161a **Not to Avoid 5.4 G** (Not Shown)
B 162 **Fright to the Finish 5.9+ PG**
- 162a **Split Rock Traverse 5.2 G** (Not Shown)
- 162b **Spinal Exam 5.10b/c PG ★★** (Not Shown)
C 163 Muriel's Nose 5.10b/c R
D 164 Hold the Mayo 5.9 G
E 165 Scrambled Legs 5.10d G
F 166 Spinal Traction 5.6 A3 PG

- 167 **Dark Side... 5.12b PG ★★** (Not Shown)
G 168 **Lean and Mean 5.8 PG**
H 169 Fat and Flabby 5.11a PG
I 170 **Short and Sassy 5.5 PG**
170a **Seniors in Motion 5.8 G** (Not Shown)
J 171 **Up in Arms 5.9 G ★**
K 172 **The Shadow Nose 5.7 PG**
L 173 Here a Bucket, There a Bucket... 5.6 G
M 174 Here a Quack, There a Quack... 5.5 G

The great Fritz Wiessner who in 1935 put up the first climb in the Gunks at Millbrook. This picture was taken atop Madame Grunnebaum's Wulst in 1980. Photo: Dick Williams

MILLBROOK
ROUTE
DESCRIPTIONS

PREFACE

Although I have climbed many of the routes at Millbrook over the years, unlike the Near Trapps, I did not get to climb or re-climb any of them in preparation for this guide. Time would not allow, plus at age 69, I did not want to lead or even follow many of the climbs out there. So, I took the route descriptions from my 1992 black guide book and upgraded many of them as best as possible, mainly with the help of Rich Romano, to who I am forever grateful. Thanks to him, there are many climb and climb grade corrections, and new route descriptions for this guide. The process of getting a consensus for the recommendation of climbs could not be completed in time for this printing, therefore there will be climbs that should be recommended but are not, due to lack of knowledge and/or input. Similarly, there are a few routes with written descriptions that are not drawn in on the photos.

MILLBROOK

Millbrook is the highest and most impressive cliff in the Shawangunks, and stands prominently on the ridge south of the Near Trapps and Bayards, about four miles from the steel bridge over Route 44-55. It is traversed by a major ledge system (it has been called The Great Traverse Ledge) which is about a third of the way up and contains much loose rock. Most of the climbs begin on, and are approached from, this traverse ledge, and are described from right (north) to left (south).

Because of its remoteness and long approaches, Millbrook has a distinct mountaineering flavor not found at the other cliffs. Weather problems and accidents are therefore much more serious affairs. Safety and help are miles away, so plan your adventure accordingly and expect to spend a full day on any excursion to this cliff.

All of this adds to the appeal of climbing there for some climbers, and is a great detraction for the majority. It is the only main cliff in the area without any bolts, which is amazing because they could have been placed to protect the many dangerous climbs; it is only the extremely high ethical standards that have prevented this from happening. There are many extremely difficult and dangerous routes that may not have been repeated for obvious reasons, for example: Route 44b Stardust Memories 5.12a R-X, and route 61 Birth of the Blues 5.11d X. In fact, there are a multitude of dangerous and scary climbs on this cliff; check out the routes tallied by the ratings chart.

Although Millbrook is presently the least popular cliff in the Gunks, it was the first one to be climbed on, by Fritz Wiessner when he discovered the area in 1935. Despite its long approaches, considerable exposure, and reputation for extremely difficult climbs with poor protection, it has many quality climbs that are well worth doing. Most of them have been established over the years by Rich Romano, who, being extremely talented and motivated, has almost single-handedly developed the area.

The most popular and recommended approach to Millbrook is via the carriage road (Trapps Carriage Road) from the steel bridge over Route 44-55, and the best access to the climbs is via the 165-foot Westward Ha! rappel in the middle of the cliff (which is identified on the cliff photo with a rappel icon, and also identified on the Millbrook Cliff Access Map).

A less popular approach is from Minnewaska State Park Preserve via the cul-de-sac (Millbrook Carriageway), which provides access to both the Westward Ha! rappel and some rappels and a 4th-Class chimney on the left (south) end of the cliff.

TRAPPS CARRIAGE ROAD APPROACH

Begin at the steel bridge over Route 44-55 and follow the carriage road (Trapps Carriage Road) south toward Minnewaska State Park Preserve for about 20 minutes to Coxing Trail (3 blue trail markings) on the left (east) side of the road. Follow the blue trail for about 20 minutes to red trail markings on the left (Millbrook Cross Path). Stay on the blue trail; in a few minutes you will find a spring on the right. Continue uphill for about another 20 minutes till a red trail is intersected (red and blue markings on tree). Go uphill on red trail for about 5 minutes and reach an intersection with the Millbrook Ridge Trail (blue trail markings). Total hiking time is about 1 hour. At this point, there are basically three cliff access options to choose from; either the Westward Ha! rappel, the south-end rappels or the 4th-Class chimney.

WESTWARD HA! RAPPEL

Cross the blue trail, work down short bands of cliffs, and head right (south) along an unmarked trail for about 100 feet, watching for a large pine tree on a ledge 25 feet below the top of the cliff. The rappel from this tree is 165 feet long and ends 10 feet to the south of Westward Ha! Most climbers leave their rappel rope(s) fixed till the end of the day. They can then provide for an escape in case of bad weather.

SOUTH-END RAPPELS AND 4th-CLASS CHIMNEY

Walk 100-150 feet south to the cul-de-sac road (Millbrook Carriageway). Walk south down the road about 800 feet (about 300 paces) to a red trail on the left (east) side. Follow the trail toward the cliff till it turns to the right (south). At this point, head down and slightly right past bushes to a pine tree at the edge of the cliff. The rappel from this tree is 80 feet long and ends at the start of Raging Bull. An alternative descent can be found by continuing south on and off the red trail for about 175 feet to the 4th-Class chimney or a 75-foot rappel from a nearby tree. The chimney offers easy access to–and escape from–the bottom of the cliff.

One can reach the cul-de-sac via the entrance to Minnewaska State Park Preserve. It was popular at one time for climbers to drive up to the highest Minnewaska parking lot and mountain bike in to the cul-de-sac.

1   THE MARCHING MORONS 5.9 A1 R

This girdle traverse of Millbrook took a day and a half to complete and involved lots of 5.8 and 5.9 climbing. The only aid was on rappel or during a pendulum. The best climbing was from New Frontier to Never Again. The climb is named after a Sci-Fi story.

Start: From just about anywhere at the right end of the cliff.

Pitches 1-20: Traverse staying high till it is possible to drop down to a left-facing corner to the right of Swinging C. Reverse the Swinging C traverse, cross Sweet Meat above its crux, and descend and traverse to a large pine tree. Rappel and tension left. Climb to the inside corner of New Frontier just above the rotten rock and continue up New Frontier and across its second-pitch traverse. Continue traversing at the same level till just before a right-facing corner system to the right of The White Corner. Then climb up and left to a ledge with a tree. Traverse at a level above the prominent corner on The White Corner and reach an even larger right-facing corner. Go around this corner to a hand traverse crack below some ceilings. Cross Rib Cracker and The High Traverse, and gain a large right-facing corner. Descend this corner and move left to the Westward Ha! belay. Traverse under more ceilings and continue at the same level till past Promises of Things to Come. Climb up a bit and cross Never Again on a large ledge above the ceiling. Follow the ledge system as it descends. Then continue at the same level to Old Route and climb up to the top.

FA 1977: Ivan Rezucha and Paul Potters

Do nothing in haste, look well to each step, and from the beginning think what may be the end.
  — Edward Whymper

2   PELVIC THRUST 5.9+ PG

START: Near the end of the ledge system 90 feet right of Garden of Allah and directly below a huge, impressive-looking left-facing corner at the top of the cliff. Scramble about 15 feet up to a ledge.

PITCH 1: 5.9 PG Climb up to the obvious overhang, step right to the broken right-facing corner and continue up the face to a belay in a cave near the large pine tree. (70 ft.)

PITCH 2: 5.9+ PG Climb to the corner above and follow it to the ceiling. Then exit right, following a crack and continue to the top. (70 ft.)

FA 1980: Rich Pleiss, Greg Collum and Morris Hershoff

2a   THE BUCK STOPS HERE 5.10d PG

Start: About 20 feet right of Hog's Breath. The first pitch is very difficult to find and follow since there are no major features.

Pitch 1: 5.10a/b PG Climb up past an overhang about 20 feet up. Continue up and left to another overhang. Climb this and up to a ledge with pine trees. (70 ft.)

Pitch 2: 5.10d PG Continue up the steep face to giant blocks on a large ledge. Above the blocks is a large overhang with a right-facing corner. Climb past the overhang and follow the corner to the top. (70 ft.)

FA 1996: Rich Romano and Matt Coleman

2b   **HOGS BREATH 5.11d PG**

START: About 50 feet right of Inshallah, (about midway between Pelvic Thrust and Inshallah) below a long overhang with a small right-facing corner in its left end, which is about 50 feet up.

PITCH 1: 5.10a/b PG Climb the face to the overhang, then work up the right-facing corner and up to a small ledge. Continue up and right, then back left and up steep rock to a shallow, right-facing corner. Follow corner to a belay ledge. (100 ft.)

PITCH 2: 5.11d PG Climb the face to a ceiling split by a thin crack. Clear the ceiling (crux, height related, easier if tall) and continue up to the top. (40ft.)

FA 1995: Rich Romano and George Peterson

3   GARDEN OF ALLAH 5.10a/b PG

Start: On a ledge at a left-facing corner with a pinkish right face, 22 feet right of Inshallah and 90 feet left of Pelvic Thrust.

Pitch 1: 5.10a/b PG Climb the corner to laurel bushes and a ceiling, move right and clear the tiered overhangs. (V1) Move right to a right-facing corner, work up the corner, and step left and up to a belay on a ledge with a pine tree. (80 ft.)

Pitch 2: 5.8 PG Climb the face to the left of the arching left-facing corner, passing an overhang and reaching the ceiling at the top of the corner. Then exit right and continue up past a short left-facing corner and another overhang to the top. (70 ft.)

Variation 1: 5.10a/b PG Climb up past a narrow right-facing corner and a pointed block to rejoin the regular route.

FA 1958: Jim McCarthy, Hans Kraus and John Rupley
FFA 1968: John Stannard

4   INSHALLAH 5.9+ PG

Height-related - easier if taller.

Start: At a short, broken, flaky left-facing corner, 115 feet right of Three Buzzards and 22 feet left of Garden of Allah.

Pitch 1: 5.9 R-X (V1) Climb past the flaky corner and blackish rock to the break in the overhangs. Continue up to the roof and traverse left about 15 feet. Then work up a left-facing corner for a while, move left and up past another short corner and up to a belay. (100 ft.)

Pitch 2: 5.9+ PG Follow a crack to the ceilings and traverse right to another crack which is climbed past some overhangs to the top. (70 ft.)

Variation 1: 5.9 PG (Original route) Follow Garden of Allah to the ceiling and then climb up left to the break in the overhangs where the regular route is joined.

FA 1977: Rich Romano and Mike Ward

5   THREE BUZZARDS 5.5 PG

START: Below a large, blocky right-facing corner with an off-width crack 15 feet right of Nothing to Write Home About and 115 feet left of Inshallah. Bushwhack and scramble up to the base of the corner.

PITCH 1: 5.5 PG Climb up right to a left-facing corner that leads up and slightly right to a chimney which is followed to a ledge. (80 ft.)

PITCH 2: 5.5 PG Continue up right to corners and cracks that slant up right past an overhang to the top. (90 ft.)

FA 1949: Hans Kraus, Ken Prestrud, Bonnie Prudden and Dick Hirschland

6   NOTHING TO WRITE HOME ABOUT 5.8 PG

Start: At some pine trees 25 feet right of Sing, Sing, Sing and 15 feet left of Three Buzzards.

Pitch 1: 5.8 PG Climb a short face past the right side of a huge laurel bush and pass the obvious off-width crack. Then diagonal up left to a belay ledge at a right-facing corner. (80 ft.)

Pitch 2: 5.8 PG Climb the corner system and continue to the top. (60 ft.)

FA 1978: Hardie Truesdale and Beau Haworth

7   SING, SING, SING 5.11b/c R

Start: At a group of pine trees 35 feet right of Brown Bomber and 25 feet left of Nothing to Write Home About.

Pitch 1: 5.11b/c R From a blocky left-facing corner, climb up past an overhang and into a shallow left-facing corner. Continue to the top of the corner, move slightly left and pass a small overhang (crux). Then work up and left to a belay stance. (100 ft.)

Pitch 2: 5.10a/b PG Climb up to the tiered ceiling, traverse right to the right end of the next overhang, and then finish up the face left of the nose. (80 ft.)

FA 1981: Rich Romano and an acquaintance

8   BROWN BOMBER 5.10a/b G

Named after the great boxer Joe Louis.

Start: Below a pine tree that is about 30 feet above the main traverse ledge, 25 feet right of Strange City and 35 feet left of Sing, Sing, Sing.

Pitch 1: 5.9 R Scramble up to the tree. Then, from its right side, climb past a blocky left-facing corner and a short face to a right-facing flake-corner that varies in size and begins on the right side of a long overhang. Follow the flake-corner past a small overhang and continue up the steepening face to a belay at a right-facing corner under a ceiling. (100 ft.)

Pitch 2: 5.10a/b G Climb the ceiling at the corner by moving left and then finish up the face above, moving slightly left. (60 ft.)

FA 1981: Rich Romano and Rich Ross

8a   THROTTLED 5.10d R

This route was named after George Peterson who, shortly before, crashed his single engine plane because the throttle cable snapped and, despite a nose dive and "off runway" landing, walked away unscathed. He just happened to be on a nearby climb during this route's first ascent.

Start: Midway between Strange City and Brown Bomber.

Pitch 1: 5.10d R Climb the face to a small (2 foot wide by 15 foot high) left-facing and left-leaning arch. Climb this, then pull the overhang (on the right side) formed by the arch's top (crux). Step right a bit and continue up the steep face till the angle lessons. Then traverse left 10 feet to a short, right-facing corner. Climb corner and the face above to a traverse that leads left to the Strange City belay. (90 ft.)

Pitch 2: Follow Explosive Bolts to the top.
FA 1993: Rich Romano, Albert Pisaneschi and Drew

9　　　　　　　　STRANGE CITY　5.7 PG
Start: Directly below a pine tree and a high, right-facing corner that begins 40 feet above the main traverse ledge, 40 feet right of Danger UXB and 25 feet left of Brown Bomber.
Pitch 1: 5.7 PG Climb the face past a small corner and some loose rock to the huge corner; follow the corner to the roof, and move left to a belay ledge. (90 ft.)
Pitch 2: 5.6 PG (Scary) Traverse left (V1) about 40 feet to the base of a large left-facing corner. (40 ft.)
Pitch 3: 5.6 PG Climb the corner and the face to its left to the top. (50 ft.)
Variation 1: 5.7+ PG Traverse left about 20 feet, climb a widening hand crack (big cams) past a ceiling, then work your way up some cracks and corners to the top.
FA 1955: Jim McCarthy, Hans Kraus and Stan Gross
FFA 1968: John Stannard and G. Livingston
FA (V1) 1985: Ivan Rezucha and Annie O'Neill

10　　　　　　　EXPLOSIVE BOLTS　5.11b/c PG-R
Climbed on May 11, 1986, the day of the Preserve's climbers meeting, when the big topic was the issue of bolts and bolting.
Start: Same as Strange City.
Pitch 1: 5.11b/c PG-R Follow Strange City for about 30 feet till just below the huge, inside corner and just above the small, right-facing corner with a chockstone. Then traverse out left on the face under the overhang and exit around the corner to a thin crack, which is followed to a right-facing corner that slants up left. Climb this corner and the face above to a belay ledge. (80 ft.)
Pitch 2: 5.10a/b PG Climb up, cross Strange City at its belay, and follow the obvious crack past the overhang and up the face for about 25 feet. Then on to the top. (70 ft.)
FA 1986: Rich Romano, Albert Pisaneschi and Jim Munson

11   DANGER UXB 5.10a/b PG

Start: On broken rock below and to the right of the short, right-facing corner that forms an offset in the long roof 60 feet up, 50 feet right of Leap Frog and 40 feet left of Strange City.

Pitch 1: 5.10a/b PG Climb broken rock to a short, broken left-facing corner. Work up past the overhang above, moving slightly left to a thin crack that leads to the short corner in the roof. Go up the corner to the upper roof and traverse out left to the lip. Then continue up past a pine tree to a belay. (100 ft.)

Pitch 2: 5.7 PG Cross the Strange City traverse, climb the left-facing corner above, step right and continue up the face to the top. (60 ft.)

FA 1981: Rich Romano and Rich Ross

12   LEAP FROG 5.11d PG

Start: Below a flaky, left-facing corner, 20 feet right of Side Pocket and 50 feet left of Danger UXB.

Pitch 1: 5.9 PG Climb broken rock to a ledge, step right and continue up more broken rock to an overhang. Step left and climb the break/fault. Then step right and work up a short left-facing corner to the roof. Traverse left and up to a short left-facing corner formed by the left end of the roof. Go up the corner, step left and pass a small overhang at a little notch. Then continue up the face past a left-facing flake to a belay ledge. (80 ft.)

Pitch 2: 5.11d PG Climb past a ceiling (crux, long reach) and left-facing corner to a ledge (optional belay). Go left, climb over the center of the overhang and continue up to the top. (60 ft.)

FA 1981: Rich Romano and Doug Strickholm

13 **SIDE POCKET 5.10d PG**

START: On the face 30 feet right of Artistry in Rhythm and 20 feet left of Leap Frog. Scramble and climb slightly up right to a pine tree about 30 feet up.

PITCH 1: 5.10d PG From the tree (V1), walk left and climb the face and a shallow, left-facing corner (crux) (this corner is about midway between two larger left-facing corners, both capped by a long roof about 60 feet up). At the top of the shallow corner, traverse right to a small overhang split by a crack. Continue up and follow a left-facing corner to the ceiling. Then step right and climb the steep face to a belay ledge. (80 ft.)

PITCH 2: 5.8 PG Move up left and climb a ramp-like corner to its top. Continue up the face to broken ledges below a large left-facing corner and then follow the corner past the ceiling to the top. (50 ft.)

Variation 1: 5.9 PG (Writhe To The Occasion) Climb up left to the large but short, left-facing corner that is capped by the long roof. Then traverse right about 30 feet to join the regular route.

FA 1980: Rich Romano and Vincent Valente
FA (V1) 1980s: Ivan Rezucha and Annie O'Neill

14 **THE TEMPEST 5.11c PG**

Start: Same as Artistry in Rhythm.

Pitch 1: 5.11c PG Follow Artistry in Rhythm to a bush below the overhang, diagonal up right till above the overhang and then climb up and left onto the face which is followed to the ceiling. Pass the ceiling (crux, long reach) about 15 feet to the right of its left end (same as Artistry) and move up the face above to a short, shallow, left-facing corner. From the top of the corner, angle up right to a belay ledge with scrub pines and bushes. (100 ft.)

Pitch 2: 5.9 PG From the right side of the bushes, climb the face to a broken ledge and continue up past tiered overhangs to the top. (50 ft.)

FA 1984: Rich Romano, Fred Yakulic and Alan Kousmanoff

15   ARTISTRY IN RHYTHM 5.10a/b R

Start: Below large, jutting, left-facing flakes with a pine tree about 20 feet up, 40 feet right of Bank Manager and 30 feet left of Side Pocket.

Pitch 1: 5.10a/b R Climb up to and then directly above the pine tree to an overhang. Step left and continue up past the break and straight up the face to some right-facing flakes. Follow the flakes to the left end of the long ceiling. Then exit left and work up a series of nondescript flakes to a ledge with a pine tree. (100 ft.)

Pitch 2: 5.10a/b R From the right side of the pine tree, diagonal up right past bulging rock (5.10a/b R) and head up to and follow a thin crack (which is about 15 feet left of the left-facing corner) past an overhang to the top. (60 ft.)

FA 1981: Rich Romano and Rich Ross

16   BANK MANAGER 5.10a/b PG

Start: Below a large pine tree about 30 feet above the main traverse ledge, 50 feet right of Hang 'Em High and 40 feet left of Artistry in Rhythm.

Pitch 1: Climb/scramble to the pine tree. (30 ft.)

Pitch 2: 5.9 R Walk right about 15 feet to some blocks that form a short, left-facing corner below the right end of an overhang 15 feet up. Climb to the right side of the overhang, move right and continue up past the left side of a small overhang. Then climb basically straight up past the left side of a long overhang to a ledge and traverse right to a large pine tree. (80 ft.)

Pitch 3: 5.10a/b PG Traverse back left about 20 feet to a left-facing corner and follow the corner till it is possible to exit right (V1). Then traverse farther right and continue to the top. (90 ft.)

Variation 1: 5.10d PG-R Don't exit right; instead, move up left and follow a clean white corner to its top. Then exit right, clear an overhang and continue up a short face to the top.

FA 1980: Rich Pleiss, Greg Collum, Ron Augustino and Morris Hershoff

FA (V1) 1980: Rich Romano and Dave Hoag

17   HANG 'EM HIGH 5.12a PG-R

Start: Behind an oak tree, 10 feet right of Swinging C and 50 feet left of Bank Manager.

Pitch 1: 5.9 PG Climb broken rock past a ledge and up a scoop to the right of a birch tree. Continue up past some small left-facing flakes to a small overhang and traverse right about 15 feet. Climb up another 10 feet and then traverse back left about 15 feet to a large right-facing corner (optional belay), which is followed to a large hanging flake. Pass the flake on its left side and belay on a large ledge. (140 ft.)

Pitch 2: 5.12a PG-R Step left, climb the black water streak, and work part way up past the tiered ceilings in the roof to a marginal rest stance (5.10b/c R) (one can escape to the left here, if necessary, 5.10b/c R). Then step right, continue up past the final tiers (crux) in the roof to a notch and continue to the top. (50 ft.)

FA 1980: Rich Romano and Russ Clune

18   **SWINGING C 5.8 PG**

START: 70 feet right of Sweet Meat and 10 feet left of the oak tree below Hang 'Em High.

PITCH 1: 5.8 PG Climb broken rock to a large ledge and then diagonal up left to the top of the prominent pedestal, that shares belays for this and the next three climbs. (70 ft.)

PITCH 2: 5.8 PG Climb the face above the pedestal, pass a small overhang on its right side and continue up to the overhangs. Then traverse right about 25 feet to a large left-facing corner. (70 ft.)

PITCH 3: 5.7 PG Follow the corner system to its top, traverse out right and finish up the face. (100 ft.)

FA 1962: Bill Goldner, Paul Karmas and Gerd Thuestad

FFA 1968: John Stannard and Don Morton

19   **SUPER SUNDAY** 5.10a/b PG

Start: Same as Swinging C

Pitch 1: Same as Swinging C

Pitch 2: 5.10a/b PG Follow Swinging C to the start of its traverse. Then traverse right 10-15 feet under the long ceiling to a right-facing corner. Climb the corner and clear the overhang to reach a ledge (optional belay). Walk right about 10 feet and climb the steep face just left of an outside corner to a left-facing corner with an overhang split by a crack. Follow the crack past the overhang and finish up a right-facing corner. (100 ft.)

FA 1981: Rich Romano and Chuck Calef

20   **SWEET MEAT** 5.9 R

Start: At a low, dirty, broken-up left-facing corner that leads to the top of the pedestal, 25 feet right of In Search Lost Time and 70 feet left of Swinging C.

Pitch 1: 5.3 PG-R Climb/scramble to the top of the pedestal. An alternate and nicer pitch one is to do Swinging C (5.8 PG). (60 ft.)

Pitch 2: 5.9 R Work up the face to an overhang, go around it on the left and continue up to a belay. (60 ft.)

Pitch 3: 5.7 PG Climb diagonally up right around the overhangs and belay at a pine tree on a ledge off to the left. (70 ft.)

Pitch 4: 5.8 PG From the right end of the ledge, move up right, then diagonal up left past some overhangs to the top. (50 ft.)

FA 1960: Art Gran and Bill Yates

FFA 1968: John Stannard and G. Livingston

20a   **KILLER BEES** 5.11b/c R
                 (APIS MELLIFERA SCUTELLATA)

Start: Same as Sweat Meat, at a low, dirty, broken-up left-facing corner that leads to the top of the pedestal, 25 feet right of In Search Lost Time and 70 feet left of Swinging C.

Pitch 1: 5.3 PG-R Climb/scramble to the top of the pedestal. An alternate and nicer pitch one is to do Swinging C (5.8 PG). (60 ft.)

Pitch 2: 5.10b/c R Fom Mission Improbable. Traverse left on small broken ledge and climb past a shallow left-facing corner and face to a double-tiered overhang. Climb past thin arching crack in second overhang and up to a crack that is followed to a large grassy ledge. Then climb a large overhang at small right-facing corner at overhang's lip. Continue straight up steep face to the notch in the long overhang. Climb past the notch and up to a tree at the roof and belay. (70 ft.)

Pitch 3: 5.11b/c R Move left and climb past a slot in the ceiling, then step left and climb the overhang where it narrows to meet left-facing flakes. Step left again and work up past the point/apex in the next overhang to the face. Continue up the steep face past a small right-facing corner and overhangs to the top. (40 ft.)

FA 1992: Rich Romano and Phil Schillaci

21   MISSION IMPROBABLE 5.10a/b PG

Start: Same as Sweet Meat, at a low, dirty, broken-up left-facing corner that leads to the top of the pedestal, 25 feet right of In Search Lost Time and 70 feet left of Swinging C.

Pitch 1: 5.3 PG-R Climb/scramble to the top of the pedestal. An alternate and nicer pitch one is to do Swinging C (5.8 PG). (60 ft.)

Pitch 2: 5.8 PG Traverse left 10-15 feet, climb to the ceiling, and continue traversing left to the notch in the overhang. Work past the notch to some left-facing flakes, move left and belay at an awkward stance (same as Time Being) above a bush in a left-facing corner. (60 ft.)

Pitch 3: 5.10a/b PG Follow a crack past some overhangs till it ends. Climb past the next overhang to a ceiling and then traverse right and up to an optional belay in a right-facing corner and up to the top. (100 ft.)

FA 1977: Rich Romano and Dave Feinberg

22   TIME BEING 5.11a PG

Some climbers downplay the seriousness of Pitch one, saying it's only PG. If you fall at the crux, or pump out just above the crux, you fall on a small wire that may or may not hold. The "good" pro (a cam) is about 25-30 feet further down. If the small wire holds, no problem; if it doesn't, well, you're in for one hell of a fall. Pitch two has sustained and well-protected climbing

Start: Just right of a broken, left-facing corner, 25 feet right of Directpissima and 25 feet left of Mission Improbable.

Pitch 1: 5.9 R-X Climb diagonally up right to the biggest bush/tree and then continue basically straight up to a clean open book. Work up the open book and the left-facing flake above, step left and belay at an awkward stance above a bush in a left-facing corner (same as Mission Improbable). (80 ft.)

Pitch 2: 5.11a PG Follow Mission Improbable to the ceiling, traverse left about 8 feet to a left-facing flake and then move up to an awkward, semi-hanging optional belay. Move left and climb a large overhang at a thin crack. Then move right on the face above and work up a left-facing corner to its top (optional belay). Finish by climbing up and left to a fault system, which is followed to the top. (120 ft.)

FA 1980: Rich Romano and Hardie Truesdale

23   IN SEARCH OF LOST TIME 5.11b/c R

Start: On the face 15 feet left of Time Being.

Pitch 1: 5.11b/c R Climb the face to a short, shallow, left-facing corner and continue past the overhang above. Then work up a shallow, groove-like left-facing corner to a belay on the left, below a right-facing corner. (70 ft.)

Pitch 2: 5.11b/c R Climb the corner, move left at the overhang, and continue up the white face to a ceiling. Traverse left to the end of the ceiling and move up steep, broken rock to a shallow right-facing corner. Traverse right about 8 feet and work up past an overhang at a short, very small left-facing corner. Then move up and right to a belay. (60 ft.)

Pitch 3: Finish on Time Being. (70 ft.)

FA 1986: Rich Romano and Albert Pisaneschi

24   DIRECTPISSIMA 5.11b/c PG-R

Start: Just left of the first broken left-facing corner, 30 feet right of Land Grab and 25 feet left of Time Being.

Pitch 1: 5.11b/c PG-R Climb the face to a short, left-facing corner with laurel bushes that is capped by an overhang about 70 feet up. Traverse left under the overhang about 10 feet and climb over it. Diagonal up left to the right side of a long ceiling; continue past the overhang and traverse left to a pine tree belay. (100 ft.)

Pitch 2: 5.9 R From tree, step right and climb straight up the face to an overhang. Then traverse right to the base of a right-facing corner and follow the corner past tiered overhangs and past a final overhang and corner to the top. (100 ft.)

FA 1981: Rich Romano, Francis Gledhill and Fred Yaculic

25   LAND GRAB 5.12a PG

Pitch one has lots of good action climbing.

Start: At a short, shallow, right-facing corner with a maple tree about 15 feet up, 20 feet right of Manifest Destiny and 30 feet left of Directpissima.

Pitch 1: 5.12a PG Climb the face, pass a black overhang and continue up to an overhang with right-facing flakes about 30 feet up. Then diagonal up left about 10 feet, angle back up right and work up the face to a short, shallow left-facing corner capped by an overhang (5.9 X). Climb the corner and the small overhang on its right side and continue up the face to a thin crack that breaks the ceiling. Then follow the crack past the ceiling and up to a pine tree belay/rap-tree. (100 ft.)

Pitch 2: 5.11d X Climb up about 20 feet and move left to reach the top of a left-facing ramp. Continue up a shallow left-facing corner past an overhang to a right-facing flake and work up and right to a short right-facing corner capped by a ceiling. Go left around the corner and continue traversing left to a short left-facing corner and an overhang. At the overhang, move right around the corner, climb past another overhang onto the face and head for the top. (100 ft.)

FA 1982: Rich Romano and Jim Munson

26   MANIFEST DESTINY 5.12d/13a G

This climb was finger-strength 5.11c before a hold broke off in Aug/Sept of 1993 or 94, it's now much more technical and difficult.

START: At a grey lichen-covered face, 45 feet right of New Frontier and 20 feet left of Land Grab.

PITCH 1: 5.10b/c PG Climb the face to a short, whitish, right-facing corner capped by an overhang. Pass this overhang and continue up to another right-facing corner capped by an even larger overhang. Then exit right and follow a broken right-facing corner to a small belay ledge. (90 ft.)

PITCH 2: 5.11d PG Traverse left about 15 feet to a hollow, left-facing flake and climb the flake past a bulge (5.10d R) and a white face to an overhang (5.9 R-X). Clear the overhang and continue up the concave face to tiered overhangs (5.10a/b R). Then move right, maneuver up past the overhangs at a crack (crux) formed by a pointed block known as the "tuning fork." Then work up till it's possible to traverse left about 10 feet to a belay stance. (100 ft.)

PITCH 3: 5.12d/13a G Traverse back right and move up to the ceiling (V1&V2). Surmount ceiling following a thin crack (crux) to the top. (50 ft.)

Variation 1: 5.10a PG (Original route) Traverse left about 10 feet and join Back To The Land Movement to the top.

Variation 2: 5.10b/c PG Traverse right about 15 feet to a left-facing corner, follow the corner to a ceiling, and move right around the corner and up to the top.

FA (P1 & P2) 1982: Rich Romano and Jim Munson
FA (P 3) 1983: Jack Mileski and Jeff Gruenberg
FA (V1) 1982: Rich Romano and Jim Munson
FA (V2) 1982: Rich Romano and Fred Yaculic

27   NEW FRONTIER 5.10d R

START: Directly below a deep cleft in the giant roof at the top of the cliff, 25 feet right of Back to the Land Movement and 45 feet left of Manifest Destiny.

PITCH 1: 5.9 PG Climb the face past a thin crack and an overhang to the obvious right-facing corner. Follow the corner past two maple trees to its top, then go left to a belay. (100 ft.)

PITCH 2: 5.8 G Traverse left to a slanting right-facing corner. (50 ft.)

PITCH 3: 5.10d R Follow the corner and crack to an overhang (V1). Then climb up left past the overhang and notch to the top. (140 ft.)

Variation 1: 5.10a PG Traverse right 30-40 feet following horizontal crack in steep face beneath large overhang to a belay at top of second pitch of Manifest Destiny. Traverse left about 10 feet and join Back To The Land Movement to the top.

FA 1962: Jim McCarthy and Ants Leemets
FFA 1969: Gary Brown and John Stannard
FA (V1) 1982: Rich Romano and Jim Munson

28   BACK TO THE LAND MOVEMENT 5.11d PG

Start: To the left of some pine trees and a maple tree about 20 feet up, 25 feet right of The New Deal and 25 feet left of New Frontier.

Pitch 1: 5.11b/c R Climb past the right side of what looks like a block about 15 feet up and continue up past some overhangs with small laurel bushes for another 10 feet to a small triangular point of rock. Work up and right to right-facing flakes under an overhang. Climb the overhang and follow a shallow, discontinuous, right-facing corner system till it ends. Then continue up the face past a small overhang and belay on a long ledge. (100 ft.)

Pitch 2: 5.11d PG Move right to a left-facing flake, climb the flake past a small overhang and continue up the steep face to the left side of a ceiling (5.9+ R-X). Move left and work up past crack that diagonals up right through the overhangs (crux) to a large left-facing corner. Then finish up the corner past a large notch-like slot in the roof to the top. (140 ft.)

FA 1979: Rich Romano, Chuck Calef and Malcolm Howells

29   THE NEW DEAL 5.11d R
Start: Just right of a pine tree growing out horizontally from a ledge about 15 feet up, 20 feet right of Schlemiel and 25 feet left of Back to the Land Movement.

Pitch 1: 5.9 R Climb past the ledge and some bushes to a bulging overhang and a black streak. Continue up the face to the left of the black streak to an open book which is followed to a right-facing flake on the right side of an overhang. Pass the overhang and set up a hanging belay on the left. (80 ft.)

Pitch 2: 5.11d R Move up, climb the right side of the overhang, and continue up to more overhangs. Then traverse left to the last pitch of Schlemeil **or** right to the last pitch of New Frontier.

FA 1981: Rich Romano and John Myers

30   NECTAR VECTOR 5.12b/c R
Start: Same as The New Deal.
Pitch 1: Same as The New Deal.
Pitch 2: 5.12b/c R Diagonal up right on the face and climb up a corner system. Move left into a "cave" with a ramp under a roof. Exit left out of the cave to a bulge (crux), move left to arête (5.11b/c R), which is followed to the top with more 5.11 run-out climbing. (60 ft.)

FA 1984: Jeff Gruenberg and Jack Mileski

31   SQUARE MEAL   5.11a PG

START: Same as for Schlemeil.

PITCH 1: 5.10b/c PG Same as Schlemeil.

PITCH 2: 5.11a PG Climb to the overhang, traverse right about 10 feet, and climb the overhang to a stance below the next overhang. Traverse right about 8 more feet and work up to a small platform (some parties belay here). Continue up the corner above to a bulging overhang, clear this, and follow the huge left-facing corner above till it is possible to hand traverse (V1) out right to a finish up the face. (100 ft.)

Variation 1: 5.6 PG Continue up the huge corner to the top.

FA 1979: Chuck Calef and Rich Romano

32   SCHLEMIEL   5.10b/c PG

As the story goes, Jim McCarthy and Burt Angrist went to Millbrook in 1971 to climb a new route. They did this one but had forgotten that they had already climbed it three years earlier, hence the name.

START: 10 feet left of a pine tree, 15 feet right of Band of Renown and 20 feet left of The New Deal.

PITCH 1: 5.10b/c PG Work up past right-facing flakes to a pine tree, move right, and climb an overhang near its right end. Continue up and slightly left to a large but short right-facing corner and a right-facing flake above. At the flake, move around left onto the face and climb up to an overhang. Move right to more overhangs and continue to a right-facing corner which is followed to a belay ledge. (100 ft.)

PITCH 2: (Unrated) Traverse left about 40 feet to a large left-facing corner.

PITCH 3: 5.7 PG Climb corner to the top. (100 ft.)

FA 1968: Jim McCarthy and Burt Angrist

FFA 1977: Rich Romano and Dave Feinberg

Rich Romano on
Square Meal 5.11a
(Route 31)
Photo: Dick Williams
1994

33   **BAND OF RENOWN 5.10d PG**

Start: Just right of an oak tree and 25 feet left of a pine tree, directly below a short, shallow, pointed right-facing corner that is just above a long overhang about 25 feet up, 120 feet right of High Plains Drifter and 15 feet left of Schlemiel.

Pitch 1: 5.10d PG Climb up loose rock for about 25 feet (5.10a R-X) to an overhang. Clear the overhang and move right to a short, shallow, flaky right-facing corner. Go up the corner and traverse back left above it to a right-facing corner capped by a large overhang. Work up this corner and traverse right under the overhang to its right end, where there is a crack-flake that leads up right. Follow the crack to another overhang, traverse left, and clear the overhang. Then continue up the face and shallow corners above to a comfortable ledge. (140 ft.)

Pitch 2: 5.10b/c PG Follow a thin crack above the belay to a small pine tree and climb up the easier face above, moving slightly right and then back left. Continue diagonally up left to an overhang with an overhanging left-facing corner. Clear the overhang at the corner and then head for the top. (120 ft.)

FA 1981: Rich Romano and Russ Clune

34   **HIGH PLAINS DRIFTER 5.10a PG-R**

Major rock fall on pitch two in Oct 1994 has made a minor change in route description.

Start: Below a large, broken right-facing corner, 100 feet right of The White Corner and 120 feet left of Band of Renown.

Pitch 1: (Fourth class) Climb the corner as best you can past very loose rock to its top, then walk left to a chimney formed by a stack of pointed blocks. (90 ft.)

Pitch 2: 5.8 R Climb to the top of the chimney and climb the shallow left-facing corner above the overhang. From the top of the corner, angle up left till beneath a ceiling. Then traverse left (this is where the rockfall was), and clear the overhang left of a short right-facing corner, and continue up the face to a belay ledge on the left. (70 ft.)

Pitch 3: 5.9+ PG Go back right and move up to a long overhang. Traverse right about 30 feet, climb a small overhang, and reach a left-facing flake that diagonals up right. Follow the flake to its top, move out right onto the steep face, and climb past some small overhangs to a large vegetated ledge at the base of a big right-facing corner. (80 ft.)

Pitch 4: 5.10a PG-R Step left to the next right-facing corner and follow it to an overhang. Then traverse around left and continue up the face past the overhangs to the top. (50 ft.)

FA 1981: Rich Romano and Chuck Calef

35   SUDDEN IMPACT 5.12b/c R
Start: From the first pitch belay of White Rose, on the ledge below the ceiling.

Pitch 1: 5.12b/c R Traverse right about 20 feet and climb over a bulge to a shallow right-facing corner which is followed to an overhang. Clear the overhang to reach an open book and belay on the left below a roof. (50 ft.)

Pitch 2: 5.11d G Climb the roof and continue to the top. (30 ft.)

FA 1984: Jeff Gruenberg and Russ Clune

36   WHITE ROSE 5.11a PG
Start: Same as The White Corner.

Pitch 1: 5.10a R Follow The White Corner to where it traverses left (at the base of the large right-facing corner) (V1). Work up into corner (crux), then up corner (no pro, 5.8 X) to the ceiling. Traverse out left to the arête and work up to a sharp right-facing corner. Belay on a ledge below a ceiling. (120 ft.)

PITCH 2: 5.11a PG Move up and around the sharp corner to an overhang with a right-facing corner. Follow the corner past the overhangs and finish up the face to the top. (100 ft.)

Variation 1: 5.10b/c PG Climb a right-facing flake that leads out right and continue up past a large pointed flake in the overhang to join High Plains Drifter or Sudden Impact.

FA 1977: Rich Romano and Fred Yaculic

37   THE WHITE CORNER 5.9 R

START: Above a grove of trees and directly below the right-hand edge of two large right-facing corners that begin about 50 feet up, 55 feet right of Big Band Era and 100 feet left of High Plains Drifter.

PITCH 1: 5.8 PG Climb up to the large white right-facing corner and traverse left about 30 feet to a flaring chimney below another large right-facing corner. Work up the chimney to a belay ledge below a large slot. (100 ft.)

PITCH 2: 5.9 R Move up past the slot, go right to a large right-facing corner, and continue up to a ceiling. Then traverse out left (**V1**) around the corner about 20 feet and climb to the top. (100 ft.)

Variation 1: 5.10d PG About halfway out the traverse, follow an inside corner up past ceilings to the top.

FA 1959: Jim McCarthy and Phil Jacobus
FFA 1968: John Stannard

37a   WHITE KNUCKLES 5.11b/c R

Start: Midway between Big Band Era and The White Corner, below a shallow right-facing discontinuous corner.

Pitch 1: 5.9 X Climb face and corner **or** the face 8 feet right of corner. Follow the corner past an overhang on the right, then hand traverse right (protection can be on Big Band Era before making the unprotected traverse), and up to a belay ledge below a large slot (same belay as for The White Corner. (100 ft.)

Pitch 2: 5.11b/c R (Height related, **a lot** harder for shorter people) Step up to the roof and traverse left to the nose, then go straight up using the arête (crux 1) and step left under an overhang to a stance. Work up past the overhang using a small right-facing corner (crux 2), then continue up the white face to finish on The White Corner. (100 ft.)

FA 1993: Rich Gottlieb and Rich Romano

38　　　　　　　BIG BAND ERA 5.10b/c PG

Start: Below a very prominent jagged, almost-pointed, right-facing corner, 75 feet right of The High Traverse and 55 feet left of The White Corner.

Pitch 1: 5.9 X Follow the corner past some overhangs to its end. Move up past right-facing flakes and into a shallow right-facing corner, climb the corner, and move left to a large right-facing flake. Work up the flake to its top and traverse left about 20 feet to where it is possible to move up and then back right to a short right-facing corner capped by an overhang. At the overhang, move left and then continue up and left to a belay stance at the base of a large right-facing corner. (120 ft.)

Pitch 2: 5.10b/c PG Step left and follow a crack past the overhang (crux) to its end. Climb straight up to a small overhang, which is passed on the left, and work up to a roof. Traverse right and clear the overhang at a right-facing flake/corner, which is followed to another roof (V1). Traverse left to a left-facing corner capped by a ceiling (some parties belay here), climb the corner to the ceiling, move out right, and continue to the top. (100 ft.)

Variation 1: 5.11b/c G (The King of Swing) Climb the flaky crack past the roof to the top.

FA 1979: Rich Romano and Chuck Calef

FA (V1) 1980: Chuck Calef and Rich Romano

38a　　　　　LOVE AND BULLETS 5.11b/c PG-R

Start: 20 feet left of Big Band Era, at a blocky right-facing corner, opposite an oak tree.

Pitch 1: 5.11b/c PG-R Climb straight up to a large overhang (V1), traverse left about 15 feet and climb bulging rock/small overhang to a small, shallow right-facing corner. Step left around corner and then diagonal up right about 15 feet (5.8 R) to a large loose flake/block (scary). From top of flake, step left, move up past small overhang and face to a thin crack in the large overhang (crux). Climb past the crack and overhang, then move up right to a belay. (90 ft.)

Pitch 2: 5.11b/c PG-R Traverse right about 8 feet into a right facing corner capped by an overhang. Move up to the overhang, exit left and go up to a short, shallow right-facing corner (pro good but strenuous and difficult to place) and up past a series of overhangs to the face above. Continue up to a small ledge and belay. (60 ft.)

Pitch 3: 5.5 PG (V2) Traverse right to finish on The White Corner. (30 ft.)

Variation 1: 5.10b/c PG-R Step left and climb a small overhang and steep rock to the flake/block and the regular route.

Variation 2: 5.11b/c PG Climb straight up past bulging rock to finish at a large pine tree 10-15 feet right of the Conflict Of Interest corner (height related, harder for shorter people).

FA 1992: Rich Romano, Jeff Colovos and Jeff Tabin
FA (V1 & V2) 1992: Rich Gottlieb and Rich Romano

38b   DANCE CARD 5.11a R

Start: Approximately 20 feet right of The High Traverse and about 10 feet left of the obvious hand crack on Big Band Era that starts 80 feet up.

Pitch 1: 5.11a R Climb easy rock to a steep red streak. Go up to a small overhang, step right, clear the overhang and go up to a ledge. From the ledge's left side, move up the face (crux-harder if short) to a finger hole, step right, and then continue up a short right-facing corner. Then either go up corner and step left onto a thin face or climb up and right to a second, similar corner capped by an overhang. (85 ft.)

Pitch 2: 5.10b/c PG Go left around a corner and up the face to a small overhang. Move left, clear the overhang, then diagonal up right to another small overhang. Move left, pass the overhang and go up a thin face (5.10) to easy rock. Diagonal left past a cleft in the overhang, then up the face to the "Dance Card" flake. Go up right to ledge, then back left on flake and straight up over ceiling (#3 steel above left edge of flake), step right and then up to the top. (100 ft.)

FA 1991: Rich Gottlieb and Rich Romano

39   CONFLICT OF INTEREST   5.9 R

Start: Same as The High Traverse.

Pitch 1: 5.9 R Follow The High Traverse to the base of the big right-facing corner. Then traverse out right and diagonal up right (crux) to a short right-facing corner, which is followed to an overhang. Step right to another short right-facing corner capped by an overhang and traverse right to a belay stance at the base of a large right-facing corner. (120 ft.)

Pitch 2: 5.8 PG Follow corner to the top. (100 ft.)

FA 1977: Rich Romano and George Willig

40   RIB CRACKER   5.9 PG

Start: Same as The High Traverse.

Pitch 1: 5.9 PG Climb the corner and face past the right side of the overhangs to the base of the big right-facing corner. Follow the big corner to its top, exit left, and continue to the top of another right-facing corner. Belay below a large loose-looking block. (130 ft.)

Pitch 2: 5.9 PG Climb past an overhang at its left end and continue up the face to a ceiling with a short right-facing corner which is followed to the top. (60 ft.)

FA 1961: Jim McCarthy, Hans Kraus and Werner Bishof

FFA 1968: John Stannard

I believe in God, only I spell it Nature.
    — Frank Lloyd Wright

41   **THE HIGH TRAVERSE 5.5 PG**

START: At a broken right-facing corner above and next to some oak trees, 70 feet right of Cruise Control and 75 feet left of Big Band Era.

PITCH 1: 5.3 PG Climb the broken corner up left to a belay at the base of the big right-facing corner. (60 ft.)

PITCH 2: 5.5 PG (V1) Climb the big corner for about 30 feet, traverse out left onto the face, and up to a large ledge. (70 ft.)

PITCH 3: 5.3 PG Climb straight to the top. (60 ft.)

Variation 1: 5.8 PG (Recollection) Climb the big corner and two parallel cracks on its left face till the cracks end (V1a). Then step left around the corner and onto the face, and continue up to rejoin the regular route.

Variation 1a: 5.8+ R (Direct Finish) Climb the steep face to the top.

FA 1937: Fritz Wiessner and Percy Olton

FA (V1) 1950: Hans Kraus and Jim McCarthy

FFA (V1) 1963: Dick Williams and John Weichsel

FA (V1a) 1970's: Rich Romano and Mike Robbins

42   **CRUISE CONTROL 5.9 PG**

START: Below a shallow left-facing corner that begins 25 feet up, a few feet right of the large block sitting on the ledge below Rags to Richs', 30 feet right of Westward Ha! and 70 feet left of The High Traverse.

PITCH 1: 5.9 PG Climb the face to a shallow corner and crack system and continue up to a small left-facing corner capped by an overhang. Pass the overhang and work up the face about 40 feet to a belay below a right-facing corner. (130 ft.)

PITCH 2: 5.8 G Follow the corner till it's possible to traverse left around the outside corner. Continue up to a thin flake/crack that leads to an overhang, step right and climb crack past overhang to the top. (60 ft.)

FA 1978: Rich Romano and Beau Hayworth

43   **RAGS TO RICHS' 5.10b/c PG-R**

START: On the face 15 feet right of the rappel landing, at a large block that sits on a ledge and is retained by a forked pine tree, 25 feet right of Westward Ha! and a few feet left of Cruise Control.

PITCH 1: 5.10a PG Climb the face to whitish-pinkish rock just left of an overhanging left-facing corner. Step up and right and work up to a weakness in the overhang above. Climb up to a very short right-facing corner, move up a bit, step right and continue up the face to the Westward Ha! belay. (130 ft.)

PITCH 2: 5.10b/c PG-R Move right till just right of a short, shallow right-facing corner. Climb up into the corner, work up a bit and traverse back left about 5 feet. Then continue up the face to an overhang and finish by traversing right to join Cruise Control. (60 ft.)

FA 1987: Rich Romano and Dick Williams

44   **WESTWARD HA! 5.7 PG**

START: On the face 10 feet left of the rappel landing, below a flaky left-facing corner, 25 feet left of Rags to Richs' and 40 feet right of Under the Wire.

PITCH 1: 5.7 PG Climb the face and flaky left-facing corner till it's possible to traverse right onto the face (it is also possible to climb directly up to this point). Continue up and right to a pine tree at the base of the large left-facing corner. Then follow the corner till it ends and step right to a belay. (130 ft.)

PITCH 2: 5.7 PG Climb a fault system that breaks the face and continue to the top. (40 ft.)

FA 1962: Jim McCarthy, Harry Daley and Hans Kraus

44a   **(TOPROPE)** 5.12a

Follow the Westward Ha! rappel line. FA 1980's Jeff Gruenberg

44b STARDUST MEMORIES 5.12a R-X
Start: Same as Westward Ha!
Pitch 1: 5.12a R-X Climb the first 35 feet of Westward Ha! to the ledge and pine tree at the base of the corner (optional belay). Walk left about 10 feet to the edge of the ledge and then diagonal up left to a steep face. Work up to a very small 2-foot-high, right-facing corner capped by a tiny overhang (5.11d or 5.12a R-X). Step left and continue straight up to a small overhang. Step right and continue up to another small overhang. Step right once again and work up past the final overhang (final crux) at a small left-facing corner, then up to a ledge and pine tree. Finish up on easy rock to the top. (120 ft.)
FA 1991: Rich Romano and Rich Gottlieb

45 UNDER THE WIRE 5.11a PG
Start: On the face 40 feet left of Westward Ha! and 25 feet right of the Wire Wizard pine tree.
Pitch 1: 5.9 R Climb to the overhang, clear it, and step right to a short flake/crack. Continue up the face, work up a leaning corner that faces right, and diagonal up left to a short right-facing flake that leads to an overhang. Undercling right, pass the center of the overhang and belay. (140 ft.)
Pitch 2: 5.11a PG Traverse right 10 feet on a small ledge beneath an overhang. Then climb the overhang at a crack and continue up a short face to a large ledge. (25 ft.)
Pitch 3: 5.8 PG Go left about 15 feet to a small right-facing corner capped by an overhang. Climb the overhang and the face above to the top. (40 ft.)
FA 1982: Rich Gottlieb, Russ Clune and Howard Doyle

46 WIRE WIZARD 5.8 R
Start: At a pine tree 25 feet left of Under the Wire and 60 feet right of Promise of Things to Come.
Pitch 1: 5.8 R Follow the crack/fault system that diagonals up right past a bulging overhang to a slabby left-facing cor-

Rich Romano on
The Time Eraser 5.10a
(Route 47)
Photo: Dick Williams 1994

ner, a blueberry bush, and an overhang. Then continue up to a pointed overhang and belay. (60 ft.)

Pitch 2: 5.7 PG Move up and around right to a shallow left-facing corner which is followed to a short right-facing corner. Continue up this corner till beneath an overhang with a jutting nose. Then step right, climb past the overhanging alcove and work up a short white face to a ledge. (130 ft.)

Pitch 3: 5.6 PG Step right, climb the face to a bush-covered ledge, and continue to the top. (40 ft.)

FA 1977: Morris Hershoff and Lindi McIlwaine

47   THE TIME ERASER 5.10a PG

Once past the initial loose rock, you'll find this to be a fine route.

START: Same as Wire Wizard.

PITCH 1: 5.10a PG Follow Wire Wizard for a few feet and then continue up and left to the left side of a small overhang with a long horizontal crack. Step left and climb the steep orange and white face, moving left to the start of a very thin crack. Follow the crack past the overhang (crux) above and continue up to a large flake and a tree belay. (100 ft.)

PITCH 2: 5.8 G From the right side of the flake, move up and right to a left-facing corner which is followed past the overhangs to the top. (70 ft.)

FA 1980: Rich Romano and Morris Hershoff

48   PROMISE OF THINGS TO COME 5.10b/c X

Start: At left-facing flakes in a left-facing corner with overhangs above, 60 feet left of Wire Wizard and 90 feet right of The Good, The Bad and The Ugly.

Pitch 1: 5.10b/c X Climb past the flakes and an overhang to the major left-facing corner above which is followed to a large ledge. (130 ft.)

Pitch 2: 5.8 PG Follow the crack above the tree to a band of ceilings on the left and then diagonal up left to the top. (90 ft.)

FA 1968: Dave Ingalls and Roy Kligfield

FFA 1973: Henry Barber and John Stannard

49   THE GOOD, THE BAD AND THE UGLY 5.10b/c R

Start: Below a loose, blocky left-facing corner system, 90 feet left of Promise of Things to Come and 65 feet right of Remembrance of Things Past.

Pitch 1: 5.10b/c R Climb past a tree to the ceiling, go right around the corner ("good"), and continue up the steep face past flakes and an overhang to a short, shallow left-facing corner ("bad"). Keep going up the face to a belay stance. (100 ft.)

Pitch 2: 5.8 PG (Ugly) (V1) Follow the obvious left-facing corner and fault system to the top. (70 ft.)

Variation 1: 5.11a R (Worst) Go left and up to the top of a very small, 6-foot-high right-facing corner (height related, harder if short–a flat leeper sky hook can be placed on finger bucket above corner, but should be tensioned down to lower gear). Continue straight up past the left side of overhang, then step right and up to the top.

FA 1981: Rich Romano and Francis Gledhill
FA (V1) 1991: Rich Gottlieb and Rich Romano

50   REMEMBRANCE OF THINGS PAST 5.10a/b PG

START: At a 10-foot-high right-facing corner with a small pine tree on its top, directly below a large right-facing corner that begins about 50 feet up, 65 feet left of The Good, The Bad and The Ugly and 25 feet right of Rings of Saturn.

PITCH 1: 5.9 PG Climb the overhang, work up the face to the corner (5.6 X) and continue up corner (crux-long reach) to a belay below the overhangs above. (90 ft.)

PITCH 2: 5.10a/b PG (V1) Traverse right around the overhang and follow the corner to the top. (80 ft.)

Variation 1: 5.10b/c PG (The Future Is Now) Climb the right-facing corner above and move out right till below a flaring right-facing corner capped by an overhang. Work up to the overhang, traverse right to an outside corner and continue to the top.

FA 1962: Jim McCarthy and Ants Leemets

FFA 1968: John Stannard
FA (V1) 1981: Rich Romano and Chuck Calef

51   RINGS OF SATURN 5.11 X

This description is somewhat vague due to lack of information.

Start: At a fairly nondescript face, 25 feet left of Remembrance of Things Past and 50 feet right of Orbit of Jupiter.

Pitch 1: 5.11 X Climb the face to a protruding 5-foot-high block and continue on, crossing the conspicuous brown band. Diagonal up left and then go straight up to the right side of a mummy-like overhang. Finish by angling up right to the top.

FA 1982: Jeff Gruenberg, John Myers and Mike Freeman, after being toproped

52   ORBIT OF JUPITER 5.11a X

Start: Below the approximate center of a long horizontal band of brown rock about 50 feet up, 50 feet left of Remembrance of Things Past and 15 feet right of Asteroid Belt.

Pitch 1: 5.11a X Climb a small overhang and continue straight up past the brown band to a very short, shallow, flake-like left-facing corner below and to the right to an overhang. Climb the overhang, move straight up a few feet, and then angle up left to another overhang with a right-leaning crack (below a block perched on a ledge). Follow the crack to a belay ledge at the base of a left-facing corner. (100 ft.)

Pitch 2: 5.9 R Follow the corner around past the overhang and continue up the steep face to a large vegetated ledge. (80 ft.)

Pitch 3: Continue to the top.

FA 1981: Rich Romano and Alex Lowe

53   ASTEROID BELT 5.11a/b X

Start: At a short, blocky right-facing corner just right of a pine tree, 15 feet left of Orbit of Jupiter and 50 feet right of Search for Tomorrow.

Pitch 1: 5.11a/b X Scramble up to a block and climb up to a small left-facing flake below the brown band. Continue up and then traverse left just above a small overhang to a left-facing corner that diagonals up right (5.9 X). Follow the corner to its end, step right, and pass a small overhang (V1). Work up another 10 feet to the left end of the Orbit of Jupiter belay ledge, traverse left under the ceiling, and move up into a left-facing corner. Follow the corner and then diagonal up left to a belay stance. (120 ft.)

Pitches 2 & 3: Follow Search for Tomorrow to top.

Variation 1: 5.10d PG Climb till just below the Orbit of Jupiter belay ledge. Then traverse left about 8 feet and follow the crack and shallow left-facing corner to the regular route.

FA 1981: Rich Romano, Chuck Calef, Rich Ross and Fred Yaculic

54   SEARCH FOR TOMORROW 5.10b/c PG

Start: Just right of an oak tree below the left side of a blocky arch-like formation, 50 feet left of Asteroid Belt and 25 feet right of Cuckoo Man.

Pitch 1: 5.10b/c PG Climb the face and a right-facing corner to an overhang, move right to the center of the overhang, clear it, and reach the base of a left-facing corner (V1). Traverse right on an overhanging wall and then diagonal up right to a shallow right-facing corner capped by an overhang. Follow the corner and step around left to a belay at the base of a long ramp that leads up right. (120 ft.)

Pitch 2: 5.8 G Follow the ramp and left-facing corners above, past overhangs to a large vegetated ledge. (80 ft.)

Pitch 3: Continue to the top.

Variation 1: 5.10b/c R (Diaper Man) Continue up the corner to a roof. Traverse out right and climb up past a small overhang. Then diagonal up right to the ramp and the regular route.

FA 1978: Rich Romano and Rod Swartz
FFA 1979: Chuck Boyd and John Maclean
FA (V1) 1981: Chuck Calef, Rich Romano and Rich Ross

55   PARAL-LAX 5.12a G

Start: Same as Cuckoo Man.

Pitch 1: 5.12a G Follow Cuckoo Man to the large ledge about 75 feet up. Then traverse right about 25 feet to the obvious fault and crack system, which is followed out right past the ceiling and up to a belay.

FA 1984: Russ Raffa

56   CUCKOO MAN 5.10b/c PG

Start: On the face 25 feet left of Search for Tomorrow and 15 feet right of a small birch tree.

Pitch 1: 5.10b/c PG Climb up to a broken ledge below an overhang with a short, shallow, flaky right-facing corner. Work up the corner, step left, and continue up the steep face to a large ledge below a right-facing corner capped by a ceiling (optional belay, loose rock (5.8 R), and about 75 feet up to this point). Then climb the right-facing corner above, step around left at the ceiling, and continue up to the next ceiling. Traverse right to the end of the ceiling and work up a shallow left-facing corner and short face to a belay at a large block. (130 ft.)

Pitch 2: 5.10b/c PG From the right side of the block, climb up to a left-facing flake on the steep face above, work up to the top of the flake, and continue past a bulge to a large horizontal crack. Traverse left to the right-facing corner on Again and Again and follow it to a ledge. Then climb past a right-facing corner, chimney past an overhang, and diagonal up left to a belay at the top of a pedestal. (90 ft.)

Pitch 3: 5.10b/c PG Continue up past an open book to a roof, traverse out right to the arête, and climb on to the top past a notch in an overhang. (60 ft.)

FA 1981: Rich Romano and Chuck Calef

57   AGAIN AND AGAIN 5.7 PG-R
Start: Same as Never Again.
Pitch 1: 5.7 PG (Same as Never Again) Climb the corner and then move up left to a ledge near another large right-facing corner (optional belay). Continue up the right face of this corner to a ledge below a large overhang. (100 ft.)
Pitch 2: 5.7 PG-R Traverse right across the steep face beneath a roof till below a large right-facing corner. Follow the corner to its top and belay on the right. (80 ft.)
Pitch 3: (Unrated) Traverse right and climb easier rock to the top. (40 ft.)
FA 1958: Art Gran and Claude Suhl

58   NEVER AGAIN 5.10b/c PG-R
Beware! Pitch two is extremely loose and scary, and thus hard to grade.
Start: At a pine tree under the ceiling formed by the very large, broken right-facing corner that has a short flaring chimney, 50 feet left of Cuckoo Man and 50 feet right of Happiness Is a 110° Wall.
Pitch 1: 5.7 PG Climb the corner and then move up left to a ledge near another large right-facing corner (optional belay). Continue up the right face of this corner to a ledge below a large overhang. (100 ft.)
Pitch 2: 5.10b/c PG-R Continue up the corner past an overhang to a large ledge (optional belay) and climb to the top. (100 ft.)
FA 1951: Hans Kraus and Bonnie Prudden
FA 1968: John Stannard

One aspect of climbing as a senior, is that one still gets the feeling of climbing 5.10's when the actual grades are a lot easier.
        — Dick Williams

59   HAPPINESS IS A 110° WALL 5.12b PG

START: At a flaky left-facing corner directly below a large right-facing corner with an overhanging left wall, 50 feet left of Never Again and 35 feet right of Agent Orange.

PITCH 1: 5.10b/c PG Climb the left face of the corner following an overhanging crack and belay on a ledge to the right. (60 ft.)

PITCH 2: 5.12b PG Traverse left to a small stance on the nose and climb the crack and face to another small stance on the nose. Then step back right and follow cracks (5.11 R) to a large ledge. (100 ft.)

PITCH 3: 5.10d PG Continue to the top. (40 ft.)

FA 1967: Art Gran and Jim McCarthy

FFA 1979: Mark Robinson and Mike Sawicky

60   AGENT ORANGE 5.11d R

Named for the orange rock on the first pitch.

Start: Directly above an oak tree on the right side of an orange face, 35 feet left of Happiness Is A 110° Wall and 30 feet right of Birth Of The Blues.

Pitch 1: 5.10d X Climb past a pointed right-facing block in the overhang (small birch up left) to a left-facing flake. From the left side of the flake move up past another overhang, traverse right 10-12 feet, and work up a steep face to a belay ledge below an overhang. (70 ft.)

Pitch 2: 5.11d R Climb a thin crack and shallow, 3-foot-high right-facing corner to a stance. Continue up the steep face, moving slightly left, to a shallow right-facing corner. Climb the corner, move right to a right-facing flake, and climb up to a belay in a broken-up area. (130 ft.)

Pitch 3: 5.5 PG Follow the large right-facing corner to the top.

FA 1981: Rich Romano, Francis Gledhill and Fred Yaculic

Lead, follow, or get out of the way.
— Thomas Paine

Mike Sawicky on
Happiness is a 110° Wall 5.12b
(Route 59)
Photo: Mark Robinson

John Bragg on
Happiness is a 110° Wall 5.12b
(Route 59)
Photo: Mark Robinson

61   BIRTH OF THE BLUES 5.11d X

Start: Behind a hemlock tree on a higher ledge system than the one at the start of Agent Orange, 30 feet left of Agent Orange and 35 feet right of Blue Streak.

Pitch 1: 5.11d X Climb a right-facing flake system past a small overhang and straight up to a large, hollow flake below a long overhang. Clear the overhang at a shallow right-facing flake-corner, and continue up the steep face past a thin crack to the right side of a long ledge which is below a left-facing corner. (90 ft.)

Pitch 2: 5.10a G Climb the left-facing corner and continue up an overhanging right-facing corner to a crack that splits an overhang. Follow the crack past the overhang and move left to a belay in a broken-up area. (60 ft.)

Pitch 3: 5.11b/c PG Walk left about 30 feet (crossing Bank Shot) and climb a shallow right-facing corner to a crack that diagonals up right past the ceiling. Follow the crack over the ceiling and continue to the top. (60 ft.)

FA 1980: Rich Romano and Russ Raffa

62   BANK SHOT 5.12a R

Start: Same as Birth of the Blues.

Pitch 1: 5.12a R Follow the right-facing flake system of Birth of the Blues to the long overhang. Traverse left about 10 feet to a shallow right-facing corner. Climb the corner and the overhang above to a second overhang and traverse right to a short right-facing corner capped by a third overhang. Work up this corner and follow a thin crack to a belay ledge at the base of a right-facing corner. (90 ft.)

Pitch 2: 5.11d PG Follow the overhanging corner past overhangs and belay in a broken area. (60 ft.)

Pitch 3: 5.9 PG Climb the crack that slants up left to the alcove in the right side of the roof. Then continue up past the notch and into a right-facing corner, and head for the top. (60 ft.)

FA 1980: Rich Romano and Doug Bower

63   BLUE STREAK 5.10b/c R

A fall on the crux of the first pitch would result in a scary but clean 60-footer.

Start: Just right of a birch tree that is below a shallow, flaky left-facing corner capped by a series of overhangs, 35 feet left of Bank Shot and 40 feet right of Little Brown Jug.

Pitch 1: 5.10b/c R Climb the face and corner to the first overhang. Clear this and reach a second overhang. Then traverse left about 8 feet and climb up to a third overhang. Move right to a short left-facing corner, step around it, and continue up the steep face to a belay ledge with a pine tree. (90 ft.)

Pitch 2: 5.10b/c R Follow a thin crack to a broken area, continue up into an alcove, and traverse out left to a small nose. Climb the overhang above to a horizontal flake and step right. Continue up the steep face and then angle up and left to a large right-facing corner. Follow the corner past overhangs and a bombay chimney to the top. (130 ft.)

FA 1980: Rich Romano and Hardie Truesdale

63a   RED'S THE COLOR (I WANNA SEE) 5.10d R

Start: Same as Blue Streak

Pitch 1: 5.10d R Climb Blue Streak till below the second overhang, then step right around the left facing corner. Diagonal up right on steep face about 10 feet to a small notch in the long overhang (crux). Work up past the overhang and follow a crack up the steep rock to a long ledge. (90 ft.)

Pitch 2: 5.10b/c PG Continue up the steep face past a short crack to a steep open book formed by an arête on its left side. Climb the open book to a ceiling. Make an exposed, cramped traverse left for 8-10 feet that leads past an outside corner or prow. Climb straight up past a small double-tiered overhang (crux) and a short, steep exposed face to the top. (130 ft.)

FA1993: Rich Romano and Al Pisaneschi

64   LITTLE BROWN JUG 5.11b/c R

Start: Directly behind a pine tree, 40 feet left of Blue Streak and 45 feet right of Realm of the Fifth-Class Climber.

Pitch 1: 5.10a X Climb past the overhangs and up the steep face past some flakes to an arch-like flake that faces right. Follow the flake to its end and continue up the face to a long ledge. Walk right to the base of a large left-facing corner that arches left. Climb corner and continue up a steep face past small overhang to a belay ledge below bulge. (120 ft.)

Pitch 2: 5.11b/c R Step left and climb left-facing flakes and bulging rock to an overhang. Traverse out right to a ceiling and follow a thin crack over it and up to a jug at the base of a shallow left-facing corner. Continue up the face above to a right-facing corner, traverse left around the corner, and finish up the final steep face. (90 ft.)

FA 1981: Rich Romano and Russ Clune

65   REALM OF THE FIFTH-CLASS CLIMBER 5.9 PG

START: At a flaky right-facing corner that is below a much larger right-facing corner, which in turn is below a triangular, pointed roof at the top of the cliff, 45 feet left of Little Brown Jug and 40 feet right of Delta Waves.

PITCH 1: 5.7 PG Climb the initial corner to a ledge at the base of the larger corner. (40 ft.)

PITCH 2: 5.9 PG Climb the large corner to the overhang, exit right, and continue up the corner to a belay ledge. (60 ft.)

PITCH 3: 5.9 PG Move left and then diagonal up left to the left edge of a large overhang. Climb the overhang and reach a second overhang. Then step left and continue to the top. (100 ft.)

FA 1964: Dick Williams, Art Gran, Jim McCarthy and Hans Kraus

Dave Leahy on
Realm of the 5th Class Climber 5.9
(Route 65)
Photo: John Okner

66 DELTA WAVES 5.10b/c PG

Start: Just right of a heavily lichen-covered face, 40 feet left of Realm Of The Fifth-Class Climber and 20 feet right of Mood Indigo.

Pitch 1: 5.10b/c PG Climb the face to an overhang with a shallow left-facing corner. Clear the overhang and follow the corner up left past another overhang to a short right-facing corner. Work up this corner and continue up to a vegetated ledge. (100 ft.)

Pitch 2: 5.8 PG Step left, climb up bulging, shattered rock, and continue up and left to a long ledge. (60 ft.)

Pitch 3: 5.10b/c PG Walk left and follow a crack that leans left up past an overhang and a bulge to a large right-facing corner that leads to the top. (60 ft.)

FA 1981: Rich Romano and Chuck Calef

67 MOOD INDIGO 5.9+ PG

Start: Directly below a short right-facing corner that has a laurel bush about 30 feet up, 20 feet left of Delta Waves and 130 feet right of Old Route.

Pitch 1: 5.9 PG Climb bulging rock to a right-facing corner which leads to a blocky ceiling. Clear the ceiling at a shallow right-facing corner and continue up to a left-facing corner. Follow this corner past another overhang and then diagonal up right to a belay ledge. (100 ft.)

Pitch 2: 5.9 PG Follow Delta Waves to the long ledge. Then, from the right side of the steep wall above, climb up right to a belay at the base of a large right-facing corner. (70 ft.)

Pitch 3: 5.9+ PG Climb about halfway up the corner, traverse around left into a steep left-facing corner which is followed passing a small overhang to the top. (50 ft.)

FA 1981: Rich Romano and Morris Hershoff

I have more respect for a climber who goes for it and falls, than I do for a climber who yells "take."
— Eric Fazio Rhicard

68   **OLD ROUTE 5.5 G**

Try to imagine doing this route in 1935 with a couple of soft iron pitons, a lousy rope, and sneakers—absolutely amazing!

START: Below a large, broken right-facing corner which is below two spectacular jutting blocks at the top of the cliff, 130 feet left of Mood Indigo and 60 feet right of Apollo Theater.

PITCH 1: 5.5 G Climb the corner till it ends at a laurel bush, traverse left on a broken ledge, and work up to and follow a shallow right-facing corner to an overhang. Then traverse right about 15 feet and continue up to a belay. (130 ft.)

PITCH 2: 5.2 PG Follow the obvious fault up left past spectacular white rock to the top. (50 ft.)

FA 1935: Fritz Wiessner and John and Peggy Navas

68a   CHAIRMAN OF THE BOARDS 5.8 PG-R

Start: About midway (25-30 ft.) between Old Route and Apollo Theater, below the long overhang that is about 8 feet up.

Pitch 1: 5.8 PG-R Climb past the overhang to a projecting block that looks loose, then continue up past a right-leaning diagonal fault into a short, shallow right-facing open book which is followed to its top and a belay on the right at a pine tree.

Pitch 2: 5.8 PG Step back left and climb up to the large right-facing corner, move left to the outside corner (arête) and climb it to join Apollo Theater to the top.

FA 1992: Rich Romano and Al Pisaneschi

69   APOLLO THEATER 5.9 PG

Start: At the base of a left-facing ramp-like trough system that diagonals up right, 60 feet left of Old Route and 60 feet right of Prelude.

Pitch 1: 5.8 PG Scramble up the ramp system till it is possible to step left and climb the steep face to the prominent right-facing corner. Follow the corner till it ends and continue up the face to a belay ledge with a pine tree at the base of a long right-facing corner. (100 ft.)

Pitch 2: 5.9 PG Climb the corner to its end and continue up the steep face past overhangs to a long ledge below another steep face and a long ceiling. From the midway point on the ledge, climb up a very short, shallow right-facing corner to a ceiling, traverse right, and finish on Old Route. (120 ft.)

FA 1981: Rich Romano and Francis Gledhill

70   PRELUDE 5.9 PG

Start: Below a big, blocky right-facing corner capped by a roof split by a crack that widens as it goes out right to the lip, 60 feet left of Apollo Theater and 35 feet right of Fugue.

Pitch 1: 5.9 PG Climb corner to the roof, traverse right to a laurel bush, and then continue up a right-facing corner to a ledge with a pine tree.

Pitch 2: 5.8 PG Continue up the right-facing corner to the base of a large tree-filled corner, step left, and follow a large, slabby low-angle ramp up left to the top.

FA 1981: Rich Romano and George Peterson

71   FUGUE 5.9 PG

Start: At a large block on the highest ledge below the double-tiered, right-pointing overhangs, 35 feet left of Prelude and 30 feet right of Allegro.

Pitch 1: 5.9 PG Climb past the overhangs at the obvious weakness and move up left to a 15-foot-wide ledge. About midway along the ledge, climb up a crack past some small bushes to a slot that leads to a whitish, concave open book. Follow crack in the open book past some bulging overhangs, continue up past another overhang, and diagonal up left to some pine trees.

Pitch 2: 5.8 PG Step right and follow the outside corner to the top.

FA 1981: Rich Romano and George Peterson

72   ALLEGRO 5.10b/c PG

Start: At a blocky, 10-foot-high, right-facing corner behind an oak tree and below a large right-facing corner capped by an overhang, 30 feet left of Fugue and 30 feet right of Top Brass.

Pitch 1: 5.8 PG Climb the corner to the overhang, move up right, and then continue up and left to a good-sized ledge with birch trees. (70 ft.)

Pitch 2: 5.9 PG Climb up right to a shallow, broken right-facing corner which is followed to its top. Step left and continue up to some bushes and a section of blocky rock that leads up left past a pine tree (on the left) to a large ledge at the base of the final headwall. Walk right about 10 feet to a belay at a pine tree. (80 ft.)

Pitch 3: 5.10b/c PG Walk right another 5 feet to a right-facing flake. Then follow this flake and some smaller right-facing flakes above to horizontal holds, step left, and continue to the top. (30 ft.)

FA 1981: Rich Romano and George Peterson

73   BETTER LATE THAN NEVER 5.8 PG

Start: Same as Allegro.

Pitch 1: 5.8 PG Same as the first pitch of Allegro.

Pitch 2: 5.8 PG From the left side of the ledge, move up onto a short slab, traverse left about 6 feet, and climb a broken left-facing corner to a ceiling. Move around the ceiling to the right and continue up to the largest ledge with trees at the base of a blocky right-facing corner. Belay at the corner or the pine tree to the right. (90 ft.)

Pitch 3: 5.3 PG Climb the corner and then diagonal up left to the top. (40 ft.)

FA 1986: Fred Polvere and Leif Savery

74   TOP BRASS 5.9 PG
    Start: At a cluster of at least six pine trees below three small pointed rocks nested together about 25 feet up, 60 feet left of Allegro.
    Pitch 1: 5. ? pro ? Climb to the obvious ledge above and walk right to blocks and pine trees on its right side, below a glacially polished face.
    Pitch 2: 5.9 PG Climb to a shallow left-facing corner and some shattered-looking overhangs. Diagonal up left to a short left-facing corner and continue up a broken corner past a small overhang to another left-facing corner, which slants up right. Follow this corner to a ledge, step right, and angle up left (5.8 R) to a larger ledge (optional belay). Continue up face and short, shallow left-facing corner to an overhang, step right and up to the top. (130 ft.)
    FA 1981: Rich Romano and Albert Pisaneschi

75   FACE-OFF 5.12a R
    Start: Just left of Top Brass, near the left end of the main traverse ledge.
    Pitch 1: 5. ? Pro ? Climb the face to a left-facing corner that leads to the Top Brass ledge.
    Pitch 2: 5.12a R Continue up past a left-facing corner to some loose, blocky rock. Step left and work up to a down-sloping overhang. Step left again and climb a short crack in a short left-facing corner. Then step right and work up a thin crack and the face above to the left side of an overhang. Angle up left to steep orange-white rock and continue up to the right side of another overhang. Step right and up to a right-facing corner. Climb this, step back around left, and continue up white rock past a bulging overhang. Then diagonal up left and climb past a crack and notch in the overhang, and head for the top. (130 ft.)
    FA 1987: Rich Romano and Albert Pisaneschi

76   M32L 5.8 PG

Start: At a small pine tree on the Top Brass ledge, 15 feet left of Face-Off and 50 feet right of a very large right-facing flake that looks like the mirror image of The Flake in the Trapps.

Pitch 1: 5.8 PG Follow the flaky left-facing corners and a crack to a "cave," then continue up left past the obvious overhang to the top. (80 ft.)

FA 1981: Rich Romano and Russ Clune

77   SAUCONY 5.9 PG

Start: On the Top Brass ledge, 20 feet left of M32L and 30 feet right of the very large right-facing flake that looks like the mirror image of The Flake in the Trapps.

Pitch 1: 5.9 PG Climb a thin crack to a flaring 3-foot-high crack. Continue following the crack system up past the left side of the ceiling to a small left-facing corner. Then climb the face on the right to the top. (80 ft.)

FA 1981: Rich Romano and Russ Clune

78   RAGING BULL 5.10c PG

Romano led this climb in an old pair of running shoes. Named in part for the movie of the same name and the great boxer Jake LaMatta.

START: On the face 45 feet left of the huge left-facing corner with the chimney on the upper part of the cliff and midway between a large oak tree and a boulder pile to the right.

PITCH 1: 5.10c PG Climb the face along a thin broken crack to the left side of a large overhang. Continue following the crack/fault system till level with a ledge on the left. Step left and work up a left-facing corner to the notch in the overhangs. Climb past the notch and up to a horizontal crack that leads out right at the next overhang (V1). Move right and layback up to another horizontal crack. Then diagonal up right past the right side of a pointed overhang, move straight up, step left, and continue to the rappel tree at the top. (90 ft.)

Variation 1: 5.10b/c PG Traverse left about 6-8 feet, climb the overhang at the break and finish up the steep face to the top.

FA 1987: Rich Romano and Dick Williams
FA (V1) 1990: Al Pisaneschi and Rich Romano

79   PRESTO 5.10b/c PG
This climb was led right after Raging Bull in the same old pair of running shoes.

Start: Just right of some blocks and directly below a large but short, white right-facing corner capped by an overhang about 50 feet up, 35 feet left of Raging Bull and 20 feet right of Air for a G-String.

Pitch 1: 5.10b/c PG Climb the face to a short ramp that leads up right. At the top of the ramp continue straight up to a corner which is followed to an overhang (V1). Then move left and finish up the steep face and the easier rock above. (80 ft.)

Variation 1: 5.11b/c PG (Prestissimo) Traverse right five to ten feet and climb the overhang at a small right-facing crack/arch at its lip and follow the steep face to the top.

FA 1987: Rich Romano and Dick Williams
FA (V1) 1990: Al Pisaneschi and Rich Romano

80   **AIR FOR A G-STRING 5.6 G-PG**
START: Between a black birch and a chestnut oak, the latter next to a large, detached flake-like boulder that points right, directly below a very obvious corner and crack system, 20 feet left of Presto.

PITCH 1: 5.6 G-PG Climb the corner and crack system to the overhang and traverse left about 10 feet along a horizontal crack to a break in the overhang. Continue up a few feet, move right, and work up past a sloping ledge to the top. (70 ft.)

FA 1987: Dick Williams and Joe Bridges

Fritz Weissner
climbing at Skytop

May the Father of all mercies scatter light, and not darkness, upon our paths, and make us in all our several vocations useful here, in His own due time and way everlasting happy.
     —George Washington

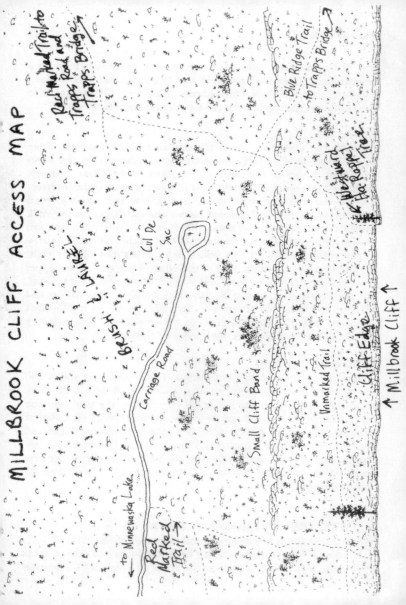

MILLBROOK CLIFF ACCESS MAP

Red Marked Trail to Trapps Road and Trapps Bridge →

Blue Ridge Trail
to Trapps Bridge →

BRUSH ↓ LAUREL

Cul De Sac

Carriage Road

← to Minnewaska Lake

Red Marked Trail →

Small Cliff Band

Unmarked Trail

Westguard

Ha-Rappel Trace

Cliff Edge

↑ Millbrook Cliff ↑

MILLBROOK
ROUTE
PHOTOGRAPHS

- I The Marching Morons 5.9 A I R (Not Shown) A 2 Pelvic Thrust 5.9+ PG

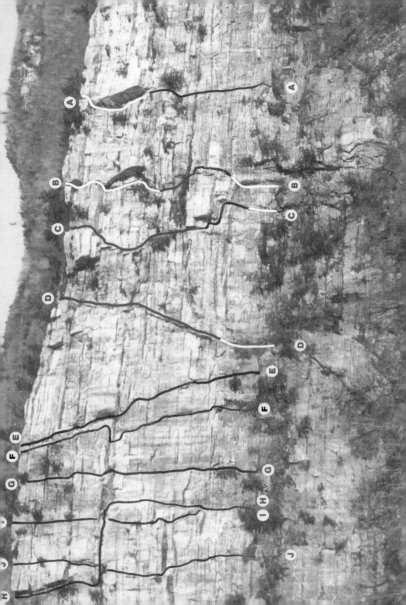

A 2 Pelvic Thrust 5.9+ PG
- 2a The Buck Stops Here 5.10d PG (Not Shown)
- **2b Hogs Breath 5.11d PG**
B 3 Garden of Alllah 5.10.a/b PG
C 4 Inshallah 5.9+ PG
D 5 Three Buzzards 5.5 PG
E 6 Nothing to Write Home About 5.8 PG

F 7 Sing, Sing, Sing 5.11b/c R
G 8 Brown Bomber 5.10a/b G
- 8a Throttled 5.10d R (Not Shown)
H 9 Strange City 5.7 PG
I 10 Explosive Bolts 5.11b/c PG-R
J 11 Danger UXB 5.10a/b PG

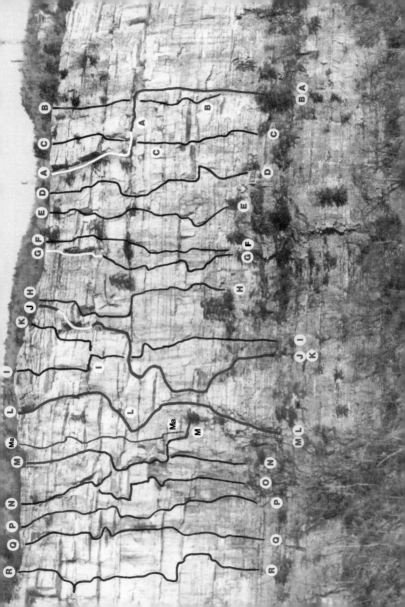

A 9   Strange City 5.7 PG
B 10 Explosive Bolts 5.11b/c PG-R
C 11 Danger UXB 5.10a/b PG
D 12 Leap Frog 5.11d PG
E 13 Side Pocket 5.10d PG
F 14 The Tempest 5.11c PG
G 15 Artistry in Rhythm 5.10a/b R
H 16 Bank Manager 5.10a/b PG
I 17 Hang 'Em High 5.12a PG-R
J 18 Swinging C 5.8 PG

K 19 Super Sunday 5.10a/b PG
L 20 Sweet Meat 5.9 R
Ma 20a Apis Mellifera Scutellata (Killer Bees) 5.11b/c R
M 21 Mission Improbable 5.10a/b PG
N 22 Time Being 5.11a PG
O 23 In Search of Lost Time 5.11b/c R
P 24 Directpissima 5.11b/c PG-R
Q 25 Land Grab 5.12a PG
R 26 Manifest Destiny 5.12d/13a G

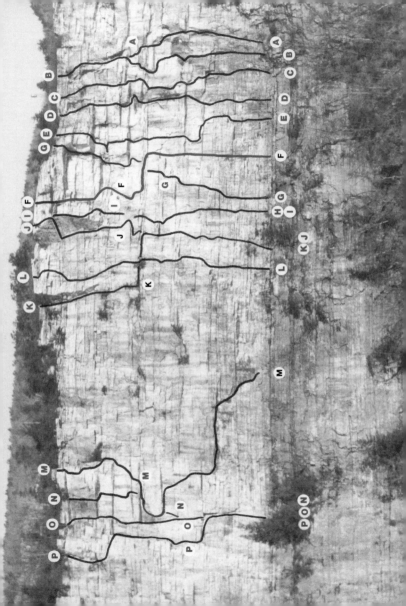

A 22 Time Being 5.11a PG
B 23 In Search of Lost Time 5.11b/c R
C 24 Directpissima 5.11b/c PG-R
D 25 Land Grab 5.12a PG
E **26 Manifest Destiny 5.12d/13a G**
F **27 New Frontier 5.10d R**
G 28 Back to the Land Movement 5.11d PG
H 29 The New Deal 5.11d R

I 30 Nectar Vector 5.12b/c R
J **31 Square Meal 5.11a PG**
K **32 Schlemiel 5.10b/c PG**
L 33 Band of Renown 5.10d PG
M 34 High Plains Drifter 5.10a PG-R
N 35 Sudden Impact 5.12b/c R
O **36 White Rose 5.11a PG**
P **37 The White Corner 5.9 R**

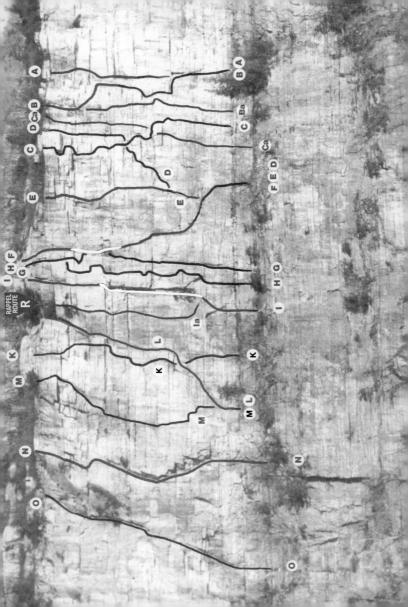

A 36 White Rose 5.11a PG
B 37 **The White Corner 5.9 R**
Ba 37a White Knuckles 5.11b/c R
C 38 Big Band Era 5.10b/c PG
Ca 38a Love and Bullets 5.11b/c PG-R
- 38b Dance Card 5.11a R (Not Shown)
D 39 Conflict of Interest 5.9 R
E 40 Rib Cracker 5.9 PG
F 41 **The High Traverse 5.5 PG**

G 42 **Cruise Control 5.9 PG**
H 43 **Rags to Richs' 5.10b/c PG-R**
I 44 **Westward Ha! 5.7 PG**
Ia 44b Stardust Memories 5.12a R-X
K 45 Under the Wire 5.11a PG
L 46 Wire Wizard 5.8 R
M 47 **The Time Eraser 5.10a PG**
N 48 Promise of Things to Come 5.10b/c X
O 49 The Good, The Bad and The Ugly 5.10b/c R

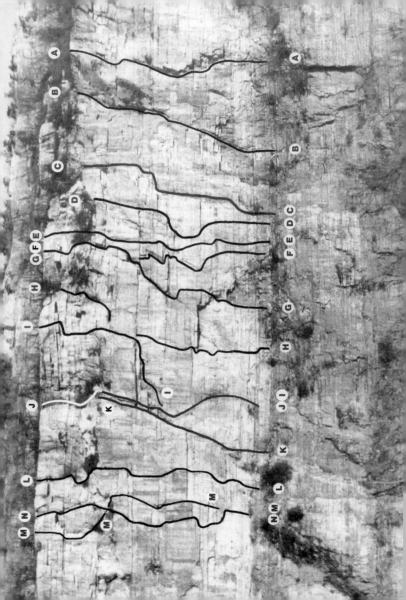

A 48 Promise of Things to Come 5.10b/c X
B 49 The Good, The Bad and The Ugly 5.10b/c R
C **50 Remembrance of Things... 5.10a/b PG**
D 51 Rings of Saturn 5.11 X
E 52 Orbit of Jupiter 5.11a X
F 53 Asteroid Belt 5.11a/b X
G 54 Search for Tomorrow 5.10b/c PG
- 55 Paral-Lax 5.12a G (Not Shown)

H 56 Cuckoo Man 5.10b/c PG
I 57 Again and Again 5.7 PG-R
J 58 Never Again 5.10b/c PG-R
K 59 Happiness is a 110° Wall 5.12b PG
L 60 Agent Orange 5.11d R
M 61 Birth of the Blues 5.11d X
N 62 Bank Shot 5.12a R

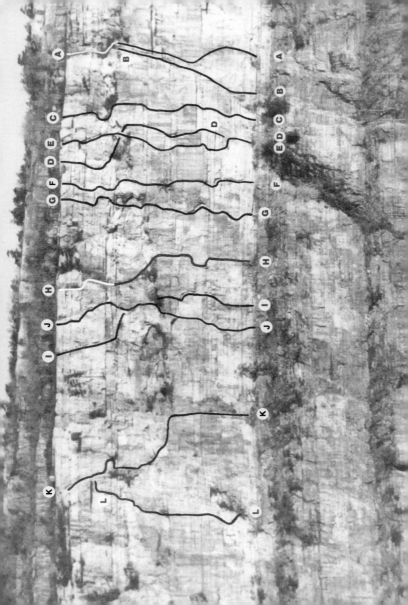

G 64 Little Brown Jug 5.11b/c R

H 65 Realm of the Fifth-Class Climber 5.9 PG

I 66 Delta Waves 5.10b/c PG

J 67 Mood Indigo 5.9+ PG

K 68 Old Route 5.5 G

- 68a Chairman of the Boards 5.8 PG-R (Not Shown)

L 69 Apollo Theater 5.9 PG

A 58 Never Again 5.10b/c PG-R

B 59 Happiness is a 110° Wall 5.12b PG

C 60 Agent Orange 5.11d R

D 61 Birth of the Blues 5.11d X

E 62 Bank Shot 5.12a R

F 63 Blue Streak 5.10b/c R

- 63a Red's the Color... 5.10d R (Not Shown)

A 68 Old Route 5.5 G

-    68a Chairman of the Boards 5.8 PG-R (Not Shown)

B   69 Apollo Theater 5.9 PG

C   70 Prelude 5.9 PG

D   71 Fugue 5.9 PG

E   72 Allegro 5.10b/c PG

F   73 Better Late Than Never 5.8 PG

G   74 Top Brass 5.9 PG

H   75 Face Off 5.12a R

I   76 M32L 5.8 PG

J   77 Saucony 5.9 PG

K   78 Raging Bull 5.10c PG

L   79 Presto 5.10b/c PG

M   80 Air For a G-String 5.6 G-PG

C 79 Presto 5.10b/c PG

D 80 Air For a G-String 5.6 G-PG

A 77 Saucony 5.9 PG

B 78 Raging Bull 5.10c PG

NEAR TRAPPS ROUTE STATISTICS

The following tables of statistics reveal the complexity of climbing available at Millbrook across all ratings, grades of protection, pitches and variations.

For example, in the first table, *Near Trapps Routes Tallied by Rating*, you can see that there are 22 routes rated 5.10 that have a PG protection rating.

Additionally, in the second table, *Near Trapps Routes Tallied by Pitch*, you can see that there are 31 pitches of 5.10 climbing that have a PG protection rating.

Finally, in the third table, *Near Trapps Routes Tallied by Variation*, you can see that there are 7 variations to 5.10 routes that have a PG protection rating.

NEAR TRAPPS ROUTES TALLIED BY RATING									
YDS	TR	G	G-PG	PG	PG-R	R	R-X	X	TOTAL
5.0									
5.1									
5.2		2							2
5.3			1	3	1				5
5.4		4	2	4		1			11
5.5		6		12					18
5.6		5		22	2	2			31
5.7	2	8	2	18	5	2		1	38
5.8	3	10	2	26	2	3			46
5.9	4	10	3	15	2	4		1	39
5.10	7	4	2	22	4	8	1		48
5.11	6	5		8	1	10		1	31
5.12	5	1		5	2	3			16
5.13	1								1
TOTAL	28	55	12	135	19	33	1	3	286

NEAR TRAPPS ROUTES TALLIED BY PITCH

YDS	TR	G	G-PG	PG	PG-R	R	R-X	X	TOTAL
5.0				1	1		1		3
5.1				3					3
5.2		2		8					10
5.3		3		17	1				21
5.4		5	2	22		2			31
5.5		13	1	39	1	1			55
5.6		11	2	48	2	3		1	67
5.7		16	2	37	6	6		2	69
5.8		15	3	40	4	5			67
5.9		15	2	19	3	5		1	45
5.10		5	2	31	5	11	1		55
5.11		5		8	1	10		1	25
5.12		1		5	2	3			11
5.13									
TOTAL		86	14	278	26	46	2	5	462

NEAR TRAPPS ROUTES TALLIED BY VARIATION

YDS	TR	G	G-PG	PG	PG-R	R	R-X	X	TOTAL
5.0				2			1		3
5.1				1					1
5.2				2					2
5.3				2					2
5.4		4	1	7	2	1			15
5.5	1	2		6		1			10
5.6		7		15	3	1			26
5.7		8	4	15	2	2			31
5.8		4	3	11	2	1			21
5.9	2	8		13	2	1	1		27
5.10	2	2	1	7	1	2			15
5.11	3	2		4	1	3			13
5.12	1	1	1						3
5.13									0
TOTAL	9	38	10	85	13	12	2		169

ROUTE NUMBER AND NAME

5.2

81a	Spic and Span 5.2 G
162a	Split Rock Traverse 5.2 G

5.3

112d	Dozy Doats 5.3 G-PG
89b	Nosey Bodies 5.3 PG-R
109a	Two Feather Flake 5.3 PG
D-Rt	Wichita 5.3 PG
73	Yum Yum Yab Yum 5.3 PG ★★★

5.4

128	Across From The Fruitstand 5.4 PG
78a	Coyote Crack 5.4 G ★
74a	Curly 5.4 G-PG
134	Eowyn 5.4 PG ★★
78b	Fisher Crack 5.4 PG
36	Gelsa 5.4 PG ★★★
B-Rt	Independence 5.4 G
161a	Not To Avoid 5.4 G
147	Roman's Climb Next To Keystone Kop 5.4 G-PG
102d	Slab Happy 5.4 R
101b	Snail's Face 5.4 G

5.5

69	Ain't Dis Yab Yum? 5.5 PG (**NR**)
101a	Antsy Oh! 5.5 PG
76a	Catch a Tiger 5.5 PG
83	Cherry's Climb 5.5 PG
112b	Drohascadam 1 5.5 PG
106c	Gardiner's Delight 5.5 G
98c	Gunks Burghers 5.5 PG
174	Here a Quack, There a Quack, Everywhere... 5.5 G
21	Layback 5.5 PG ★★

ROUTE NUMBER AND NAME

5.5

82	Orc Stone 5.5 PG
139	Punch and Judy 5.5 PG ★
130	Roman's Climb...Across From The Fruitstand 5.5 PG
170	Short and Sassy 5.5 PG
98e	Spring Reigns 5.5 G
C-Rt	St. Louis 5.5 G
98d	Summer Breeze 5.5 G
86c	Summer Brie 5.5 G
88	Three Generations 5.5 PG (**NR**)

5.6

148	Aftermath 5.6 PG
103	Animal Farm 5.6 PG (**NR**)
105a	Annie Dotes 5.6 PG
102c	Beauty and the Skink 5.6 PG ★
108a	Benadryl Daze 5.6 PG
117a	Birch Beer Crack 5.6 G
77a	Catnip 5.6 G ★★
144	De Colores 5.6 PG
14	Disneyland 5.6 PG ★★★
108	Eat Here and Get Gas 5.6+ PG
139a	Fossil Fools 5.6 G ★
115	Giddah 5.6 R
142	Gil-Galad 5.6 PG
59	Grease Gun Groove 5.6 PG ★★
60c	Grey Hair Arete 5.6 PG
173	Here a Bucket, There a Bucket... 5.6 G
133	Interlewd 5.6 PG ★
118	Just Allow Me One More Chance 5.6 PG
140a	King of P 5.6 PG ★
141	Little White Mushroom 5.6 PG
62	Lonely Challenge 5.6 PG
67	Loose Goose 5.6 PG ★★

ROUTE NUMBER AND NAME

5.6 (continued)

152 Positively 4th Street 5.6- PG ★
116 Rock Around the Clock 5.6 R (**NR**)
117b Root Beer Crack 5.6 G
166 Spinal Traction 5.6 A3 PG
129 To Come or Become 5.6 PG
125 Tree-Filled Chimney 5.6 PG-R (**NR**)
127a Up Root 5.6 PG
 87 Vulga-Tits 5.6 PG (**NR**)

5.6 VARIATION

124a TFC Nein 5.6 PG-R

5.7

 72 After You 5.7 PG-R
137 Akidlleativytoowouldn'tyou? 5.7 G ★★
 34 Baskerville Terrace 5.7 PG ★★
64a Bee Bite 5.7 G-PG ★★
111a Bush League Too 5.7 PG
112a Bush Lite 5.7 G
101 Deception 5.7 PG (**NR**)
102a Double Quacks 5.7 PG
 75 Eenie Meenie 5.7 PG
60b Fat and Weak 5.7 PG-R
117 Flake, Rattle and Roll 5.7 R (**NR**)
109 Highway 51 5.7 PG
 63 Horney 5.7 PG
143 Keystone Kop 5.7 PG
  4 Le Plie 5.7- PG ★
 17 Leftovers 5.7 PG
98f Mud, Sweat and Beers 5.7 G (**NR**)
78e Old and Mossy 5.7 G
159 Outsider 5.7 G ★★

ROUTE NUMBER AND NAME

5.7 (continued)

131 Parsifal and Potato Chips 5.7 PG-R
85 Phalladio 5.7 PG-R **(NR)**
89a Route Awakening 5.7 G
113b Saving Grace 5.7+ G-PG
98 Scuttlebutt 5.7 R
106d Serf's Up 5.7 PG
73a Silver Bullet 5.7 G
18 Te Dum 5.7 G ★★
172 The Shadow Nose 5.7 PG
121 The White Pillar 5.7 PG-R
145 Trick or Treat 5.7 PG
66 Up Yours 5.7+ PG ★
78c What? Are You Nuts? 5.7 PG **(NR)**
29 Yellow Ridge 5.7 PG ★★★

5.7 LINK-UP

103a Animal Farm Link-Up 5.7 PG
34a Basking Ridge 5.7 PG ★★★

5.7 AS A TOPROPE

149 Omega 12 Clausthaler 5.7 X

5.7 TOPROPE

102b Frau's Prow 5.7
117c TurtleFly 5.7

5.8

24 Alphonse 5.8 G ★★★
114a Amazing Grace 5.8 PG ★
106 B M 5.8 PG
74 B. Warewolf 5.8 PG
61a Back to The Future 5.8 G ★
92 Between a Rock and a Hard Place 5.8 R

ROUTE NUMBER AND NAME

5.8 (continued)

52	Birdland 5.8 PG ★★★
95	Boston Tree Party 5.8 G ★
12	Broken Sling 5.8 PG ★★★
112	Bush League 5.8 PG
146	D.S.B. 5.8+ PG ★
96	Day-Tripper 5.8 PG ★★
94	Easter Time Too 5.8 G ★★
100	Energy Crunch 5.8 R (**NR**)
138	Far From the Madding Crowd 5.8 PG ★
54	Farewell to Arms 5.8 PG ★★
31	Fat Stick 5.8 G-PG ★
67a	5.8 Crack Climb 5.8 G ★
99	Gold Flakes 5.8 PG
86b	Gouda Climb 5.8 PG
61	Grey Gully 5.8 PG-R
150	Grim and Tonic 5.8+ R
98b	Halfbeak 5.8 G
127	Just For The Record 5.8 PG
168	Lean and Mean 5.8 PG
76b	Left Meets Right 5.8 G
127b	Like a Box of Chocolates 5.8 PG
155	Main Line 5.8 PG ★★★
74c	Moe 5.8 G
89	Nowhereland 5.8 PG
107d	One Way or Another 5.8 PG-R
2	Outer Space 5.8 PG ★
136a	R2-OK? 5.8 PG
113a	Saving Face 5.8- PG
170a	Seniors in Motion 5.8 G
107	Slab Shtick 5.8 PG
68	Swissair 5.8 PG
80a	Whet Stone 5.8 PG ★
28	Yellow Belly 5.8 PG ★★
80	You're in the Wrong Place, My Friend 5.8 PG

ROUTE NUMBER AND NAME

5.8 LINK-UP

32a Dog-Stick-Ridge 5.8 PG ★★★
37a G-String Giants 5.8 G ★★
155a Main Line/Mac-Reppy 5.8 G-PG ★

5.8 TOPROPE

142a Barely Memorable 5.8
86a Cam-n-Bearit 5.8
106b Nickel And Timing 5.8

5.9

107b Ambien Knights 5.9 G-PG ★
 97 As the Cliff Turns 5.9 G ★★
 77 By the Toe 5.9+ PG
105 Cherokee 5.9 G ★★
 60 Corporate Conglomerate 5.9+ R
113 Drohascadamfubast 5.9 G
  3 Easy Rider 5.9- G ★★
162 Fright to The Finish 5.9+ PG
 38 G-String 5.9 PG
 86 Gold Rush 5.9 PG
 93 Good Friday Climb 5.9+ PG
 22 Grand Central 5.9 PG ★★★
153 Ground Control 5.9 PG ★★
164 Hold the Mayo 5.9 G
120 Honky Tonk Woman 5.9 R ★
136 I'm OK-You're OK 5.9 PG ★
158 Inside Out 5.9 G ★
132 Interplanetary Agents 5.9+ PG
 19 Inverted Layback 5.9 PG ★★★
140 L P 5.9 R
129a Miss Mantle 5.9 PG

ROUTE NUMBER AND NAME

5.9 (continued)

- 114 Moxie 5.9 G-PG ★
- 76 My-Knee Moe 5.9 G-PG ★
- 77d Nutzville 5.9 PG
- 61b Princess Leia 5.9 PG-R
- 44 Roseland 5.9 PG ★★★
- 126 The Near Side of Far 5.9 G
- 110 3,4,5,6, Over and Out Porkypine 5.9 G
- 171 Up In Arms 5.9 G ★
- 112e Whatayamacallit 5.9 PG
- 102 Wolf and the Swine 5.9 PG-R
- 90 Zachariah 5.9 G ★★

5.9 LINK-UP

- 90a Interiah 5.9+ G ★★

5.9 AS A TOPROPE

- 156 High Anxiety 5.9 R
- 119 She's the Boss 5.9+ X

5.9 TOPROPE

- 106a In the Nick of Time 5.9
- 74b Larry 5.9
- 112c Liddle Lamzy Divey 5.9
- 60a Quack'n-Up 5.9+

5.10

- 53 Birdcage 5.10b PG
- 27 Bongos and Beached Whales 5.10a R
- 66a Boob Job 5.10b PG ★
- 64b Born Again 5.10b/c G-PG
- 77c By the Claw 5.10b G
- 5a Crass 5.10b PG
- 8 Criss Cross 5.10a PG

ROUTE NUMBER AND NAME

5.10 (continued)

9	Criss Cross Direct 5.10a PG ★★★
65	Elder Cleavage Direct 5.10b PG ★★★
81	Elf Stone Direct 5.10b/c PG
35	Fat City Direct 5.10d G-PG ★★★
30	Fat Stick Direct 5.10b PG ★★★
113c	Graceland 5.10a PG
124	Hang Ten 5.10a PG ★
91	International Harvesters 5.10a PG-R
37	Land of the Giants 5.10a/b PG
135	Live and Let Die 5.10b/c PG-R
163	Muriel's Nose 5.10b/c R
78	Nazgul 5.10b/c R
26	No Slings Attached 5.10b/c R
23	Penn Station 5.10b/c PG
70a	Preying Mantle 5.10a PG
70b	Predator 5.10a PG-R
43	Revolving Eyeballs 5.10b/c R
165	Scrambled Legs 5.10d G
151	Shirley Tumble 5.10c R
123a	Shootin' the Curl 5.10b/c PG
25	Sissy Boys 5.10d R
42	Shitface 5.10c PG ★★
162b	Spinal Exam 5.10b/c PG ★★
32b	The Hounds 5.10b PG
A1	Topeka 5.10a G ★
48	Transcontinental Nailway 5.10b PG ★★★
59a	Tulip Mussel Garden 5.10d G ★
71	Vultures Know 5.10b/c R-X
127c	Whatever 5.10a PG ★
70	Where the Wild Things Are 5.10d PG
64	Wildmere 5.10a PG-R
94a	Woolly Clam Taco 5.10c PG ★

ROUTE NUMBER AND NAME

5.10 LINK-UP

5   Crass/Outer Space Direct Finish 5.10b PG ★

5.10 AS A TOPROPE

79   Wrong Place, Right Time 5.10d R

5.10 TOPROPE

77b   Bridges to Knowhere 5.10a
115a   Git-Git Giddah 5.10a
98a   Here's the Scoop 5.10b
89c   Nip & Tuck 5.10b/c
78d   P/L 5.10a
111b   Raven's Run 5.10a
107a   Shtick It 5.10c/d

5.11

160   Avoid Where Inhibited 5.11a G ★★
21a   Ba-Ba Moran 5.11a PG ★
10   Between the Lines 5.11a/b R
125a   Boogy Bored 5.11b/c R
59b   Broken Spring 5.11a PG-R
20   Burning Babies 5.11b/c PG
7   Criss 5.11a PG
46   El Camino Real 5.11b PG ★★
41   Eraserhead 5.11d/12a R
169   Fat and Flabby 5.11a PG
32   Generation Gap 5.11b/c PG
122   Harvest Moon 5.11a G ★★
84   Lost World 5.11b/c R
157   Mac-Reppy 5.11c G ★
39   Pain Strain 5.11a/b PG
15   Sling Time 5.11d G
57   Son of Stem 5.11d R
58   Soylent Green 5.11a R

ROUTE NUMBER AND NAME

5.11 (continued)

154 Strange Customs 5.11d R
16 Swing Time 5.11a PG ★★
161 Void Where Prohibited 5.11d G ★★

5.11 AS A TOPROPE

51 Bird Brain 5.11d X
45 Boogeyman 5.11d R
104 Raven and the Cat 5.11a R
49 Road Warrior 5.11d R

5.11 TOPROPE

76c 5.11d/12a
111 Mighty White of Us 5.11d
66b Nice Job 5.11a
107c Pump Ethyl 5.11d
11 Sling Line 5.11a
54a The Boys from Above 5.11d

5.12

167 Dark Side of The Moon 5.12b PG ★★
5c Double Cross-issima 5.12d R
47 El Kabong 5.12b/c R
6 Iron Cross 5.12d PG
1 Kansas City 5.12b G ★★
33 Requiem For a Heavyweight 5.12d PG-R
56 To Have or Have Not 5.12a/b R
13 Squat Thrust 5.12a PG
123 The Mincer 5.12a PG-R

5.12 VARIATION

5b Infinite Space 5.12a PG ★★

ROUTE NUMBER AND NAME

55 **5.12 AS A TOPROPE**
To Be or Not To Be 5.12a PG ★★★

5.12 TOPROPE

55a Believe It or Not 5.12a
53a Birdjuice 5.12a
12a Bumpkey 5.12a
40 Forbidden Zone 5.12a/b
50 Slammin' the Salmon 5.12b

5.13

45a Dyno-Soar 5.13a

MILLBROOK ROUTE STATISTICS

The following tables of statistics reveal the complexity of climbing available at Millbrook across all ratings, grades of protection, pitches and variations.

For example, in the first table, *Millbrook Routes Tallied by Rating*, you can see that there are 18 routes rated 5.10 that have a PG protection rating.

Additionally, in the second table, *Millbrook Routes Tallied by Pitch*, you can see that there are 32 pitches of 5.10 climbing that have a PG protection rating.

Finally, in the third table, *Millbrook Routes Tallied by Variation*, you can see that there are 7 variations to 5.10 routes that have a PG protection rating.

MILLBROOK ROUTES TALLIED BY RATING								
YDS	TR	G	G-PG	PG	PG-R	R	R-X	X	TOTAL
5.0									
5.1									
5.2									
5.3									
5.4									
5.5		2		1					3
5.6			1						1
5.7				2	1				3
5.8				4	1	1			6
5.9				11		4			15
5.10		1		18	3	6		1	29
5.11				8	3	8		4	23
5.12	1	2		2	1	4	1		11
5.13									
TOTAL	*1*	*5*	*1*	*46*	*9*	*23*	*1*	*5*	*91*

MILLBROOK ROUTES TALLIED BY PITCH									
YDS	TR	G	G-PG	PG	PG-R	R	R-X	X	TOTAL
5.0									
5.1									
5.2				1					1
5.3				3	2				5
5.4									
5.5		1		5					6
5.6			1	3					4
5.7				10	1				11
5.8		4		19	1	1			25
5.9				20		10	2	2	34
5.10		2		32	2	10		2	48
5.11				10	4	10		5	29
5.12		2		2	1	4	1		10
5.13									
TOTAL	0	9	1	105	11	35	3	9	203

MILLBROOK ROUTES TALLIED BY VARIATION									
YDS	TR	G	G-PG	PG	PG-R	R	R-X	X	TOTAL
5.0									
5.1									
5.2									
5.3									
5.4									
5.5									
5.6				1					1
5.7				1					1
5.8				1					2
5.9				2					2
5.10				7	2	1			10
5.11		1		2	1	1			5
5.12									
5.13									
TOTAL	0	1	0	14	3	2	0	0	21

ROUTE NUMBER AND NAME

5.5

68   Old Route 5.5 G
41   The High Traverse 5.5 PG
5   Three Buzzards 5.5 PG

5.6

80   Air For a G-String 5.6 G-PG

5.7

57   Again and Again 5.7 PG-R
9   Strange City 5.7 PG
44   Westward Ha! 5.7 PG

5.8

73   Better Late Than Never 5.8 PG
68a   Chairman of the Boards 5.8 PG-R
76   M32L 5.8 PG
6   Nothing to Write Home About 5.8 PG
18   Swinging C 5.8 PG
46   Wire Wizard 5.8 R

5.9

69   Apollo Theater 5.9 PG
39   Conflict of Interest 5.9 R
42   Cruise Control 5.9 PG
71   Fugue 5.9 PG
4   Inshallah 5.9+ PG
67   Mood Indigo 5.9+ PG
2   Pelvic Thrust 5.9+ PG
70   Prelude 5.9 PG
65   Realm of The Fifth-Class Climber 5.9 PG
40   Rib Cracker 5.9 PG
77   Saucony 5.9 PG
20   Sweet Meat 5.9 R

ROUTE NUMBER AND NAME

5.9 (continued)

1	The Marching Morons 5.9 A1 R
37	The White Corner 5.9 R
74	Top Brass 5.9 PG

5.10

72	Allegro 5.10b/c PG
15	Artistry in Rhythm 5.10a/b R
33	Band of Renown 5.10d PG
16	Bank Manager 5.10a/b PG
38	Big Band Era 5.10b/c PG
63	Blue Streak 5.10b/c R
8	Brown Bomber 5.10a/b G
56	Cuckoo Man 5.10b/c PG
66	Delta Waves 5.10b/c PG
11	Danger UXB 5.10a/b PG
3	Garden of Allah 5.10a/b PG
34	High Plains Drifter 5.10a PG-R
21	Mission Improbable 5.10a/b PG
58	Never Again 5.10b/c PG-R
27	New Frontier 5.10d R
79	Presto 5.10b/c PG
48	Promise of Things to Come 5.10b/c X
78	Raging Bull 5.10c PG
43	Rags to Richs' 5.10b/c PG-R
63a	Red's the Color (I Wanna See) 5.10d R
50	Remembrance of Things Past 5.10a/b PG
32	Schlemiel 5.10b/c PG
54	Search for Tomorrow 5.10b/c PG
13	Side Pocket 5.10d PG
19	Super Sunday 5.10a/b PG
2a	The Buck Stops Here 5.10d PG
49	The Good, The Bad and The Ugly 5.10b/c R
47	The Time Eraser 5.10a PG
8a	Throttled 5.10d R

ROUTE NUMBER AND NAME

5.11

60	Agent Orange 5.11d R
53	Asteroid Belt 5.11a/b X
28	Back to The Land Movement 5.11d PG
61	Birth of The Blues 5.11d X
38b	Dance Card 5.11a R
24	Directpissima 5.11b/c PG-R
10	Explosive Bolts 5.11b/c PG-R
2b	Hogs Breath 5.11d PG
23	In Search of Lost Time 5.11b/c R
20a	Killer Bees 5.11b/c R
12	Leap Frog 5.11d PG
64	Little Brown Jug 5.11b/c R
38a	Love and Bullits 5.11b/c PG-R
52	Orbit of Jupiter 5.11a X
51	Rings of Saturn 5.11 X
7	Sing, Sing, Sing 5.11b/c R
31	Square Meal 5.11a PG
29	The New Deal 5.11d R
14	The Tempest 5.11c PG
22	Time Being 5.11a PG
45	Under the Wire 5.11a PG
37a	White Knuckles 5.11b/c R
36	White Rose 5.11a PG

5.12

62	Bank Shot 5.12a R
75	Face-Off 5.12a R
17	Hang 'em High 5.12a PG-R
59	Happiness is a 110° Wall 5.12b PG
25	Land Grab 5.12a PG
26	Manifest Destiny 5.12d/13a G
30	Nectar Vector 5.12b/c R
55	Paral-Lax 5.12a G
44b	Stardust Memories 5.12a R-X

ROUTE NUMBER AND NAME

5.12 (continued)

35 Sudden Impact 5.12b/c R

5.12 TOPROPE

44a 5.12a

the ACCESS FUND

...preserving America's diverse climbing resources.

The Access Fund, a national, non-profit climbers' organization, is working to keep you climbing. The Access Fund works to preserve access and protect the environment by buying land, funding climber-support facilities, financing scientific studies, helping develop land management policy, publishing educational materials, and providing resources to local climbers' coalitions.

Every climber can help preserve access!

- **Commit yourself to "'leaving no trace."**
  Remove litter, old slings, etc., from crags and the base of walls.

- **Dispose of human waste properly.**
  Use toilets whenever possible. If none are available, dig a six-inch-deep hole at least 50 meters from water and bury waste. Always pack out toilet paper (use zip-lock plastic bags).

- **Use existing trails.**
  Avoid cutting switchbacks and trampling vegetation.

- **Use discretion when placing bolts & fixed protection.**
  Camouflage all anchors. Bolting above public trails is discouraged.

- **Respect restrictions to protect natural resources and cultural artifacts.**
  Be aware of seasonal closures to protect nesting raptors.
  Power drills are illegal in wilderness areas.
  Never manufacture holds in natural rock. No other activity so seriously threatens climbers' access.

- **Park in designated areas.**
  Try not to park in undeveloped, vegetated areas.

- **Maintain a low profile.**

- **Respect private property.**
  Consult landowners before developing new crags.

- **Join or form a local group to deal with access issues.**

- **Join the Access Fund. To become a member, make a tax-deductible donation of any amount.**

THE ACCESS FUND • PO BOX 17010 • BOULDER, CO 80308

ROUTE NAME, *PAGE*, **ROUTE NUMBER**

A

Across...Fruitstand, *161*, **128**
After You, *79*, **72**
Aftermath, *175*, **148**
Ain't Dis Yab Yum?, *74*, **69**
Akidlleativytoo...?, *167*, **137**
Alphonse, *22*, **24**
Amazing Grace, *148*, **114a**
Ambien Knights, *137*, **107b**
Animal Farm, *127*, **103**
Animal Farm Link-Up, *128*, **103a**
Annie Dotes, *133*, **105a**
Antsy Oh!, *123*, **101a**
As the Cliff Turns, *117*, **97**
Avoid Where..., *183*, **160**

B

B M, *133*, **106**
B. Warewolf, *82*, **74**
Ba-Ba Moran, *20*, **21a**
Back to the Future, *59*, **61a**
Barely Memorable, *172*, **142a**
Baskerville Terrace, *34*, **34**
Basking Ridge, *34*, **34a**
Beauty and...Skink, *126*, **102c**
Bee Bite, *65*, **64a**
Believe it or Not, *52*, **55a**
Benadryl Daze, *138*, **108a**
Between...Hard Place, *113*, **92**
Between the Lines, *11*, **10**
Birch Beer Crack, *152*, **117a**
Bird Brain, *48*, **51**
Birdcage, *49*, **53**
Birdjuice, *49*, **53a**

Birdland, *48*, **52**
Bongos and...Whales, *24*, **27**
Boob Job, *70*, **66a**
Boogeyman, *44*, **45**
Boogy Bored, *158*, **125a**
Born Again, *67*, **64b**
Boston Tree Party, *116*, **95**
Bridges to Knowhere, *91*, **77b**
Broken Sling, *12*, **12**
Broken Spring, *55*, **59b**
Bumpkey, *13*, **12a**
Burning Babies, *18*, **20**
Bush League, *142*, **112**
Bush League Too, *141*, **111a**
Bush Lite, *143*, **112a**
By the Claw, *91*, **77c**
By the Toe, *88*, **77**

C

Cam-n-Bearit, *105*, **86a**
Catch a Tiger, *87*, **76a**
Catnip, *90*, **77a**
Cherokee, *132*, **105**
Cherry's Climb, *102*, **83**
Corporate Con..., *55*, **60**
Coyote Crack, *93*, **78a**
Crass, *8*, **5a**
Crass/Outer Space..., *7*, **5**
Criss, *10*, **7**
Criss Cross, *10*, **8**
Criss Cross Direct, *11*, **9**
Curly, *83*, **74a**

ROUTE NAME, *PAGE*, **ROUTE NUMBER**

D

D.S.B., *174*, **146**
Dark Side of the Moon, *188*, **167**
Day-Tripper, *116*, **96**
De Colores, *173*, **144**
Deception, *122*, **101**
Disneyland, *13*, **14**
Dog-Stick-Ridge, *31*, **32a**
Double Cross-Issima, *8*, **5c**
Double Quacks, *125*, **102a**
Dozy Doats, *145*, **112d**
Drohascadam 1, *143*, **112b**
Drohascadamfubast, *146*, **113**
Dyno-Soar, *44*, **45a**

E

Easter Time Too, *115*, **94**
Easy Rider, *4*, **3**
Eat Here and Get Gas, *138*, **108**
Eenie Meenie, *84*, **75**
El Camino Real, *44*, **46**
El Kabong, *45*, **47**
Elder Cleavage Direct, *67*, **65**
Elf Stone Direct, *98*, **81**
Energy Crunch, *122*, **100**
Eowyn, *165*, **134**
Eraserhead, *42*, **41**

F

Far From the..., *168*, **138**
Farewell to Arms, *51*, **54**
Fat and Flabby, *188*, **169**
Fat and Weak, *58*, **60b**
Fat City Direct, *35*, **35**
Fat Stick, *28*, **31**

Fat Stick Direct, *28*, **30**
Fisher Crack, *93*, **78b**
5.8 Crack Climb, *72*, **67a**
5.11d/5.12a, *88*, **76c**
Flake, Rattle and Roll, *151*, **117**
Forbidden Zone, *42*, **40**
Fossil Fools, *169*, **139a**
Frau's Prow, *126*, **102b**
Fright to the Finish, *184*, **162**

G

G-String, *40*, **38**
G-String Giants, *40*, **37a**
Gardiner's Delight, *134*, **106c**
Gelsa, *37*, **36**
Generation Gap, *29*, **32**
Giddah, *149*, **115**
Gil-Galad, *172*, **142**
Git-Git Giddah, *149*, **115a**
Gold Flakes, *121*, **99**
Gold Rush, *104*, **86**
Good Friday Climb, *114*, **93**
Gouda Climb, *105*, **86b**
Graceland, *147*, **113c**
Grand Central, *20*, **22**
Grease Gun Groove, *54*, **59**
Grey Gully, *58*, **61**
Grey Hair Arete, *58*, **60c**
Grim and Tonic, *176*, **150**
Ground Control, *178*, **153**
Gunks Burghers, *120*, **98c**

H

Halfbeak, *119*, **98b**
Hang Ten, *157*, **124**

ROUTE NAME, *PAGE*, **ROUTE NUMBER**

Harvest Moon, *156*, **122**
Here a Bucket..., *191*, **173**
Here a Quack..., *193*, **174**
Here's the Scoop, *119*, **98a**
High Anxiety, *181*, **156**
Highway 51, *138*, **109**
Hold the Mayo, *187*, **164**
Honky Tonk Woman, *154*, **120**
Horney, *63*, **63**

I

I'm OK-You're OK, *166*, **136**
In the Nick of Time, *134*, **106a**
Independence, *1*, **B-Right**
Infinite Space, *8*, **5b**
Inside Out, *182*, **158**
Interiah, *112*, **90a**
Interlewd, *164*, **133**
International Harvesters, *112*, **91**
Interplanetary Agents, *164*, **132**
Inverted Layback, *17*, **19**
Iron Cross, *10*, **6**

J

Just Allow Me..., *153*, **118**
Just For the Record, *159*, **127**

K

Kansas City, *3*, **1**
Keystone Kop, *172*, **143**
King of P, *170*, **140a**

L

L P, *169*, **140**
Land of the Giants, *39*, **37**

Larry, *83*, **74b**
Layback, *18*, **21**
Le Plie, *7*, **4**
Lean and Mean, *188*, **168**
Left Meets Right, *87*, **76b**
Leftovers, *16*, **17**
Liddle Lamzy Divey, *143*, **112c**
Like a Box..., *160*, **127b**
Little White..., *171*, **141**
Live and Let Die, *166*, **135**
Lonely Challenge, *60*, **62**
Loose Goose, *71*, **67**
Lost World, *102*, **84**

M

Mac-Reppy, *181*, **157**
Main Line, *180*, **155**
Main Line/Mac-Reppy, *180*, **155a**
Mighty White of Us, *141*, **111**
Miss Mantle, *162*, **129a**
Moe, *83*, **74c**
Moxie, *148*, **114**
Mud, Sweat and Beers, *121*, **98f**
Muriel's Nose, *185*, **163**
My-Knee Moe, *85*, **76**

N

Nazgul, *92*, **78**
Nice Job, *71*, **66b**
Nickel and Timing, *134*, **106b**
Nip & Tuck, *110*, **89c**
No Slings Attached, *23*, **26**
Nosey Bodies, *110*, **89b**
Not to Avoid, *184*, **161a**

ROUTE NAME, *PAGE*, **ROUTE NUMBER**

Nowhereland, *107*, **89**
Nutzville, *91*, **77d**

O

Old and Mossy, *94*, **78e**
Omega 12..., *176*, **149**
One Way or Another, *137*, **107d**
Orc Stone, *101*, **82**
Outer Space, *4*, **2**
Outsider, *182*, **159**

P

P/L, *94*, **78d**
Pain Strain, *41*, **39**
Parsifal and..., *163*, **131**
Penn Station, *21*, **23**
Phalladio, *103*, **85**
Positively 4th Street, *178*, **152**
Predator, *76*, **70b**
Preying Mantle, *76*, **70a**
Princess Leia, *60*, **61b**
Pump Ethyl, *137*, **107c**
Punch and Judy, *168*, **139**

Q

Quack'n-Up, *57*, **60a**

R

R2-OK?, *167*, **136a**
Raven and the Cat, *131*, **104**
Raven's Run, *141*, **111b**
Requiem for a..., *32*, **33**
Revolving Eyeballs, *42*, **43**
Road Warrior, *47*, **49**

Rock Around the Clock, *151*, **116**
Roman's Climb Next..., *163*, **130**
Roman's Climb...Kop, *175*, **147**
Root Beer Crack, *152*, **117b**
Roseland, *43*, **44**
Route Awakening, *109*, **89a**

S

Saving Face, *147*, **113a**
Saving Grace, *147*, **113b**
Scrambled Legs, *187*, **165**
Scuttlebutt, *118*, **98**
Seniors in Motion, *189*, **170a**
Serf's Up, *135*, **106d**
She's the Boss, *154*, **119**
Shirley Tumble, *177*, **151**
Shitface, *42*, **42**
Shootin' the Curl, *157*, **123a**
Short and Sassy, *189*, **170**
Shtick It, *137*, **107a**
Silver Bullet, *82*, **73a**
Sissy Boys, *22*, **25**
Slab Happy, *126*, **102d**
Slab Shtick, *136*, **107**
Slammin' the Salmon, *48*, **50**
Sling Line, *12*, **11**
Sling Time, *15*, **15**
Snail's Face, *124*, **101b**
Son of Stem, *53*, **57**
Soylent Green, *53*, **58**
Spic and Span, *100*, **81a**
Spinal Exam, *185*, **162b**
Spinal Traction, *187*, **166**
Split Rock Traverse, *184*, **162a**
Spring Reigns, *120*, **98e**

ROUTE NAME, *PAGE,* **ROUTE NUMBER**

Squat Thrust, *13,* **13**
St. Louis, *1,* **C-Right**
Strange Customs, *179,* **154**
Summer Breeze, *120,* **98d**
Summer Brie, *106,* **86c**
Swing Time, *15,* **16**
Swissair, *72,* **68**

T

Te Dum, *16,* **18**
TFC Nein, *158,* **124a**
The Boys...Above, *52,* **54a**
The Hounds, *31,* **32b**
The Mincer, *157,* **123**
The Near Side..., *158,* **126**
The Shadow Nose, *190,* **172**
The White Pillar, *156,* **121**
3,4...Over and Out, *140,* **110**
Three Generations, *106,* **88**
To Be or Not to Be, *52,* **55**
To Come or Become, *162,* **129**
To Have or Have Not, *52,* **56**
Topeka, *3,* **A1**
Transcontinental..., *47,* **48**
Tree-Filled Chimney, *158,* **125**
Trick or Treat, *174,* **145**
Tulip Mussel..., *55,* **59a**
TurtleFly, *153,* **117c**
Two Feather Flake, *139,* **109a**

U

Up in Arms, *190,* **171**
Up Root, *160,***127a**
Up Yours, *70,* **66**

V

Void Where..., *183,* **161**
Vulga-Tits, *106,* **87**
Vultures Know, *77,* **71**

W

What? Are You Nuts?, *94,* **78c**
Whatayamacallit, *145,* **112e**
Whatever, *160,* **127c**
Where the Wild..., *75,* **70**
Whet Stone, *98,* **80a**
Wichita, *1,* **D-Right**
Wildmere, *64,* **64**
Wolf and the Swine, *124,* **102**
Woolly Clam Taco, *115,* **94a**
Wrong Place, Right Time, *95,* **79**

Y

Yellow Belly, *24,* **28**
Yellow Ridge, *26,* **29**
You're in... My Friend, *96,* **80**
Yum Yum Yab Yum, *80,* **73**

Z

Zachariah, *111,* **90**

ROUTE NAME, *PAGE*, **ROUTE NUMBER**

A

Again and Again, *267*, **57**
Agent Orange, *268*, **60**
Air for a G-String, *281*, **80**
Allegro, *278*, **72**
Apollo Theater, *276*, **69**
Artistry in Rhythm, *241*, **15**
Asteroid Belt, *265*, **53**

B

Back to the Land..., *248*, **28**
Band of Renown, *252*, **33**
Bank Manager, *241*, **16**
Bank Shot, *271*, **62**
Better Late than..., *278*, **73**
Big Band Era, *255*, **38**
Birth of the Blues, *271*, **61**
Blue Streak, *272*, **63**
Brown Bomber, *237*, **8**

C

Chairman of..., *276*, **68a**
Conflict of Interest, *257*, **39**
Cruise Control, *258*, **42**
Cuckoo Man, *266*, **56**

D

Dance Card, *256*, **38b**
Danger UXB, *239*, **11**
Delta Waves, *275*, **66**
Directpissima, *246*, **24**

E

Explosive Bolts, *238*, **10**

F

Face-Off, *279*, **75**
5.12a, *259*, **44a**
Fugue, *277*, **71**

G

Garden of Allah, *235*, **3**

H

Hang 'em High, *242*, **17**
Happiness is a 110°..., *268*, **59**
High Plains Drifter, *252*, **34**
Hogs Breath, *234*, **2b**

I

In Search of Lost..., *245*, **23**
Inshallah, *235*, **4**

J

Explosive Bolts, *238*, **10**

K

Killer Bees, *243*, **20a**

L

Land Grab, *246*, **25**
Leap Frog, *239*, **12**
Little Brown Jug, *273*, **64**
Love and Bullits, *255*, **38a**

ROUTE NAME, *PAGE*, **ROUTE NUMBER**

M

M32L, *280*, **76**
Manifest Destiny, *247*, **26**
Mission Improbable, *244*, **21**
Mood Indigo, *275*, **67**

N

Nectar Vector, *249*, **30**
Never Again, *267*, **58**
New Frontier, *248*, **27**
Nothing to Write..., *236*, **6**

O

Old Route, *276*, **68**
Orbit of Jupiter, *264*, **52**

P

Paral-Lax, *266*, **55**
Pelvic Thrust, *234*, **2**
Prelude, *277*, **70**
Presto, *281*, **79**
Promise of Things..., *262*, **48**

R

Raging Bull, *280*, **78**
Rags to Richs', *259*, **43**
Realm of the Fifth..., *273*, **65**
Red's the Color..., *272*, **63a**
Remembrance of..., *263*, **50**
Rib Cracker, *257*, **40**
Rings of Saturn, *264*, **51**

S

Saucony, *280*, **77**
Schlemiel, *250*, **32**
Search for Tomorrow, *265*, **54**
Side Pocket, *240*, **13**
Sing, Sing, Sing, *236*, **7**
Square Meal, *250*, **31**
Stardust Memories, *260*, **44b**
Strange City, *238*, **9**
Sudden Impact, *253*, **35**
Super Sunday, *243*, **19**
Sweet Meat, *243*, **20**
Swinging C, *242*, **18**

T

The Buck Stops Here, *234*, **2a**
The Good, the Bad..., *263*, **49**
The High Traverse, *258*, **41**
The Marching Morons, *233*, **1**
The New Deal, *249*, **29**
The Tempest, *240*, **14**
The Time Eraser, *262*, **47**
The White Corner, *254*, **37**
Three Buzzards, *236*, **5**
Throttled, *237*, **8a**
Time Being, *245*, **22**
Top Brass, *279*, **74**

U

Under the Wire, *260*, **45**
Unnamed, 259, 44a

ROUTE NAME, *PAGE*, **ROUTE NUMBER**

W

Westward Ha!, *259*, **44**
White Knuckles, *254*, **37a**
White Rose, *253*, **36**
Wire Wizard, *260*, **46**

The author and his son Richard in 2008.

To my climbing friends and partners, I want to thank you all from the bottom of my heart for your wonderful friendship on and off the cliffs. We've shared so many years of great adventures, great climbs and just plain good times. Thank you all!

ABOUT THE AUTHOR

by Julie Seyfert Lillis

In 51 years of climbing in the Gunks, Dick Williams has seen it all. He has worn both knickers and lycra, used both body belays and Gri-Gris, and carried racks of pitons and racks of Aliens. In the '60s he made his mark by putting up scores of inspiring first ascents and first free ascents. It was also during this time that Dick and friends formed the legendary band of climbers called the Vulgarians—a renegade crew that followed up wild nights with long days of climbing overhangs with hangovers. Besides his first ascents, which now number in the hundreds, he was the first in the East to climb dynamically; something he brought to the sport from his years as a competitive gymnast.

Dick has climbed all over the United States and Europe but has always returned to his home crag. His dedication to the area and the community shows in countless ways. In 1970, he opened Rock and Snow, a climbing equipment shop in New Paltz, retiring after 30 years of service to the climbing community. More recently, seeing the deterioration of the trails at the base of the crag caused by the increase in crowds resulting from the growing popularity of the sport, he initiated a volunteer trail restoration crew. For his work, the Mohonk Preserve awarded him the Tom Scheuer Stewardship Award in 2001.

His guidebooks set a standard by which all others may be measured. He has published 8, but this guide–along with the 2005 Trapps guide–is a significant improvement over the rest. He spent more than three years re-climbing nearly every route in the Near Trapps. Thanks to his tireless efforts, we now have definitive route descriptions with pitch-by-pitch grades and protection ratings.

The author in 2007

Photo: Annie O'Neill

The guide you are holding is the definitive guide to the Near Trapps. Dick literally wrote the book on climbing in the Gunks. Perhaps one day he will retire. He will find his old tapes of whale songs recorded under the polar ice-cap while he was in the US Submarine Service. However, from the looks of things, that day is a long way off. More likely, you will see him on the sharp-end of the rope, or on the sharp turn below The Near Trapps pursuing his other major passion—riding his very fast Yamaha FJR13R motorcycle.

In Memory of my beloved dogs, Leia and Cruz, who for 11 and 14 years respectively were always at my side with a smile, rain or shine regardless of my mood. After each climb they would always greet me like they hadn't seen me for a month.

Even as Leia was dying of cancer she hung on to life long enough for me to be there, to hold her in my arms and to comfort her in our last moments together. What love, what a friend, I will always remember her and her loving smile.

I was not as fortunate to be with Cruz; I heard her chase some critter one night and never return. I will always suffer for that time.

Shawangunk Rock Climbs, First Edition, 1972, American Alpine Club. (The Blue Guide)

Shawangunk Rock Climbs, Second Edition, 1980, American Alpine Club. (The Red Guide)

Shawangunk Rock Climbs, The Trapps, 1991, American Alpine Club Press. (One of the Black Guides)

Shawangunk Rock Climbs, The Near Trapps, Millbrook, 1991, American Alpine Club Press. (One of the Black Guides)

Shawangunk Rock Climbs, Skytop, 1991, American Alpine Club Press. (One of the Black Guides)

The Gunks Select, First Edition, 1996, The Vulgarian Press.

The Gunks Select, Second Edition, 2001, Dick Williams.

The Climber's Guide to the Shawangunks, The Trapps, 2004, The Vulgarian Press. (The Grey Guide)